After the Fall

After the Fall

The Legacy of Fascism in Rome's Architectural and Urban History

FLAVIA MARCELLO

BLOOMSBURY VISUAL ARTS
LONDON • NEW YORK • OXFORD • NEW DELHI • SYDNEY

BLOOMSBURY VISUAL ARTS
Bloomsbury Publishing Plc
50 Bedford Square, London, WC1B 3DP, UK
1385 Broadway, New York, NY 10018, USA
29 Earlsfort Terrace, Dublin 2, Ireland

BLOOMSBURY, BLOOMSBURY VISUAL ARTS and the Diana logo are trademarks of Bloomsbury Publishing Plc

First published in Great Britain 2024

Copyright © Flavia Marcello, 2024

Flavia Marcello has asserted her right under the Copyright, Designs and Patents Act, 1988, to be identified as Author of this work.

For legal purposes the Acknowledgements on pp. xv–xvi constitute an extension of this copyright page.

Cover design: Eleanor Rose
Cover images: *Monument to Anita Garibaldi* by Mario Rutelli, 1932. Janiculum Hill, Rome. Photographs © Ian Woodcock

All rights reserved. No part of this publication may be reproduced or transmitted in any form or by any means, electronic or mechanical, including photocopying, recording, or any information storage or retrieval system, without prior permission in writing from the publishers.

Bloomsbury Publishing Plc does not have any control over, or responsibility for, any third-party websites referred to or in this book. All internet addresses given in this book were correct at the time of going to press. The author and publisher regret any inconvenience caused if addresses have changed or sites have ceased to exist, but can accept no responsibility for any such changes.

A catalogue record for this book is available from the British Library.

A catalogue record for this book is available from the Library of Congress.

ISBN: HB: 978-1-3501-2059-4
       PB: 978-1-3501-2058-7
       ePDF: 978-1-3501-2060-0
       eBook: 978-1-3501-2061-7

Typeset by Integra Software Services Pvt. Ltd.
Printed and bound in India

To find out more about our authors and books visit www.bloomsbury.com and sign up for our newsletters.

CONTENTS

List of Figures vi
Acknowledgements xv
A note on terms and acronyms xvii

1. Introduction 1
2. Mussolini's mark 16
3. The architecture of Fascist Rome between politics and practicality 51
4. The Fascist phoenix: Virgilio Testa and the resurrection of EUR 81
5. Mothers, martyrs and military men: The changing meanings of Rome's Fascist monuments 113
6. Aspirations and illusions of control: Re-contextualizing Rome's Fascist epigraphy 140
7. A conclusion for a centenary 171

Notes 177
Bibliography 208
Index 222

FIGURES

1.1 Map showing Nodes of Fascist Rome. Drawing by Kylie Burns and author 4
1.2 Elements of political rhetoric in the Fascist and post-Fascist eras. Diagram by author 5
1.3 The relationship between nodes and political rhetoric in the Fascist and post-Fascist eras. Diagram by author 6
1.4 Examples of *Romanità* in Fascist era public art in Rome. Montage by author of photographs by Ian Woodcock and author. a. Unknown, Trophies, bas relief, Janiculum Ossuary; b. Corrado Vigni, Castor/Pollux, bas relief, Faculty of Arts, *Città Universitaria*; c. Publio Morbiducci, Castor/Pollux, statue, Italian Civilisation Building, E42/EUR; d. Italo Griselli, Genius of Fascism/Sport, statue, Office Building, E42/EUR; e. Arturo Martini, Minerva, statue, *Città Universitaria*; f. Dino Basaldella, Lion and Centaur, statue, Office Building, E42/EUR; Unknown, EUR logo, bas relief, E42/EUR; h. Giulio Rosso, *Inchoata Roma forma leonis*, mosaic, Piazzale dell'impero/Foro Italico 7
2.1 1941/2 General Variant of 1931 Regulatory Plan for Rome (VG41/2) as reconstructed by Insolera and Mancini. Drawing by Kylie Burns and author 21
2.2 *Comitato di Elaborazione Tecnica* (Technical Drafting Committee – CET), Perspective drawing of Social

Infrastructure Axis (*Asse attrezzato*) From *Il Giornale d'Italia*, 25–26 September 1970. Testa archive, Box 8. Archivio Centrale di Stato, Rome 23

2.3 Technical Drafting Committee, schematic representation of plan for Rome, 1956. Drawing by Kylie Burns and author 24

2.4 1962 Regulatory Plan for Rome (PR62). From *Urbanistica*, 1959. Courtesy of Arthur and Janet C. Ross Library, American Academy in Rome 27

2.5 1931 Regulatory Plan for Rome (PR31), schematic plan showing rail systems. From *Planimetrie del Piano Regolatore 1931 IX. Riproduzione ridotta delle planimetrie allegate at R. decreto legge 6 luglio 1931, n. 981*. Courtesy of Library of British School at Rome 28

2.6 Map of unplanned or rogue development (*abusivismo*) in relation to Node 7 (*quartieri* and *borgate*) between 1952 and 1961 as reconstructed by Gigli Padellaro and Panizza. Drawing by Kylie Burns and author 31

2.7 The 'oceanic masses' gather in Piazza Venezia to hear Mussolini announce Italy's entry into the Second World War, January 1941. Scherl/Süddeutschezeitung Photo/Alamy. Used with permission 34

2.8 The *Bersaglieri* run liltingly down Via dei Fori Imperiali. From *Italy Today*, Presidency of the Council of Ministers Information Service, 1962 35

2.9 Via della Conciliazione. Photograph by author 38

2.10 Enrico Del Debbio, Academy of Sports 1929, proudly displaying its new name 'Foro Italico' in 1958. Luce Historical Archive 39

2.11 An aerial view of the *Foro Italico* for the 1960 Olympic Games in Rome, showing the main Olympic Stadium, with smaller stadiums and arenas and the new Ministry of Foreign Affairs on the left. 22 June 1959. Smith Archive/Alamy Stock 40

2.12 Schematic plan of *E42/EUR* showing principal buildings and four axes. Drawing by Brandon Gardiner and author 44

2.13 'A little sovereign state for Prof. Virgilio Testa'. Testa archive, Box 8. Archivio Centrale di Stato, Rome 46

3.1 Just another day at Villa Torlonia for Mussolini at the wheel of an Alfa Romeo hobnobbing with famous racing car driver Tazio Nuvolari. Prospero Gianferrari Archive owned by his son Vincenzo. Public domain. 57

3.2 Angiolo Mazzoni and later Leo Calini, Massimo Castellazzi, Vasco Fadigati, Eugenio Montuori, Achille Pintonello, Annibale Vitellozzi, Rome Termini Railway Station, the ticket hall and internal street in the 1950s. Images by kind permission of Archivio Fotografico Fondazione FS Italiane 61

3.3 Marcello Piacentini, National Association of War Wounded. Photograph by Ian Woodcock 62

3.4 Enrico Del Debbio, Arnaldo Foschini, Vittorio Morpurgo, Ministry of Foreign Affairs (formerly *Palazzo Littorio*) with Arnaldo Pomodoro's *Sfera grande* in the foreground. Photo by Gianni, Wikimedia Commons 64

3.5 Luigi Moretti, Fencing Academy. The cages for the accused fitted into the main hall while being used as the *Aula Bunker* for high security trials. Roberto Koch Agenzia Contrasto, Immagini del Novecento dall'Archivio fotografico del PCI 67

3.6 Sets under construction at *Cinecittà* for the swords and sandals blockbuster *Quo Vadis* with 700 refugees still on site. Luce Historical Archive, Rome 71

3.7 Ettore Rossi, Nanni Moretti's *Nuovo Sacher* cinema (formerly After-work circle for employees of the State Monopolies). Photograph by Ian Woodcock 73

3.8 Gaetano Minnucci, Montesacro Post Office, Middle School, Regional Offices Sport and Community Centre (formerly *Casa GIL* Montesacro). Photograph by Ian Woodcock 76

3.9 Luigi Moretti, WeGIL and Sports Centre (formerly *Casa GIL* Trastevere). Photograph by Ian Woodcock 77

3.10 Roberto Narducci, Ostiense Station as decorated for Adolf Hitler's state visit to Italy, May 1938. From *Architettura*, 16 August 1938, 490. Courtesy of American Academy Library 78

3.11 President Gronchi leans out of the window of the Presidential train at Ostiense Station on his way to Germany in December 1956. Luce Historical Archive 79

4.1 Aerial views of EUR in 1951 and 1961. From Virgilio Testa, *Relazione sull'attività svolta nel decennio 1951–1961*. Testa Archive Box 31. Archivio Centrale di Stato, Rome 84

4.2 Map of EUR showing pre and post-Fascist era buildings. Drawing by Kylie Burns and author 86

4.3 Mario Paniconi, Giulio Pediconi and Giovanni Muzio, INPS Exedra showing 1950s extension in background. Photograph by author 88

4.4 Adalberto Libera, Conference and Receptions Building. Photograph by Ian Woodcock 89

4.5 Giovanni Guerrini, Bruno La Padula, Mario Romano, Italian Civilisation Building. Photograph by Ian Woodcock 90

4.6 Gaetano Minnucci, Office Building showing quote by Mussolini and statue of the 'Genius of Sport'. Photograph by author 92

4.7 Aerial view of Piazza Marconi looking towards Museum of Roman Civilisation. Arrows by author indicate (left to right) Conference and Receptions Building, Piazza of Museum of Roman Civilisation, Alitalia/INAIL Skyscraper and 'Nuvola' Conference Centre. Photo by Andrea Ricci 93

4.8 Luigi Brusa, Gino Cancellotti, Eugenio Muntuori and Alfredo Scalpelli, Museum of Civilisations (formerly Science Museum). Photograph by author 95

4.9 Pietro Aschieri, Domenico Bernardini, Cesare Pascoletti, Gino Peressutti. Museum of Roman Civilisation. Photograph by Ian Woodcock 97

4.10 Luigi Figini and Gino Pollini with Mario De Renzi, Piazzale degli Archivi. Photographs taken from the central building along the Society Axis in 1951 and 1961. From Virgilio Testa, *Relazione sull'attività svolta nel decennio*. Testa Archive Box 31. Archivio Centrale di Stato, Rome 99

4.11 Basilica of Saints Peter and Paul with statues of the Saints by Domenico Ponzi and Francesco Nagni. Photograph by Ian Woodcock 101

4.12 Final model of the Housing Exhibition/residential area around the Basilica of Saints Peter and Paul, 1943. From: ASFE42 0683 – Archivio Storico Fotografico di EUR SpA 101

4.13 Park and Lake showing a collection of post-war buildings. From left to right: Telecom Italia Tower, *Grattacielo Italia*, Ministry of Finance, INAIL and ENI Skyscraper. Author: Dueduezerosettesettequattro. Wikimedia Commons 103

4.14 Marco Bacigalupo and Ugo Ratti, ENI Skyscraper. Cover of *Il gatto selvatico*, 7, 9 (1962) 105

4.15 Former Mayor Umberto Tupini, President Giovanni Gronchi, Public Works Minister Giuseppe Togni, Defense Minister Giulio Andreotti, Mayor Urbano Cioccetti and others in front of the model of the Palace of Sport, May 1959. Luce Historical Archive 107

4.16 Saverio Muratori, Former Christian Democrat Party Headquarters. Photograph by Ian Woodcock 110

4.17 Massimiliano Fuksas, The 'Cloud' Congress Centre. During the 2021 G20 meeting in Rome, Italy. LSF Photo/Alamy Stock 111

5.1 Richard Meier, *Ara Pacis* Museum 2006. Photograph by Palickap. Wikimedia commons 117

5.2 Giovanni Jacobucci, Janiculum Ossuary. Photograph by Ian Woodcock 119

5.3 Postcard of the Dogali monument with the lion of Judas in place, 1936. Author's collection 121

5.4 Postcard of the Aksum Stele before and after the completion of the World Headquarters of the United Nations' Food and Agriculture Organisation (former Ministry of Italian Africa) Author's collection 123

5.5 Arturo Dazzi, Marconi Obelisk. Photograph by author 125

5.6 Guglielmo Marconi in his *Accademico d'Italia* uniform with Marchioness Maria Cristina Marconi in a rather fetching turban at the Piazza del Campidoglio after being awarded the Mussolini Prize. Luce Historical Archive 127

5.7 Monument to Anita Garibaldi. Photograph by Ian Woodcock 128

5.8 Altar of the Fascist Martyrs all forlorn in the back blocks of the *Campidoglio*. Photograph by Francesca de Caprariis 130

5.9 Mausoleum of the Fascist Martyrs, Verano Cemetery. Photograph by author 131

5.10 Giuseppe Sacconi, Monument to Victor Emanuel and Altar of the Fatherland with some presidential pomp and ceremony in progress. February 2022, Presidenza della Repubblica 135

5.11 Constantino Costantini, Mussolini Obelisk, *Foro Italico/Mussolini, c.* 1944 while in use as the United States Army Rest Centre with flags of the Allies: Great Britain, the United States of America and France in the foreground. From *The United States Army Rest Center, Foro d'Italia, Rome 1944–45* pamphlet, Casa Editrice Dalmatia di Luciano Morpurgo, Rome 1945. No page number 137

6.1 Gallery of (Contradictory) fasces. Montage and photographs by author. a. Extant fasces and inscription on Ministry of Aeronautics; b. extant fasces on the Mausoleum of Fascist Martyrs, Verano Cemetery; c. fasces hacked off a lamp post on the Via dei Fori Imperiali; d. fasces hacked off a sign for Lot 21, Garbatella 144

6.2   Assemblage of inscriptions at Piazza Augusto Imperatore. Montage and photographs by author. a. Extant quote in Italian by Mussolini; b. Restored quote in Latin by Mussolini; c. Extract of Augustus's *Res gestae* re-installed on the side of Richard Meier's *Ara Pacis* Museum (with admirer)   147

6.3   Arnaldo Foschini, Entrance Portico of *Città Universitaria* with Fascist-era inscription framed either side with stylised fasces. From *Architettura. Numero speciale – La Città Universitaria di Roma*, 1935, p. 25   148

6.4   Arnaldo Foschini, Entrance Portico of *Città Universitaria* with new post-war inscription. Zoonar/Valerio Rosati, Alamy Foto Stock, PHCG7C, Zoonar GmbH   149

6.5   Gabriele d'Annunzio inscription around altar at the Janiculum Ossuary. Photograph by Ian Woodcock   150

6.6   Italian quote attributed to Mussolini and Latin quote by Livy in the crypt of the Janiculum Ossuary. Photograph by author   151

6.7   Marcello Piacentini, National Association of War Wounded, side façade showing a triad of mottoes above the windows. Photograph by Ian Woodcock   152

6.8   Diagrammatic plan indicating dates shown on the marble blocks at Piazzale dell'Impero/Foro Italico. Drawing by author   156

6.9   Luigi Moretti, Piazzale dell'Impero/Foro Italico. Marble block displaying extract from Mussolini's Proclamation of Empire speech. Photograph by author   157

6.10 Luigi Moretti, Piazzale dell'Impero/Foro Italico. Marble block displaying freshly minted inscription to commemorate the referendum for the republic. Luce Historical Archive, Rome   159

6.11 Luigi Moretti, Piazzale dell'Impero/Foro Italico. Marble block displaying graffiti denying the fall of the Fascist regime and exalting the Duce. Photograph by Edward Schröter. Foto: Bibliotheca Hertziana – Max-Planck-Institut für Kunstgeschichte, Rom 160

6.12 Arnaldo Foschini, INA Building, Corso Rinascimento displaying an inscription about Empire. Photograph by author 161

6.13 Latin inscriptions for all classes. a. 'LABOR OMVIA VINCIT' on an apartment building in Via dei Ciceli, Quadraro. b. 'DOMINUS CUSTODIAT DOMUM' on a Villa in Via dei Monti Parioli. Photographs by author 165

6.14 Marcello Piacentini, Rectory Building, *Città Universitaria*. Rear façade with extract from Horace's *Odes* on the virtues of education. Photograph by author 167

6.15 Restored graffiti at the back of an apartment building Garbatella. It reads 'Down with the Nazi fasces' and 'Down with Adolf Hitler'. Photograph by author 169

7.1 1944 Proposal to the President to draft a set of norms and set up an inter-ministerial commission to remove monuments and artworks exalting Fascism. PCM44-47 1/7 f.11240/2. Archivio Centrale di Stato, Rome 175

ACKNOWLEDGEMENTS

There may be the name of a single author on the cover of this book but, like many works, it has been a collective effort. I will start by thanking Ian Woodcock who has been by my side throughout the whole process: listening to me talk about it endlessly and offering invaluable insights and advice. He also drove around Rome in my aunt Chiara's car and sidestepped the passing traffic while I double-parked, emergency lights flashing, so he could leap out to take many of the photographs that illustrate this book.

You can read its pages thanks to the unflagging enthusiasm and encouragement of my writing buddy, Simone Taffe. She and my colleagues from the Centre for Design Innovation writing workshops, Kay's Shut Up and Write sessions and our own Thank God It's (Shut Up and Write) Fridays have supported (and kept me company) all the way, especially during COVID lockdowns. Thanks also go to Nick Carter who reassured me over Chinese lunches that I was not the only one in Australia obsessed with the heritage of Fascism.

In Rome I'd like to thank Simon Martin for all our great discussions over dry crackers and juice from the vending machines at the Archivio Centrale di Stato, Noa Steimatsky and Fabio Barry for their company during my fieldwork, Paul Gwynne for the Latin translations, Francesca de Caprariis for her proficiency in Roman topography and all the wonderful 'fellow Fellows' and staff of the British School at Rome.

To the Roman list I'd also like to add Francesco Innamorati of Eur Spa who has been of invaluable assistance from the very early days of my fascination with the Fascist legacy in the mid-1990s when he took a young PhD candidate from Australia down the haunted hallways of the Square Colosseum.

The Rome list would not be complete without my family. My mother whose stories of growing up in Montesacro made me want to find out more, my grandfather who instilled a love of the city's history into me from a young age, my aunts Chiara and Titti Marcello who fed and watered me between archive and library visits. On that note it is time to thank the many people in the archives and libraries I used to collect the material for this book: the Archivio Centrale di Stato, the Arthur and Janet C Ross Library at the American Academy in Rome, the Deutsches Historiches Institut, the Biblioteca Hertziana and the wonderful Mez Wilkinson at Swinburne library who hunted high and low for the many books I borrowed on inter-library loan.

Thanks also go to my research assistants Petra Cipriani, Kylie Burns and Daria Gradusova who really went the extra mile in the final throes of getting the manuscript together as well as Rick Mohr whose OCD-driven proofreading got the footnotes into shape.

Finally I'd like to dedicate this book to the memory of Professor Jennifer Taylor with whom I began a PhD on this topic in the early 1990s and who inspired me to become the architectural historian I am today.

A NOTE ON TERMS AND ACRONYMS

As a number of the examples in this book have changed names since the fall of the regime, I have opted to use a dual naming system throughout. For example, E42/EUR refers to the planned incarnation of the 1942 Expo, the renaming of the Expo to EUR (*Esposizione Universale Roma:* Rome Universal Exposition) after it was indefinitely postponed and the name of the suburb as it is known today. The same goes for the *Foro Mussolini/ Italico*.

The book also uses the Italian name for the various streets, buildings and monuments as well as a number of Italian terms when the English translation does not fully render its nuances. A similar convention is used for acronyms. For those unfamiliar with Italian, a glossary and list of acronyms is provided below.

Acronyms

ACS	*Archivio Centrale di Stato,* State Central Archives
ANMIG	*Associazione Nazionale Mutilati e Invalidi di Guerra,* National Association of War Wounded
CET	*Comitato di Elaborazione Tecnica,* Technical Drafting Committee
CLN	*Comitato di Liberazione Nazionale,* National Liberation Committee
DC	*Democrazia Cristiana,* Christian Democrat Party
E42/EUR	*Esposizione42/Esposizione Universale Roma,* 1942 Exposition/Rome Universal Exposition
FIFA	*Fédération Internationale de Football Association,* International Federation of Football Associations
GIL	*Gioventù Italiana del Littorio,* Fascist Youth Organisation
IACP	*Istituto Autonomo per Case Popolari,* Autonomous Worker Housing Institute

ICP	*Istituto per Case Popolari*, Worker Housing Institute
INA	*Istituto Nazionale Assicurazioni*, National Insurance Institute
INA-Casa	*Istituto Nazionale Assicurazioni-Casa*, National Insurance Housing Institute
INCIS	*Istituto Nazionale Case per Impiegati di Stato*: National Housing Institute for Public Servants
INPS	*Istituto Nazionale di Previdenza Sociale*, National Social Security Institute
INU	*Istituto Nazionale di Urbanistica*, National Institute of Urban Planning/Design
MVSN	*Milizia Volontaria per la Sicurezza Nazionale*, Voluntary Militia for National Security
ONB	*Opera Nazionale Balilla*, Fascist Youth Organisation catering for boys between the ages of eight and fourteen named after the nickname of young Genoese boy, G. B. Perasso who, according to legend, sparked an insurrection against Austrian troops by throwing a stone at them.
OND	*Opera Nazionale Dopolavoro*, National After-work Organisation
PCM	*Presidenza del Consiglio dei Ministri*, Presidency of the Council of Ministers
PNF	*Partito Nazionale Fascista*, National Fascist Party
PR31	*Piano Regolatore 1931*, 1931 Regulatory Plan
PR62	*Piano Regolatore 1962*, 1962 Regulatory Plan
SGI	*Società Generale Immobiliare*, General Real Estate Development Agency
UNRRA	United Nations Relief and Rehabilitation Administration
USNPR	*Ufficio Speciale per il Nuovo Piano Regolatore*, Special Office for the New Regulatory Plan
VG41-2	*Variante Generale 1941–2*, 1941–2 General Variant

Italian terms

abusivismo: unplanned or rogue development outside the limits of regulatory plans. Also any unauthorized building work or buildings in breach of planning regulations.

anni di piombo: sometimes translated to the Lead Years it does not allow for the dual meaning of the word to also mean bullet, hence my translation to Lead/Bullet Years.

anti-fascistizzazione: the process of de-fascistizing.

arengario: tribune, platform, balcony or other elevated position used for official or public speeches, from the verb *arringare* – to make a speech in front of a crowd in the form of an oratory intended to persuade or motivate the audience.

asse attrezzato: translated to Social Infrastructure Axis this was an element of urban design that was essentially a high-speed road provided with cultural, government and commercial services on multiple levels.

autarchia: literally autarky or self-sufficiency. PNF policy of economic independence that was given particular impetus after the League of Nations imposed sanctions on Italy due to their invasion of Ethiopia.

bastone: literally stick and used as the preferred font for Fascist-era inscriptions (see also *manganello* below).

Battaglia del Grano: the PNF's Battle for Grain policy enacted to counteract migration to the cities and keep bread on the nation's tables.

bersagliere: riflemen of the Italian army infantry corps known for their storming of Porta Pia (and rather festive feathered hats).

borgate: a term adapted from the word *borgo* meaning small rural town but essentially outer residential suburbs with none of their history, charm or even essential services.

Caduti per la Rivoluzione: the Fallen for the [Fascist] Revolution.

Campidoglio: literally one of the seven hills of Rome but used metonymically to refer to Rome City Council located thereon.

carabinieri: Italian Military/Security Police, originally soldiers armed with short rifles.

cardo: main north-south axis in Roman town planning.

Casa delle Armi: literally Arms House but used to give a military air to Luigi Moretti's Fencing Academy at the *Foro Mussolini/Italico*.

Casale Balilla: literally House of the *Balilla*, these were local headquarters of the original National Fascist Youth Organisation in each town or city (see ONB, above).

Casale del Dopolavoro: literally House of the After-work circle, usually referred to simply as a *dopolavoro* (see OND, above).

Casale del Fascio: literally House of the Fasces, local National Fascist Party Headquarters built in each Italian town and city. Also known as *Casa del Littorio* or *Casa Littoria* (see littorio/a below).

Casale del Mutilato: literally House of the War Wounded, local ANMIG Headquarters built in each Italian town and city (see ANMIG, above).

Casa Madre: literally Mother House, used to refer to the national headquarters of the above *Case*.

centro direzionale: development centre or new residential, commercial and institutional hub to allow for polycentric urban development.

centro storico: Rome's historic city as bounded by the Aurelian walls.

Cinecittà: new cinema studios built on the outskirts of Rome in 1937.

Città Giardino: Garden City, used to refer to Rome's Montesacro quarter begun in 1924 and expanded during the Fascist period.

Città Universitaria: the new campus of Rome's *La Sapienza* university completed in 1935.

Comune di Roma: Rome Municipal/City Council (see *Campidoglio*).

Corporativismo: uniquely Fascist economic policy conceived as a 'Third Way' between Communism and Capitalism that allowed the regime to gain control over industry and commerce.

decumanus: main east-west axis in Roman town planning.

defensor civitatis: Latin for defender of the city used in reference to Pope Pius XII who came out of the Vatican after the Allied bombings.

Duce: Italian translation of the Latin word for leader made eponymous for Mussolini.

Ente: para-governmental organization, body or authority with its own internal structure but reporting to government.

Farnesina: the popular name (and also metonymy) for the Ministry of Foreign Affairs named after the site on which it was built that once belonged to the noble Farnese family.

Fasci di Combattimento: earliest provincial groups of Fascism founded by Mussolini in Milan on 21 March 1919 dedicated to a range of issues from

Nationalism to destruction of Socialism. Later wrangled under national control with the establishment of the dictatorship in 1925.

fascio: literally meaning organization or group, it is also known as the *fascio littorio* the ancient Roman symbol of magisterial power, this was a bundle of sticks tied together with red ribbons with an axe inserted into the top during times of war. It was adopted by the Italian Fascist Party as its symbol with the added emphasis on the strength of collective thought and action.

Fratelli d'Italia: political party formed in 2012 and allied first centre-right and right-wing parties inspired by Nationalist, liberal and populist values. Named after the first line of the National Anthem by Gofredo Mameli it gained an extraordinary 26% of the vote in the 2022 elections under the leadership of Giovanna Meloni.

Giunta: Council, in this specific context Rome City or Municipal Council.

Italiani brava gente: literally the Italians are a good people. A form of patriotism and *apologia* for participation in the Holocaust and Colonialism based on the myth of Italian soldiers as innocuous and un-warlike who fitted Mediterranean stereotypes as lovers of women, music and soccer/football, always ready to joke and fraternise with the locals.

Littorio/a: literally the lictor but used as another word for fasces as the lictor was the person who accompanied magistrates to the Roman senate with the fasces upon their shoulders.

leva fascista: literally the Fascist draft, a new form of yearly ritual modelled on Catholic confirmation that confirmed an adolescent's Fascist faith and subsequent entry into the PNF.

manganello: the stick or truncheon used by Fascist crack squads.

miracolo economico: literally the Economic Miracle. Refers to the period of the 1950s and 1960s when Italy underwent an unprecedented period of economic growth that transformed the country from a mainly rural economy to a major Western industrial power.

palazzo: large-scale urban building usually associated with nobility, Popes, leaders or institutions.

Palazzo Littorio: literally Palace of the Lictors, the national headquarters of the PNF.

partito di raccolta: Catch-all Party.

passo romano: literally Roman step, a form of military march or goosestep, renamed as such during Fascism as part of the general rhetoric of *Romanità* (see below).

pater familias: Latin for father of the family to mean the head of the family.

patria: literally Fatherland but can also stand for nation or country.

piano nobile: literally the noble floor or storey of a *palazzo* that contained the most important rooms, ceremonial halls and balcony.

piano particolareggiato: detailed structure plan that applies the general terms of the city-scale regulatory plan.

piano regolatore: city-scale regulatory plan.

quadriga: four-horse chariot, usually driven by Sun Gods, the Roman Goddess Victory and the triumphant generals of Imperial Rome.

quartieri: inner residential suburbs for the middle classes.

Risorgimento: literally resurgence, the name given to Italy's process of unification (c. 1861–70).

Romanità: literally Roman-ness. Of or pertaining to the city of Rome and by extension to the culture and history of ancient Rome. A key element of Fascist rhetoric, pillar of the framework of political religion and powerful force behind the will to power.

Sacrario: sacred space or shrine usually dedicated to Fascist martyrs or those who died during the Fascist Revolution.

salone d'onore: Hall of Honour, a large space reserved for ceremonies and other important events, often richly decorated.

sanatoria: literally amnesty but used in the context of urban planning as regularisation procedure for unauthorized building work or buildings in breach of planning regulations (see *abusivismo*).

Sfollare le città: literally clearing out or 'de-crowding' the cities. A PNF policy to entice internal migrants away from the city and back to tilling the lands. Closely tied to rural ideology, demographic policy, land reclamation projects (*bonifica integrale*) such as the draining of the Pontine Marshes and the foundation of new towns such as Sabaudia and Littoria (see also *Battaglia del Grano*).

Squadristi/squadrista: Fascist crack (or action) squads.

Stile littorio: a special architectural style developed under Fascism whose symmetry, monumentality and severity brought Roman-style Classicism into the twentieth century.

sventramenti: literally gutting or disembowelment, a term used by architects and urbanists of the time to refer to whatever cuts into the urban fabric deemed necessary to accommodate city life.

tangenti: kick-backs or bribes given to politicians and Party bureaucrats to obtain preferential treatment, jobs or government contracts.

Tangentopoli: a city known for its system based on *tangenti* and subjected to the *mani pulite* (clean hands) inquests that began in 1992 bringing down the old party system and, with it, the First Republic.

Torre littoria: Lictory Tower or Tower of the Lictors. An important formal and symbolic feature used on *Case del Fascio* and *Case Balilla*, usually featuring an *arengario* (see above) and a quote by Mussolini.

urbanista: literally urbanist or urbanologist. Usually an architect with experience and training in city planning and/or urban design.

ventennio: the twenty years of the Fascist regime from 1922 to 1943.

Vittoriano: the name popularly given to the Victor Emanuel Monument at Piazza Venezia

Wehrmacht: the Germany army under Nazism.

Translations are a combination of author's knowledge, the *Treccani Enciclopedia* and *Dictionary* and the Forum at wordreference.com.

CHAPTER ONE

Introduction

A chi Roma? (E un urlo risponde 'A noi!')
A chi l'Italia? ('A noi!')
A chi la vittoria? ('A noi!')
To whom Rome? (and a cry answers 'To us!')
To whom Italy ('To us!')
To whom Victory ('To us!')
Mussolini – On the First Anniversary of the
March on Rome, 28 October 1923.[1]

Rome the eternal city is an entity that has morphed and materialized over millennia, its many layers, its many faces and its many identities continue to be a source of fascination, not least for me who considers it one of her home towns. A town where my mother was born, where my father grew up and where I lived with my family for many years. The book tells the story of its Fascist layer and how it has impacted the city we see today. As an assemblage of urban development, buildings and monuments, it also acts as a matrix that plots the shameful and ennobling events that define both individual and national identities.[2] What traces have the *ventennio* (the twenty years of the Fascist regime from 1922 to 1943) left on this unique repository for iconic overproduction? Where can this surfeit of visual markers of a dead regime be found? How do they manifest? The answers can be found by using three different perspectives: the when, the where and the what, or chronology, location and meaning. Brought together, this can lead us to address the elusive (and most important) question: why?

Chronology or the when

Attitudes towards past historical periods – especially those not everyone cares to remember – are affected by changing social and political contexts, as each decade brings us further away in time. To borrow from Maurice Halbwachs, society represents the past to itself in different ways in relation to its own circumstances according to particular points in time. Conventions for how to remember the past also change and society will accept (or not accept) these conventions as they form what he calls their collective memory.[3] Since its legendary foundation in 753 BCE there have been many Romes: the Rome of the Kings, the Rome of the Republic, the Rome of the Caesars and the Rome of the Popes, although only the last two were of significance to the Fascist imaginary which determined the First Rome to belong to the Caesars and the Second to the Popes. We are concerned with the legacy of Mussolini's Rome as the Third Rome of Fascism. Following on from this we can delineate the post-war Romes through key periods linked to political change. The Fourth Rome of the 1940s begins with the fall of the regime and was marked by Nazi occupation and civil war. It was a time of immense upheaval, uncertainty, privation and violence when reactions to the heritage of Fascism were at their most intense. The Fifth Rome begins in 1948 with the foundation of the First Republic and continues into the 1960s with the *miracolo economico* (Economic Miracle) when the capital of a democratic nation was building a new identity with a clean slate that considered the *ventennio* as a blip in history disconnected from the present. The Sixth Rome began with the *autunno caldo* (Hot Autumn) of 1969 which marked an end to this golden era and is defined by the dark and violent *anni di piombo* (Lead/Bullet Years) when the Fascist past made a return through open hostility between anti-Fascist and Fascist groups. The advent of the Seventh Rome was more gradual and is more closely defined by the *Tangentopoli* (Bribesville or Kickback City) scandals that tore through all levels of government signalling the end of First Republic. The 1990s began with the Second Republic, a new set of political alliances that gave more room to the far right and ushered in the era of a new brand of directly elected mayor for whom Rome and its image were stepping stones of a political career. Each of these Romes related back to the Third Rome of Fascism in its own way: the Fourth Rome was reactive; it was visceral, a time when anything Fascist was to be fought against and/or destroyed. The Fifth Rome was concerned with rebuilding and although it maintained a repugnance towards the most overt and symbolic aspects of the Third Rome it took a necessarily pragmatic attitude towards it. The city needed to grow, people needed to work and be housed, and if the matrix of the Fascist city and its different nodes were going to help rebuild the nation socially, politically and economically then so be it. The Sixth Rome brought to a head the political tensions of the Fourth Rome that had been smoothed over in the name of rebuilding the nation and debates on what its heritage meant to different political groups came out into the open. This was also fuelled by concentrations of citizens in the new residential areas built during the regime (Node 7) with precise political leanings that were a direct result of the Third Rome. The Seventh Rome also provided a context for far-Right sentiments about the value of the Third Rome to be expressed and this also coincided with enough historical distance for the architecture of the Third Rome to be judged for its aesthetic merits.

Location or the where

Italy's confrontation and reckoning with the past is tied, secondly, to location – to what I have called the Seven Nodes of Fascist Rome. The Fascist legacy of Node 1: the *centro storico* and Node 2: the Vatican were carved out of the existing city and vied with the symbolism and physicality of the First Rome of the Caesars and the Second Rome of the Popes. In the case of the newly built nodes of the Third Rome, the Fascist legacy occurs at different scales among a larger assemblage of urban planning, architecture, art and epigraphy that operated at multiple scales to communicate political messages. Two nodes dedicated to building the future of Fascism were: Node 3: the City of Sport, or *Foro Mussolini* (Mussolini Forum), a sports complex on the Western side of the Tiber near the Via Flaminia later renamed *Foro Italico* and Node 4: the City of Learning, a new campus for Rome's *La Sapienza* University (or *Città Universitaria*) northeast of Termini Station. These were joined by two more nodes with a stronger propaganda focus, Node 5: *Cinecittà*, a massive cinema studio on the city fringe along the Via Tuscolana and Node 6: the E42/EUR Expo founded in 1937 on a greenfield site to the southwest, roughly halfway between the city centre and the Tyrrhenian coast. Among these nodes were new housing developments closer to the centre called *quartieri* and estates located in the urban periphery called *borgate* which collectively form Node 7 (see Figure 1.1). Each node, both as assemblage and in its constituent parts, also functioned as physical manifestations of eight key elements of political rhetoric central to Fascism: *Romanità*, Militarism, Empire, Modernity/Fascist Achievement, Moral Behaviour/Social Control, National Unity, the Cult of the *Duce* and Catholic Power. Each node was dealt with differently by post-war governments at local, regional and national levels to represent those elements of political rhetoric that carried over more or less modified from the Fascist period (Figures 1.2 and 1.3).

Meaning or the what

Finally there is the lens of meaning which is closely connected to the eight key elements of Fascism's political rhetoric that relate to the unique representational function of Rome as national capital. They act as a

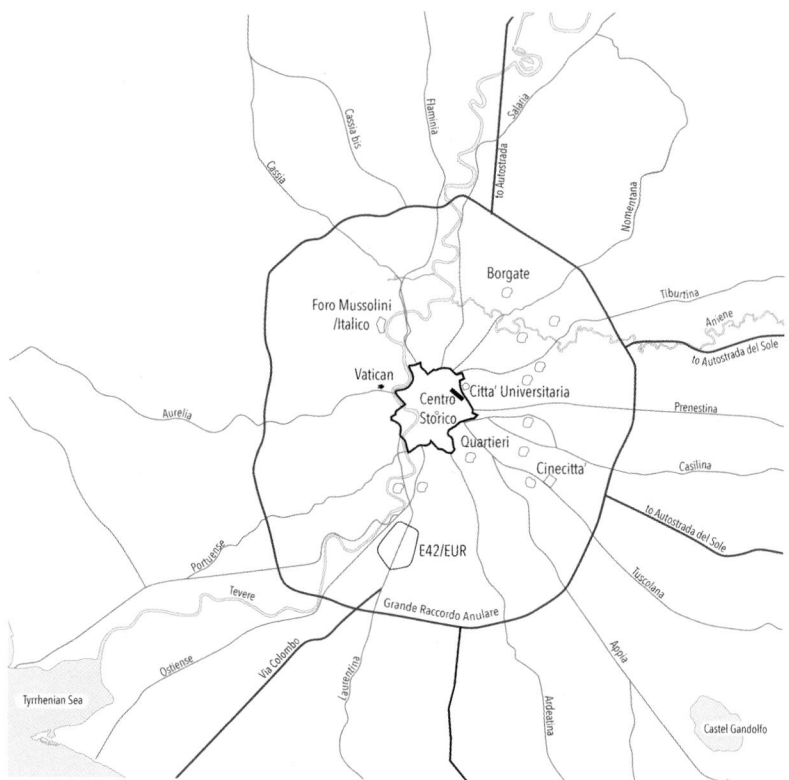

FIGURE 1.1 Map showing Nodes of Fascist Rome: 1. *Centro storico*, 2. the Vatican, 3. *Foro Mussolini/Italico*, 4. *Città Universitaria*, 5. *Cinecittà*, 6. E42/EUR, 7. *Quartieri & Borgate*. Drawing by Kylie Burns and author.

framework for understanding both the genesis and the legacy of the urban planning, architecture, monuments and epigraphy of Fascist Rome. These were used throughout the regime to underpin the propaganda efforts directed towards the processes and techniques of fabricating consent for a Fascist dictatorship. The first, *Romanità*, has frequent crossovers with Militarism and Empire which are nested within it. Militarism also contains National Unity and overlaps with Moral Behaviour/Social Control. These are overseen by the Cult of the *Duce* that was used to foster a sense of National Unity underpinned by Catholic Power. Each of these elements was brought under the umbrella concept of Modernity/Fascist Achievement. In the post-war era, the Cult of the *Duce* was repudiated and *Romanità* was stripped of its political garb placing it outside the realm of political rhetoric.

INTRODUCTION

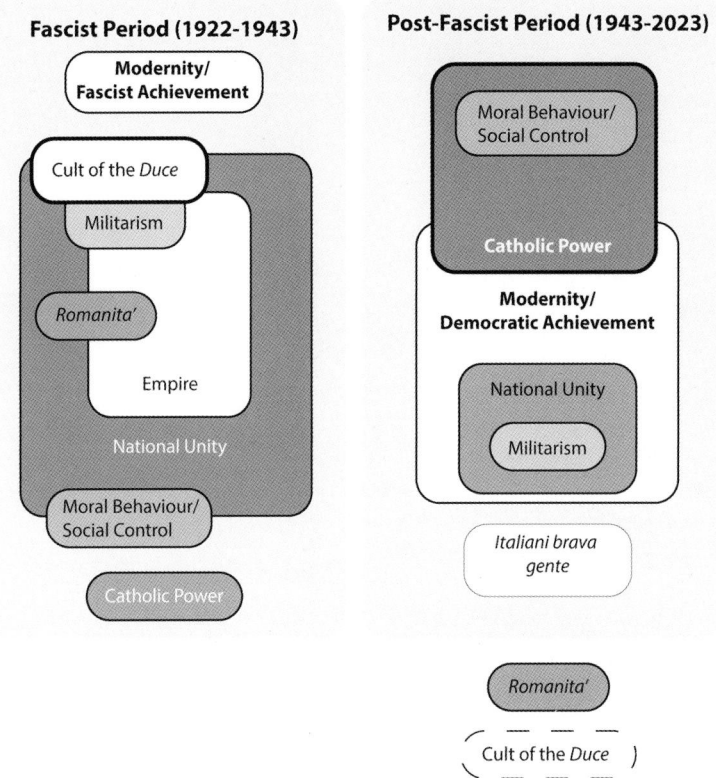

FIGURE 1.2 Elements of political rhetoric in the Fascist and post-Fascist eras. Diagram by author.

The others were remediated, recycled and repurposed to rebuild the image of a Democratic Republic with Catholic Power at its centre (Figure 1.2). This helps us identify and interpret the traces of the regime as manifest in the contemporary city, consider what they may have meant to the people of the time and reflect on how their shifting meanings impact the twenty-first century.

Romanità *(Roman-ness)*

Romanità situates Rome as the capital of Western civilization. For the Fascist Regime Rome, as both city and concept, was past, present and future together. Because the Roman past was a time of order and discipline distinguished by human, artistic, literary and technological achievement, it

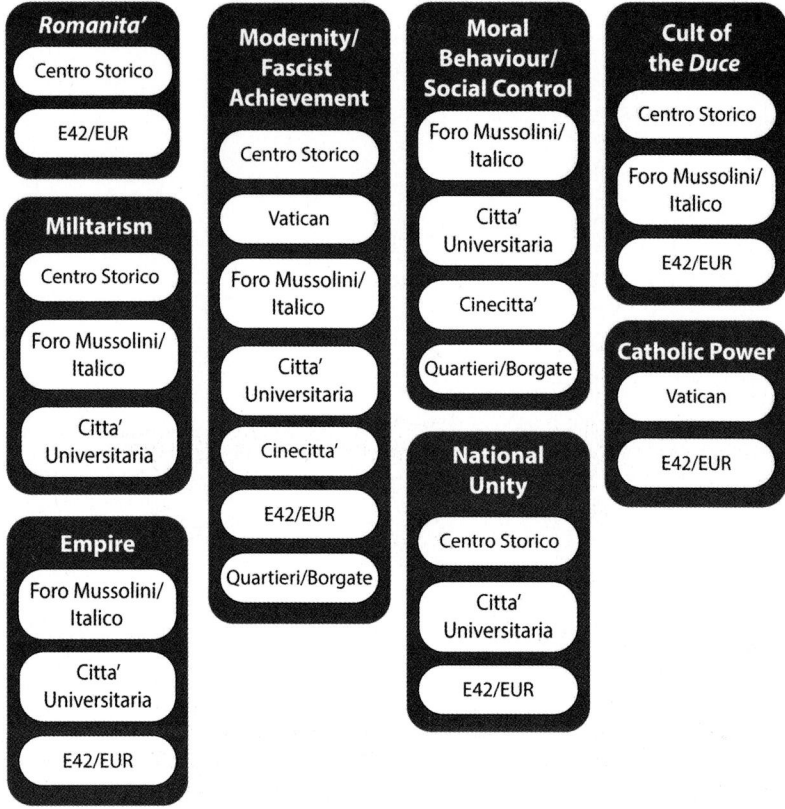

FIGURE 1.3 The relationship between nodes and political rhetoric in the Fascist and post-Fascist eras. Diagram by author.

was mobilized in the service of propaganda. *Romanità* was a key pillar of the framework of political religion and a powerful force behind the will to power. It achieved consistency by intervening in civic space through urban planning principles, architectural form, as subject for art and in the practice of epigraphy. There was a revival of ancient Roman techniques such as mosaic and fresco embedded into the architecture turning Rome into a

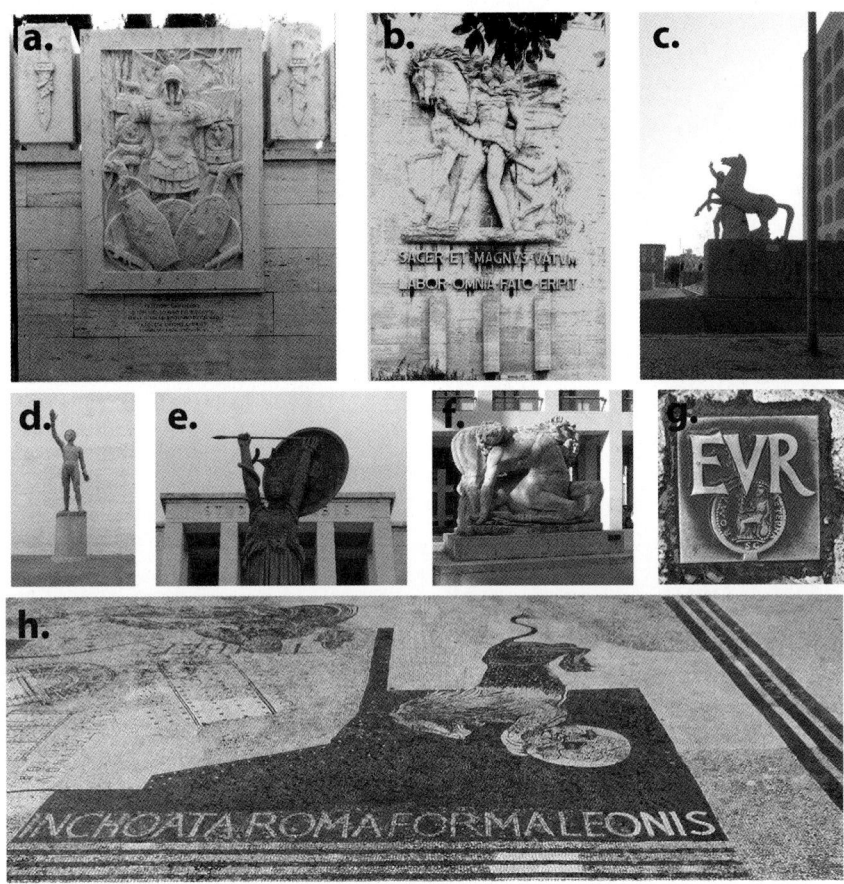

FIGURE 1.4 Examples of *Romanità* in Fascist-era public art in Rome. Montage by author of photographs by Ian Woodcock and author. a. Unknown, Trophies, bas relief, Janiculum Ossuary; b. Corrado Vigni, Castor/Pollux, bas relief, Faculty of Arts, *Città Universitaria*; c. Publio Morbiducci, Castor/Pollux, statue, Italian Civilisation Building, E42/EUR; d. Italo Griselli, Genius of Fascism/Sport, statue, Office Building, E42/EUR; e. Arturo Martini, Minerva, statue, *Città Universitaria*; f. Dino Basaldella, Lion and Centaur, statue, Office Building, E42/EUR; Unknown, EUR logo, bas relief, E42/EUR; h. Giulio Rosso, *Inchoata Roma forma leonis*, mosaic, Piazzale dell'Impero/Foro Italico.

twenty-four-hour public art gallery (Figure 1.4).[4] This was further bolstered by capillary dissemination into the hearts and minds of all Italians with the symbol of the Party – the lictoral fasces, through journals, newspapers, radio and cinema and, at a more ephemeral level, through parades and rituals such as the Fascist salute and the *passo romano* (Roman goosestep). Fascism wanted to realize a new Italy that was at the same time a 'Roman Italy': strong, disciplined and imperial. In this way, the past could act as a regenerative force to both define and secure the future.

Nowhere was *Romanità* more present than in the ancient ruins of Node 1: the *centro storico*. Their excavation, restoration and reconstruction were key to fashioning Fascist Rome. First, they presented an opportunity to undertake a series of major demolition projects. Second, they allowed for the physical (and conceptual) removal of a period of urban and architectural history without a readily perceptible governing order. Third, they provided a scenic background of an idealized imperial past to bolster the rhetorics of Militarism and Empire. And finally, they symbolized a glorious past to be matched (if not outstripped) by the grand monuments of the Fascist era itself. It was also central to the layout and overall architectural style of Node 6: E42/EUR, the site of the unrealized Olympics of Civilisation Expo of 1942.

In the post-war period, *Romanità* was divested of the political trappings added to give legitimacy to the regime and its leader and simply claimed back as belonging to the Italian nation. The *centro storico* continues to be the central node expressing *Romanità* and, in what became the suburb of EUR, *Romanità* remains studded throughout what is primarily 1950s and 1960s building stock. Thanks to our continued fascination and veneration for the world of ancient Rome, this element of Fascist rhetoric has enjoyed the greatest continuity and, with the exception of most (but not all) the fasces, has neither been erased nor cancelled (Figure 6.1).

Militarism

Militarism was a key aspect of Fascism beginning with its very foundation in 1919 as the *Fasci di combattimento* (Battle Fasces) and was connected to both the Futurist war credo and the interventionist campaigns that led Italy into the First World War. Militarism was woven into Fascism's secular religion with its own set of myths, rites and symbols based on *Romanità* that also translated into the Cult of the *Duce*. Militarism's dual aim was to govern Italians and shape them into a new (Fascist) humanity. Militaristic language was used in Mussolini's speeches from the early 1920s reaching its peak during the colonial campaigns when it merged with the rhetoric of Empire.[5] The martial climate was also kept alive with continued references to battles of the *Risorgimento*, Italy's triumphs in the First World War, the blood spilt in the name of the Fascist Revolution, Italy's involvement in the

Spanish Civil War alongside Franco and the invasion of Ethiopia. It was manifest in Node 1: the *centro storico* with the exaltation of the Tomb of the Unknown Soldier in the *Vittoriano* (Victor Emanuel Monument) and the many military parades and rallies held in the new, wide straight avenues that were driven through it.

To ensure the perpetuity of the regime Militarism was inculcated into the next generation of Fascists and was core to the symbolic apparatus of both Node 3: the *Foro Mussolini/Italico* and Node 4: the *Città Universitaria*. Dressed in awkward uniforms with mini muskets draped across their shoulders, they were taught gestures, fed a steady diet of *Heroes and Martyrs* and learned slogans like *Libro e moschetto, fascista perfetto* (Book and musket, Perfect Fascist).[6] Outside school they belonged to the *Opera Nazionale Balilla* (the Fascist Youth Organisation) which began as a semi-independent youth organization not dissimilar to the Boy Scouts and was later absorbed into the *Gioventù Italiana del Littorio (GIL)*. The GIL organized the lives of young Italians as part of the *leva fascista* (Fascist conscription), training them in military-style gymnastics, taking them on excursions to military bases and building military culture into the school curriculum.[7] For a select elite this continued into their university education.

After the fall of the regime, militarist culture did an about-face and became the foundation of the armed Resistance. As with *Romanità*, the *Risorgimento* belonged once more to Democracy and the martyrs of the Resistance were celebrated in place of the martyrs of the Fascist Revolution. Although the First Republic was founded on the ideals of peace and democracy, the post-war period continued to celebrate Italian success in the First World War in Node 1: the *centro storico* with military parades that reclaimed the monuments appropriated by Fascism and spaces wrought around them. Many monuments and memorials were also built to Resistance heroes and events but that is material for its own book. Militarism also made a return during the so-called *anni di piombo* (Lead/Bullet Years) when bombings and assassinations on the part of extremist left- and right-wing groups, who had been marginalized by the dominant centrist politics, created a whole new type of martial climate that cast a veil of darkness over much of the 1970s and 1980s.

Empire

Closely connected to the themes of *Romanità* and Militarism, the Empire theme became especially popular in 1936 when Fascist troops invaded Ethiopia and Mussolini proclaimed Fascist Italy an empire. But imperialism was not unique to Mussolini. Italy's Liberal State had had its eye on colonial possessions since the 1860s, Eritrea became an Italian colony in 1887 and Somalia was taken six years later. Italy craved Ethiopia's mineral riches but failed to secure them after a crushing defeat at Adowa in 1896, a humiliation only partly assuaged by the taking of Libya after the Italo-Turkish War of 1911–12. Ethiopia was like a big slice of colonial pie that Italy had bitten into and could not swallow. Decades later Fascist Imperialism provided the impetus for the next attempt to take Ethiopia fuelled by hyperkinetic Nationalism, resurrected *Romanità*, an obsession with colonial conquest as manifest destiny, a need to find receptacles for excess population, a desire for vengeance and a thirst to establish Italy as a bellicose and virile nation.[8] The centrality of Empire for Fascist society was expressed in Node 1: the *centro storico* with the Stele of Aksum, Node 3: the *Foro Mussolini/Italico*'s Piazzale dell'Impero, Node 4: the *Città Universitaria*, was inaugurated as Italian troops were invading Ethiopia and in the very DNA of Node 6: E42/EUR, conceived as the Fascist empire was declared in 1936.

As a former ally of Nazi Germany, Italy relinquished its colonial possessions at the 1946/47 Paris Peace Conference and agreed to give back much of its war booty. But Rome still has many traces connected to this time and their relative obscurity has nonetheless facilitated a dangerous process of conveniently forgetting Imperialist sentiment turned in to an apologist myth of *Italiani brava gente* or the 'good imperialists' that remains either hidden or absent throughout the *centro storico*.

Modernity/Fascist achievement

Much of Fascism's political rhetoric was centred on the concept of its own special take on modernity or in Mussolini's own words 'marching into the future with one foot firmly planted on the past'. Fascism's ideas of its own future – whether it be hyper-technological or dynamic, cosmopolitan or defined by rural idylls – were inextricably linked to a range of idealized pasts: from the pre-Roman to the Renaissance, from the imperial Roman to the *Risorgimento*.[9] With this brand of modernity and an inordinate amount of government expenditure, the Fascist regime was able to chalk up substantial achievements and all seven nodes were presented as physical proof thereof. With the collaboration of Italy's chief industrialists, much of Italy's modern communication and transport networks over road, rail and sea were built in the twenties and thirties.

The *ventennio* was also a boon for state-backed cultural production: the Venice Biennale and Rome Quadriennale of Art, the Milan Triennale of Decorative Arts and two exhibitions of Rationalist architecture. Then there was the establishment of Italy's national *Enciclopedia italiana*, the Istituto LUCE – (*L'Unione Cinematografia Educativa* – Union of Educational Cinema), a new campus for Rome's *La Sapienza* university – the *Città Universitaria* (Node 4) and state-of-the-art film studios at *Cinecittà* (Node 5). Despite attempts at creating unitary expression, Fascist culture was both heterogeneous and highly instrumentalized. It was shaped by modernist socio-political ethic and displayed a high degree of originality, artistry, creativity and visionary passion[10]. It is important to keep these two points in mind when understanding how it was then dealt with in the post-war period because historical distance separates instrumentality from originality, artistry and creativity.

There was also socio-economic transformation brought about by the Corporative State. This so-called 'Third Way' between Communism and Capitalism allowed the regime to gain control over industry and commerce in a way that simultaneously rejected left-wing politics and gave market forces free rein.[11] This economic reform, together with significant financial input from the United States' Marshall Plan, paved the way for the *miracolo economico* (Economic Miracle) that brought Italy back into the club of modern, industrialized democracies.

On the one hand, these Fascist achievements, in their various states of completion, provided the much-needed housing stock, infrastructure and services for a city under reconstruction and continued expansion. This allowed the government of the First Republic to pick up the vestiges of the Third Rome and either complete or transform them in the name of reconstructing their democratic, peace-loving and Catholic nation built on honest labour. This can also be seen in the rebirth of E42/EUR and its use, along with the *Foro Mussolini/Italico* for the 1960 Olympics. On the other hand, it provided fodder for an *apologia* of the *ventennio* for that minority who continued believing in the Fascist faith.

Moral behaviour/social control

Fascism's social order was also predicated on new norms of moral behaviour and control. It was manifest in public space with new forms of Fascist ritual connected to martyrs for the Revolution, a suite of new anniversaries and national holidays with the requisite parades and rallies to celebrate them. Under Fascism public space went from being a space for the people into a space of symbolism and ceremony.[12]

A new society called for a new Moral Behaviour, and this was reinforced through newspapers, magazines, literature, popular songs, newsreels and cinema. It was embodied in how people moved through coordinated gymnastic displays, goose step marching and gestures like the Fascist salute. It was heard in how they spoke with the catechism of slogans like *credere obbedire combattere* or the use of the *voi* address in place of the bourgeois *lei*. It was seen in the men's blackshirts, the children's uniforms and even women's hairdos. These new forms of behaviour were both underpinned and surveilled by a capillary distribution of *Case del Fascio* (local Party headquarters) and *Dopolavoro* (after-work circles) together with a reformed education system working in tandem with *Case Balilla/GIL* (local Fascist youth headquarters) and the *Opera Nazionale Maternità e Infanzia* (Maternal and Child Health Centres – OMNI).

In the post-war period, public space was reclaimed by the people who celebrated new national holidays in the streets or poured out into the piazzas to protest. The populations of Node 7 in the *quartieri* and *borgate* burgeoned after the war and their Fascist institutions, once stripped of their regalia, were happily repurposed for the needs of the population and could both contribute to the *miracolo economico* (Economic Miracle) and act as evidence for Modernity/Democratic Achievement while Moral Behaviour/Social Control became once more the sole province of Catholic Power.

National Unity

The idea of National Unity under Fascism was strongly tied to Militarism, Empire and the Cult of the *Duce*. Where the Monarchy and the Liberal State had failed, the War effort and the Fascist State would succeed. Italy's process of unification, known as the *Risorgimento* (literally, resurgence), gave the nation a modern democratic system with a king as head of state and was harnessed as an element of Fascist propaganda, broadly by couching it as an incomplete or failed revolution and specifically by appropriating its heroes. The Fascist concept of National Unity was also built upon the interventionist movement that was lobbying the Salandra government to enter the First World War. The 'fraternity of the trenches' united the men and the sacrifice of their sons and husbands united the women. National Unity was also encapsulated in slogans such as *Tutto nello Stato, niente al di fuori dello Stato, nulla contro lo Stato* (Everything in the State, nothing outside the State, nothing against the State).

After the fall of the regime, National Unity and the notion of the *patria* (Fatherland) remained, its principles exchanged with a new set of values at the core of the new Republic: peace, democracy, anti-Fascism, Labour and Catholicism. It is mostly expressed in Node 1: the *centro storico* around the *Vittoriano* on the parades and celebrations that go with the Republic's new set of national holidays.

The Cult of the Duce

The Cult of the *Duce* relied heavily on the mythologization of Mussolini as thinker and man of action, artist and statesman, messiah and prophet propped up by drawing long bows to illustrious figures of the past.[13] He was compared to Socrates and Plato, Julius Caesar and Augustus, Saint Francis, Machiavelli, Napoleon, Mazzini and Garibaldi and why stop there? Even Christ and God because if Fascism is a religion, Mussolini is its central deity.[14] He was in the eyes and ears, the hearts and minds of all Italians. Children learned of his life from their earliest school days, read about him in the newspapers, heard him on the radio, watched him in newsreels, stood for hours in Piazza Venezia to catch a glimpse of him on the balcony and his gaze struck them from portraits in public buildings and living rooms. His face was on key fobs and bottle openers, medals and statuettes. Artists portrayed him in many guises and styles, often on horseback like an emperor, and usually at the apex of the composition.[15]

This concentration of power and authority into the single body of Mussolini contributed to his own and the regime's downfall. Without Mussolini there could be no Fascism and without Fascism there was no regime. As a result, images of the *Duce* were the first to be subjected to widespread iconoclasm. As soon as the fall of Fascism was announced on the very radios he had provided in nearly every home, the streets were littered with broken glass for the 1000s of framed portraits of the *Duce* that flew, with a flourish of freedom, out of apartment windows up and down the country. The face that, for two decades, had watched over the life of an entire nation from the walls of schools, offices and living rooms was being trampled under the heels of those dancing for joy.

In the post-war period, any veneration of images of the *Duce* and other forms of Fascist paraphernalia was effectively outlawed by the 1952 Scelba Law but that only drove enthusiasts underground. Aside from the rare extant examples of monumental art images of Mussolini were not shown to the public until 1997 while underground trade and veneration of these objects continues apace on eBay.

Catholic power

By 1929 Fascism had erased all existing political and civic organizations connected to Democracy, the next step was to ally itself strategically with the Church. The Pope was still smarting from the loss of temporal power after unification, the Vatican was almost bankrupt and its spiritual leadership was being slowly eroded by the Cult of the *Duce*, so the Church agreed to recognize the Kingdom of Italy under the House of Savoy with Rome as its capital and resume diplomatic rapport with the Fascist state. This conciliation was achieved through the Lateran Pacts signed between Mussolini and Cardinal Gasparri on 11 February 1929. By recognizing a reciprocal sovereignty of the Church via an internationally recognized Holy See and the Italian Fascist State the Pacts became one of the definitive acts consolidating the regime's power.[16]

In 'exchange' for sanctioning the reinsertion of both the Catholic hierarchy and the community into Italian political life, the Vatican would receive: a compensation payment of 1.750.000.000 lire (over 1.5bn euros in today's money) for lost revenue, the payment of all priests' salaries by the State, the establishment of Catholicism as the State religion along with its teaching in public schools and the protection of Catholic Action.[17] The Pope was given sovereign rule and tax exemptions for the Vatican as a State in its own right which included the area around St. Peter's and a number of other territorial possessions in Rome.[18]

The Pacts were one of the few pieces of legislation left intact by the First Republic and their anniversary was celebrated as a public ritual until 1977. The pacts embedded the Church into the structure of government and later created the conditions for their new party *Democrazia Cristiana* (DC – Christian Democrats) – founded in 1942 – to take on a key role in Italian post-war politics.[19] Catholic Power sailed through the fall of the regime and into the First Republic on the winds of a uniting faith. They supported the Resistance and, despite accusations that he turned a blind eye to the Holocaust, Pius XII was able to redeem his image by coming out as the *defensor civitatis* (defender of the city) after the Allied bombings of 1944.[20] The DC became the dominant political force by acting as a *partito di raccolta* (Catch-all Party) for people of various political persuasions from ex-Fascists to social conservatives, from ex-Monarchists to moderates and anyone looking for a familiar reference point in a country that had been at war with itself for many years.[21]

It remains manifest in Node 2: the Vatican, the Basilica of Sts. Peter and Paul towering over E42/EUR and the swathes of residential development around the *Quartieri/Borgate* nodes by the Vatican's real estate arm, the *Società Generale Immobiliare* (General Real Estate Development Agency). The extraordinary Holy Year of 2015 (to commemorate fifty years of Vatican II) and preparations for 2025 Holy Year indicate that Catholic Power continues to shape the urban development of Rome. 8.2 bn euros have been set aside for everything from skate parks to 150 km of new roads to the completion of the Metro C station at the Colosseum.[22]

A road map through Fascist Rome

This book is neither chronological nor topographic, it is neither history nor guide book, it chooses instead to look at the difficult heritage of Fascist Rome through the lens of shifting meaning. It considers the post-regime city as an assemblage of many parts, from the large-scale urban entity made of plans and realizations, to buildings and monuments all the way down to the writing upon their walls.

Chapter 1 is this introduction. Chapter 2 frames Rome's post-war urban development as the result of an enduring matrix of many threads: planning legislation, public transport networks, continuity in the reins of power, funding models and the Fascist construction of the past. Each of the seven nodes of Fascist Rome originates where two or more of these threads intersect and by tracing them through each node we can measure two things. First, the extent to which the plans and visions of the Fascists were realized and, second, the different approaches taken by the post-war democratic government to harness the legacy left by the fallen regime to rebuild its new capital.

Working its way through the seven nodes, Chapter 3 traces the post-war fate of Fascist era architecture from the most politically charged government institutions to everyday buildings like apartments and schools and how this was connected to their expression of one or more elements of Fascist rhetoric. Once they had been completed or cleansed of overtly Fascist elements they have either continued their functions or have been repurposed into a range of uses to match the historical climate.

Because it is such a rich and complex node of Fascist Rome, Chapter 4 is dedicated entirely to the architecture of Rome's EUR quarter. As the incomplete and abandoned site of the 1942 International Expo it is often considered the lost fantasy of an ideal Fascist city. This chapter uses a narrative walk to propose a different reality: a building-by-building story of how this assemblage of Italy's most identifiably Fascist architecture is immersed in a collection of post-war urban and architectural vicissitudes that paint a fascinating picture of Italy's post-war history.

Chapter 5 focusses on the changing meanings of Rome's Fascist era monuments that were used to shore up Fascist rhetoric. First, by appropriating pre-existing monuments for their own propaganda ends; second, by building new monuments to figures and events from the past namely ancient Rome, the *Risorgimento*, the 19th C colonial enterprise or the First World War and third, by creating monuments dedicated to the heroes, anniversaries and important events of the Fascist regime. Many were reclaimed, some deleted and others remain.

Chapter 6 focusses right down to the scale of epigraphy and inscriptions whose genesis, changing meaning, re-inscription and erasure tell a story of politics and counter-politics, heroes and villains, memory and forgetting. Told through the lens of Fascist rhetoric, the many inscriptions, symbols and plaques from this era still continue to act as testimonials of the aspirations, mandates and illusions of the fallen regime.

The final chapter reflects on how this assemblage makes up the city of Rome and shows its continuing capacity to communicate and encapsulate changing political climates by tracing their fate over different post-war periods we can reveal the many facets of Italy's complex relationship with its Fascist past.

CHAPTER TWO

Mussolini's mark

Tracing the legacy of Fascism in Rome's post-war urban planning

Alla periferia si costruiscono i nuovi quartieri, si disegnano le strade al termine delle quali i riverberi del gas brillano melanconicamente e segnano la fine del sobborgo. È una nuova città che sorge e cinge la vecchia. Non più le viuzze del centro strette, sudicie, paurose: ma ampi viali alberati, le strade che si lanciano nella distesa verde della campagna, quasi a sollecitare la plebe rurale a dar l'assalto alla città

In the outskirts new suburbs are being built, new roads are being traced. Where they end gas lamps shine a melancholy light as if to mark the edge of the city. It is a new city, one that rises and encircles the old one. No more narrow, filthy, frightening laneways but wide tree-lined avenues that launch into the green expanse of the countryside as if inviting the peasants to storm the city.

MUSSOLINI – THE SPRAWLING CITIES, 12 AUGUST 1909.[1]

Introduction

According to the 2019 census, there are nearly 3,000,000 people living in Rome within a metropolitan area of nearly 1,300 square kilometres. In 1920, just two years before Mussolini came to power the city was the same as when it had become capital of a united Italy in 1870 with its population of 500,000 concentrated in the *centro storico* (the historic centre). By 1931 the city had doubled in size and ten years later its population had gone past the million mark, with the biggest area of growth in the new *quartieri* (inner suburbs). By 1961, when the phoenix of the *miracolo economico* (Economic Miracle) had risen from the ashes of the war, Rome's population had more than doubled again to 2,256,000. The city had grown exponentially to match with a significant redistribution of the population: inhabitants of the *centro storico* virtually halved while those in the *quartieri* nearly doubled.[2] In this way, Rome continued its 'oil stain' expansion with unregulated speculative development despite the best intentions of urban growth plans.[3]

In July 1943 when the Grand Council of Fascism voted to divest Mussolini of his executive powers, Rome was a very different city to the one he had ostensibly seized in the name of his new Party in October 1922. Like Augustus who 'found a city of brick and left it a city of marble',[4] so did Mussolini find a capital 'of a little people of antiquarians' that he intended to leave 'vast, ordered, powerful, as it was in the times of Augustus' first empire [...] the pulsating centre of a renewed Italian nation [...] the marvellous capital of the entire Latin world.'[5] Like Augustus before him, the *Duce* was to be inscribed into the very fabric of the city.[6] To that end the *ventennio* (the twenty years of the Fascist regime) saw an unprecedented scale of demolition, excavation and construction enabled by swiftly drawn up (and approved) structure plans, special legislation and outright autocratic decisions made by a new city administration called a *governatorato* (governorate).[7]

In 1925 the former mayor Filippo Cremonesi was instated as the first governor in a pompous ceremony held on the Anniversary of the Birth of Rome where Mussolini handed him a list of tasks:

> You will continue to free the great oak from all that still overshadows it. You will create space around the Augustan Mausoleum, the Theatre of Marcellus, the Capitoline, the Pantheon. Everything that has grown in the centuries of decadence must disappear. In five years, the Pantheon, thanks to a large opening, must be visible from Piazza Colonna. You will also free the majestic temples of Christian Rome from the parasitic and profane constructions around them. The thousand-year-old monuments of our own history must stand like giants in their necessary solitude. In this way the Third Rome will expand over other hills, along the banks of the sacred river, down to the beaches of the Tyrrhenian Sea.[8]

As we will discover, the last sentence has proved to be eerily prophetic and is still visible today above the colonnade of the E42/EUR's *Palazzo Uffici* (Office Building).

The threads of the Fascist matrix

Rome's post-war urban development was the result of a complex interplay of legal, economic, political and social factors or threads which wove together into what I have called a Fascist matrix that has continued to shape the contemporary city beyond the existence of the regime itself. These threads intersect at significant nodes, like cities within the city, that have left behind significant architectural, urban and symbolic legacies. These nodes are the Node 1: *centro storico* (or Historic City as bounded by the Aurelian walls), Node 2: the Vatican State (or City of Religion), Node 3: the *Foro Mussolini/Italico* (or City of Sport on the northern edge of the city at the feet of the untouched Monte Mario), Node 4: the *Città Universitaria* (or City of Learning), Node 5: *Cinecittà* (or City of Cinema, the massive complex of studios built to feed the propaganda machine along the Via Tuscolana), Node 6: E42/EUR (the suburb built on the framework of the planned World Expo of 1942) and Node 7: a more distributed residential node made up of additive interventions to absorb the city's demographic and topographical expansion: the *quartieri* and *borgate* (a term adapted from the word *borgo* meaning small rural town but essentially outer suburbs with none of their history or charm) (Figure 1.1). Public and private actors worked together to build the new *quartieri* (inner suburbs) for the middle classes each with its own after-work circle, maternal health centre, youth organizations and party headquarters and, further out the *borgate* (outer suburbs), for the urban poor either rendered homeless by the demolitions or flocking to the capital in search of work. This set up a social geography that continues to this day. Inner *quartieri* like Parioli, Trieste and Quartiere Africano remain predominantly middle class and lean politically to the right if not declaredly neo-Fascist while others like the Tufello, Pietralata and Quadraro are for the most part working class and are firmly left-wing if not outright Communists.[9] In the post-war period each node had a different effect on the city's post-war urban development and identity. E42/EUR and the housing nodes had the most impact on urban development while the *centro storico* and the Vatican were re-used for their symbolic power in a bid to re-forge a new national identity.

The Fascist matrix is made up of the following threads: planning legislation, regulatory plans and development control, public transport infrastructure, concentrated landownership, continuities of power, public-private as well as foreign-local funding models, *abusivismo* (rogue development), internal migration and special events that gave access to both extraordinary funding and exemption from development control.

Of these threads, I have chosen to focus on the pervasive power of Fascist-era planning legislation and development control to give a history of Rome's post-war city planning. I will then discuss the seven nodes of Fascist Rome, their generation and their continued impact on Rome's urban development.

Planning legislation

Of the many threads of the Fascist matrix, the instruments of planning legislation and development control were the 'thickest' and most prevalent. They were the 1942 planning law n. 1150 which is incidentally, still in force and was amended eight times throughout the 1950s and 1960s mostly to change the validity of the existing plans and their mode of implementation.[10]

City planning in the Fascist era was about selective execution and harnessing the image of the city for political ends made possible by a totalitarian structure called a governorate. Its governor (directly appointed by and answerable to Mussolini) had an unprecedented level of authority and executive power which, given the aristocratic string of governors, was of great advantage to large landowners.[11] As we will see, this advantage did not disappear when Rome went back to being a democratically elected council.

Piano Regolatore *1931 (1931 Regulatory Plan – PR31)*

Catering for a projected population of two million, the PR31 was less a plan and more a 'collage' of a series of preceding ones: four independent plans drawn up by groups of architects and a significant *variante* (modification) of the pre-existing 1909 plan, the *Variante Generale* 1925-6 (1925-6 General Variant – VG25-6).[12] It was drawn up and approved in the space of six months and effectively remained in force until the 1960s. It aimed to create a modern city based on order and efficiency through the lens of *Romanità* with new parts built and old parts selectively demolished to represent the vision presented to the governor five years before. Despite the PR31's directives for controlled urban growth, Rome continued to expand like an 'oil stain' thanks to the matrix thread of unregulated speculative development that responded to continued population increase and was facilitated by new expropriation provisions in the *piani particolareggiati* (detailed plans).[13]

The PR31 had to solve two types of problems for twentieth-century Rome, as outlined by Mussolini in a 1924 speech, those related to necessity and those related to grandeur that also aligned with key themes of Fascist rhetoric: *Romanità*, Fascist Modernity/Achievement and Moral Behaviour/Social Control.[14] These were solved by the parallel processes of destroying the old and creating the new. The 'centuries of decadence' were done away with by *sventramenti* (literally gutting or disembowelment), a term used by architects and urbanists of the time to refer to whatever 'cuts' into the urban fabric were deemed necessary to accommodate city life.

With the upcoming tenth anniversary of the March on Rome, the other priority was to lay bare the Rome of the Caesars for the world to see, while the 'misery' of the working classes was banished from the *centro storico* node to the urban periphery, out of sight and out of mind. A total of two million cubic metres of buildings were demolished between 1922 and 1937 with 50,000 homes razed to the ground between 1927 and 1931.[15] This added 50,000 families to the list of people needing a home along with a growing influx of people to the Capital despite the best efforts of the Party's rural ideology. These families had enjoyed the advantage of living in the heart of the *centro storico* but the misfortune to live in homes deemed by Mussolini to be 'parasitic and profane constructions'. The *sventramenti* had a dual function: to create clean, ordered avenues for staging the theatre of consent and 'cleansing' the city centre of its disorderly and unsightly housing stock, inhabited, for the most part, by working poor who often eked out a living with a handcraft or trade and whose shop was on the very street that they lived in, if not directly above it. When entire city blocks near the centres of power at Piazza Venezia and St. Peter's were razed to the ground to make way for the Via dell'Impero, the Via del Mare or Via della Conciliazione the inhabitants were forcibly relocated to the *borgate*. Despite evoking a romanticized rural life, they were what the outspoken critic of all Fascist urban design, Antonio Cederna described as 'out and out architectural and urban planning obscenities, concentration camps for workers not considered worthy to be living in the city centre'.[16]

The avenues and piazzas of the *centro storico* became spaces for the pomp and ceremony of Fascist ritual or stage set for the theatre of consent. These spaces were later appropriated for a new kind of pomp and ceremony of the democratic state and its new national holidays: 25 April, the anniversary of Italy's liberation from Fascism (in 1946), and 2 June, the declaration of the Italian Republic.

Variante Generale *1941–2* (*1941–2 General Variant – VG41-2)*

Rome grew so fast in the 1930s that the PR31 was quickly superseded and new areas of planned expansion needed to be provided. Mussolini called together a new planning committee to draw up the *Piano Regolatore del Ventennale* (20th Anniversary Regulatory Plan) to celebrate the twenty-year anniversary of the March on Rome, little did they know that it would continue to determine the future development of the city for more than twenty years after his death (Figure 2.1). Then Governorate Secretary Virgilio Testa

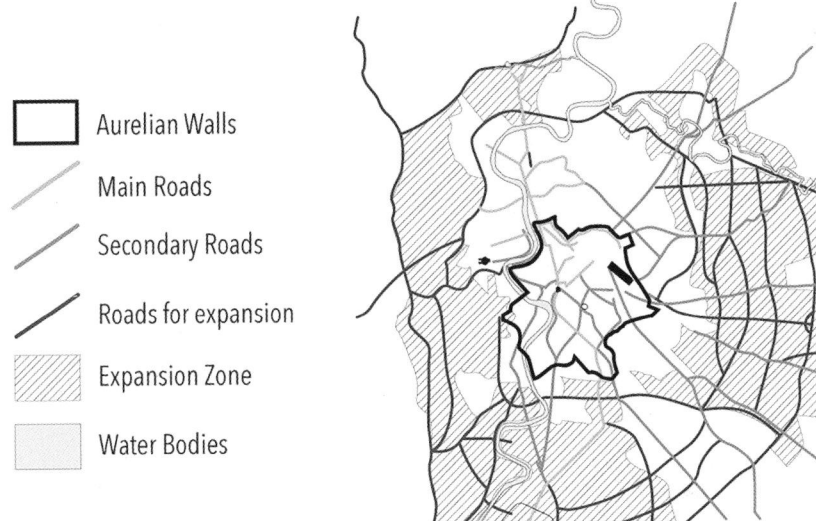

FIGURE 2.1 1941/2 General Variant of 1931 Regulatory Plan for Rome (VG41/2) as reconstructed by Insolera and Mancini. Drawing by Kylie Burns and author.

had been angling for Rome's expansion towards the southwest since 1935 and was finally able to make it happen in the 1950s as the commissioner of EUR.[17] What was imagined by Governor Bottai, Testa, Piacentini and Mussolini as the foundation for the Third Rome of Fascism became – after its rebirth – *Città parco della Roma moderna* (the Park-City of Modern Rome).

Ultimately the VG41-2 threaded itself through all of Rome's succeeding planning efforts and its persistent afterlife together with elements of the PR31 and the reins of power in the hands of characters like Testa prompted Rome's most prominent urban historian, Italo Insolera, to pose the poignant questions: how did the anti-Fascism of the post-war period manage to skip urban planning?[18] If we have refused and revised so much of the Fascist past why have we let its planning frameworks stay in place? Ardent Marxist that he was, he saw the answer in the continuity of landownership and speculative interests but as we will discover in this chapter, both the questions and the answers are rather more complex.

Piano Regolatore *1962 (1962 Regulatory Plan – PR62)*

To answer Insolera's question, attempts were made to 'de-fascistise' the cities. In 1946, while Rome was transitioning from Governorate to an elected city council under Prince Doria Pamphilj, Rome's only anti-Fascist aristocrat saw the need to update both the PR31 and the VG41-2. *Anti-fascistazzione* (de-fascistization) was sweeping the nation with fasces chiselled off buildings, plaques and statues being taken down and entire ministries dissolved and reorganized. But to 'de-fascistise' Italian cities, whose future urban development was enshrined in law via Fascist Regulatory Plans, was a far more complex proposition. Planners and urban designers had to regroup and work out, first, how to erase the most grandiose and scenographic parts of these plans and Rome's was the most grandiose of all. Second, they had to undo those elements that signalled Rome as the Capital of the Fascist empire and, third, they needed to realize the post-war Capital of a Democratic Republic. All this whilst recovering from the devastation of war with a virtually non-functioning public transport network, an exacerbated housing crisis and no real demographic data. Fascism's attempts to impose a modern road system onto an ancient centre had not only failed but had actually made things worse by concentrating more vehicular traffic within the city's politically symbolic centre, Piazza Venezia. Internal migration of unskilled workers had created an underclass whose needs went beyond housing and would adversely affect the urban development if the City Council did not also address employment and training.[19]

Luigi Piccinato, in what turned out to be an admirable but unrealistic spurt of optimism, declared: 'At the threshold of a new cycle in [Roman] life, we need to, at least this time, get serious'.[20] The journey towards the 1962 plan had a number of 'stops along the way' and consisted in a back and forth of plans and resolutions which reflected who had control of City Council. But drawing up a new plan that could do all this (and do it with a democratic process) took several years, and while the fate of Rome's new regulatory plan was subject to ever more complex negotiations, E42/EUR was going full steam ahead subverting more optimal urban growth zones, the Vatican's *Società Generale Immobiliare* – (General Real Estate Company – SGI) and other real estate consortia had risen in power and were taking advantage of a succession of *piani particolareggiati* (detailed structure plans) that, combined with elements of the national planning law, allowed for higher and higher densities.[21]

The first step towards the PR62 was the 1946 Traffic Plan. It came out of the anti-Fascist *Comitato Liberazione Nazionale* (National Liberation Committee – CLN) rule and went against the pre-existing plans by removing traffic in the city centre and improving conditions in the *borgate*.[22] Then, after gaining some breathing space by extending the PR31's validity, a succession of Centre-right (1947–1952) and Centre (1952–1956) coalitions put together the people and process necessary for a new plan. They set up an *Ufficio Speciale Nuovo Piano Regolatore* (Special Office for the New Regulatory Plan – USNPR) who would work with an 80-member special commission and an 8-member *Comitato di Elaborazione Tecnica* (Technical Drafting Committee – CET) who presented a new plan by 1955. The CET proposed *centri direzionali* (decentralized business districts) in the East at Pietralata and Centocelle and an expressway called the *asse attrezzato*

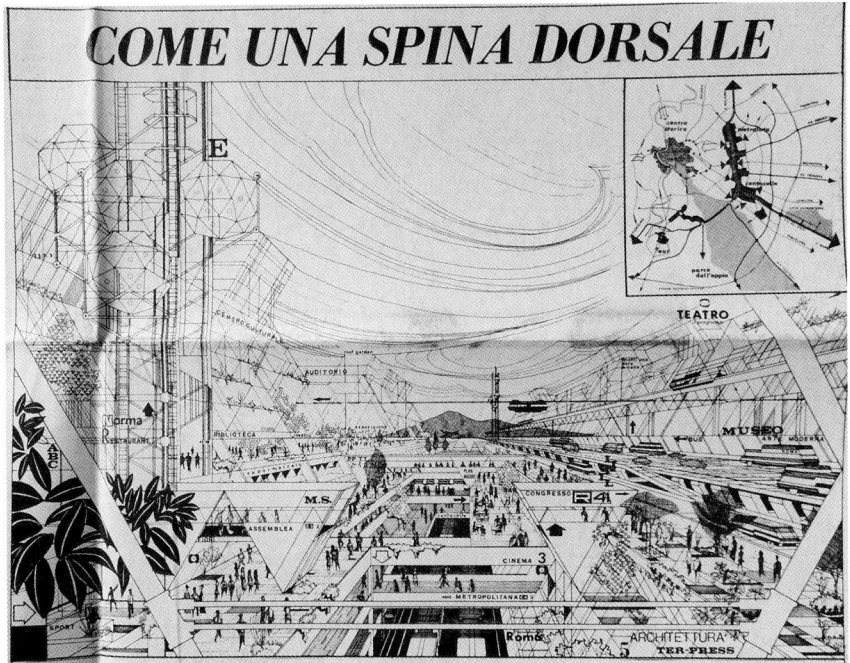

FIGURE 2.2 *Comitato di Elaborazione Tecnica* (Technical Drafting Committee – CET), Perspective drawing of Social Infrastructure Axis (*Asse attrezzato*) From *Il Giornale d'Italia*, 25–26 September 1970. Testa archive, Box 8. Archivio Centrale di Stato, Rome.

(social infrastructure axis) which connected to new arterial roads and would feed into Italy's first major post-war infrastructure project: the *Autostrada del Sole* connecting Milan to Naples via Rome and inaugurated in 1964 (Figure 2.2). The *Asse* would also improve access to *borgate* in the north-east like Tufello and San Basilio and Gordiani on the Via Prenestina then onwards to serve EUR and (paradoxically) help realize many aspects of Fascist-era planning.[23] To gain approval the CET had to allow for the majority of new development (40 per cent) in the south to favour EUR as the major *centro direzionale*, followed by 30 per cent towards the east and 15 per cent each for the north and the west (Figure 2.3).

But by 1957, just as the CET plan was due to be ratified, a political shift to the right, combined with intense lobbying from landowners, developers and the Minister for Aviation, dissolved the entire set up. The new centre-right coalition (1956–1960) further extended the validity of the PR31 and decided to draw up the 1959 *Giunta* plan (Council Plan) to bring more focus to EUR and more general development towards the sea much to the delight of Testa who was busily resurrecting it, not to mention the

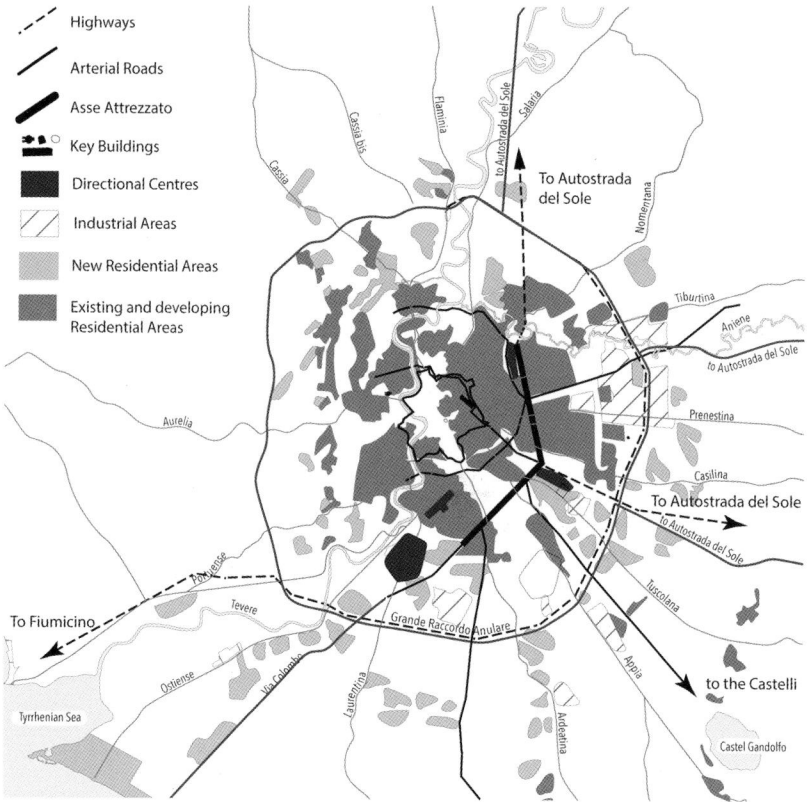

FIGURE 2.3 Technical Drafting Committee, schematic representation of plan for Rome, 1956. Drawing by Kylie Burns and author.

minister who could begin construction of 'his' new international airport at Fiumicino with impunity. The 1959 *Giunta* plan was speedily superseded by the 'Olympic Plan' which used extraordinary infrastructure funding to build new facilities around two key nodes of the Fascist City: *Foro Mussolini/Italico* and E42/EUR.

The centre-right coalition was dissolved following scandals surrounding the new airport so even the *Giunta* Plan failed. Ironically the 1962 Plan was finally completed during a mini-dictatorship with Rome under a prefectoral commissioner, Francesco Diana, that allowed the centre-left Fanfani national Government (1960–2) to intervene in city planning matters. Diana quickly set up a new planning committee who picked up many of the old threads of the CET Plan and wove them around the then fully resurrected E42/EUR to produce the PR62 (Figure 2.4). This plan, finally ratified with modifications five years later, became the PR67 and signalled the final demise of the PR31 and VG41-2. But by then it was too late, with more than twenty years to fully entrench themselves into the very physical, practical and political fabric of the city the effects of both plans will never be fully undone. Like Mussolini, who had to relinquish transforming the First and Second Rome into a Third Rome of Fascism, so did his successors have to give up on transforming Fascist Rome into their Fourth Rome of the First Republic.

The 1962 plan effectively legalized *abusivismo* and put laws in practice to put a brake on it but, by 1977, it became evident that it was not able to stop more than 1,000,000 instances of illegal construction outside of planning criteria.[24] In 1976, the first item on the agenda of Rome's first Communist Party mayor, the art historian Giulio Carlo Argan, was finding ways to undo the effect of Fascism on the city. He went out to fix the *borgate*, deal with the 28 per cent of the city built outside of planning regulations, stitch together the Roman Forums and revive culture with the *Estate Romana* (Roman Summer) Festival.[25]

Public transport networks

Rome's public transport infrastructure is also a legacy of the Fascist period. Today's buses and trams may have different route numbers but they operate down the same streets out to the same neighbourhoods. In 1929 transport was centralized and brought under a single body, the *Azienda Tramvie e Autobus del Governatorato* – (Tram and Bus Agency of the Governorate – ATAG). After the fall of the regime, it became ATAC when the G of Governorate was replaced by the C of *Comune di Roma* (Rome City Council). Reforming and organizing Rome's public transport was part of the rhetoric of modernity and Fascist achievement.[26] In a less quoted section of his *Grande Roma* speech, Mussolini had also charged the Governor with 'removing the stupid contamination of the trams and giving the most modern forms of transport to the new cities which will rise in a ring around the ancient centre'.[27]

Rome was given a radial transport network that traversed the centre and operated across four concentric zones linking opposite ends of the city that later underpinned a continued pattern of oil-stain expansion (Figure 2.5). Rome's principal metro system forms a cross that continues to serve residential areas in the four main cardinal directions. Its initial trunk also came into being thanks to the existence of E42/EUR. What we now know as the Metro B runs from a station called Laurentina, just beyond the boundary of the Expo's initial area and continues all the way out to the Rebibbia jail in the north-east without quite reaching San Basilio, one of the early *borgate* of the 1930s. In the early 2020s extensions to the A, B and C lines and a new D line are under way to take pressure off the Via Olimpica.

Work on tunnels between E42/EUR and Termini began in 1937, they served as air-raid shelters during the Second World War and work began again in 1948.[28] The *Ferrovia dell'E42* (the E42 train) was inaugurated in

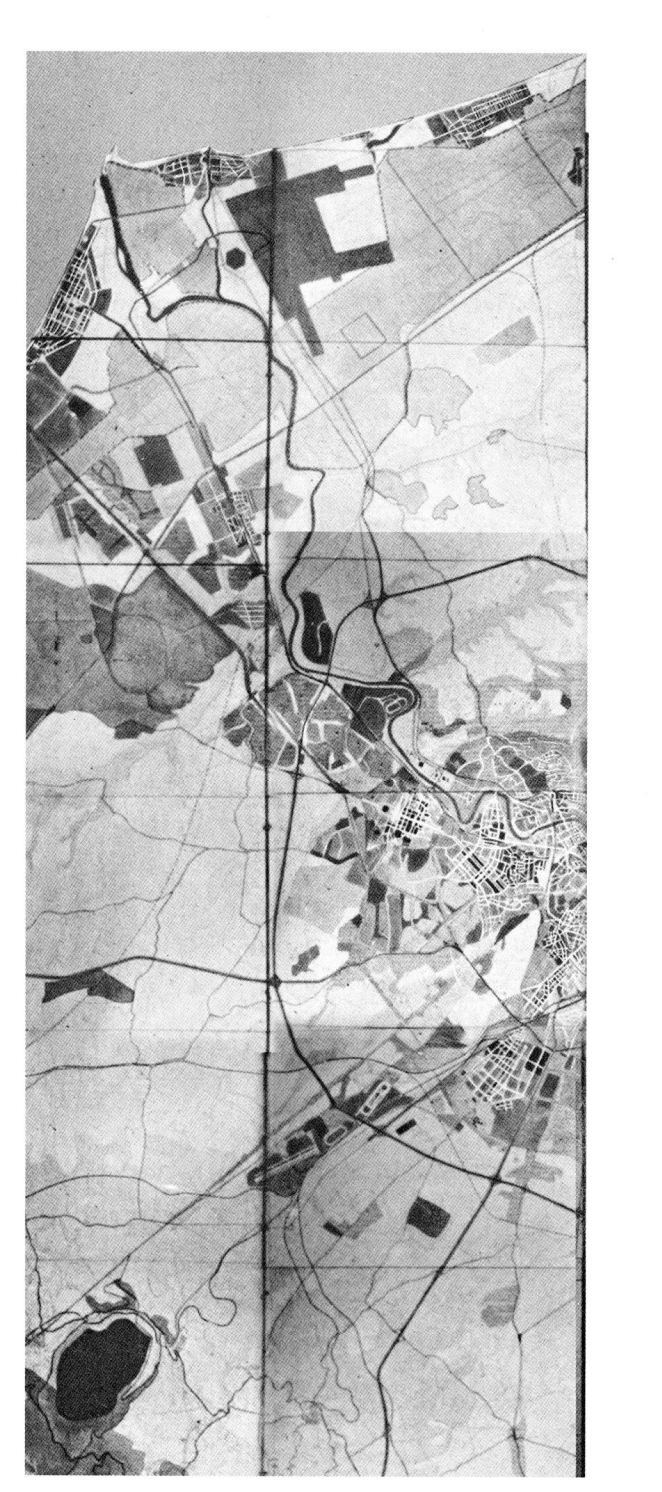

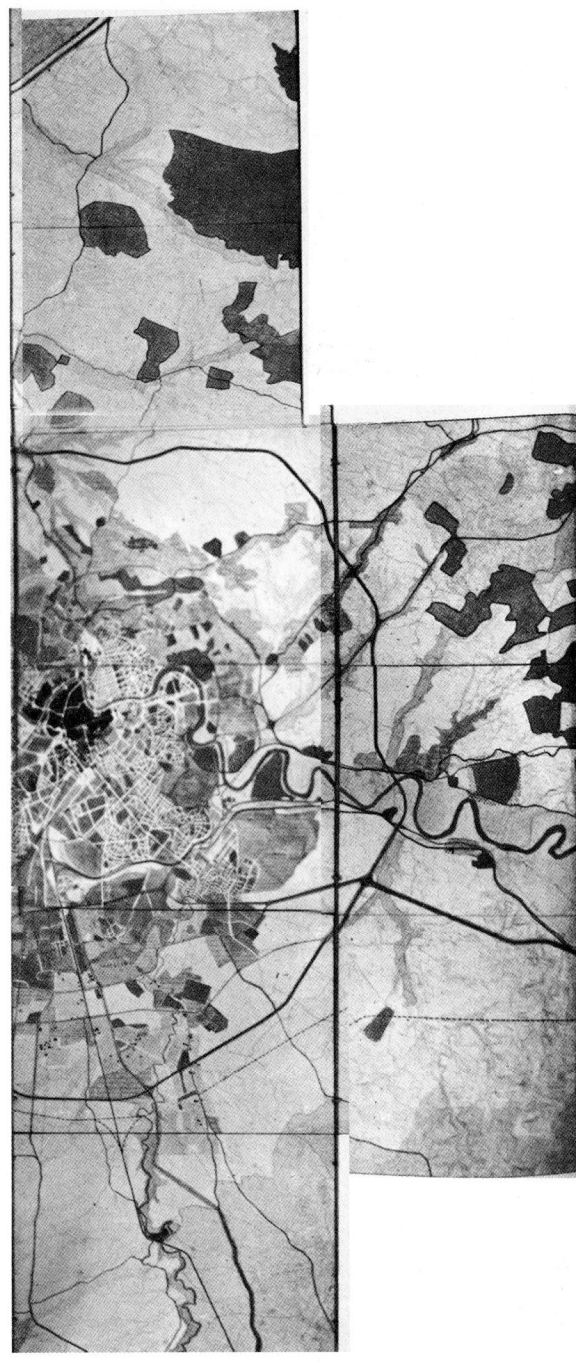

FIGURE 2.4 1962 Regulatory Plan for Rome (PR62). From *Urbanistica*, 1959. Courtesy of Arthur and Janet C. Ross Library, American Academy in Rome.

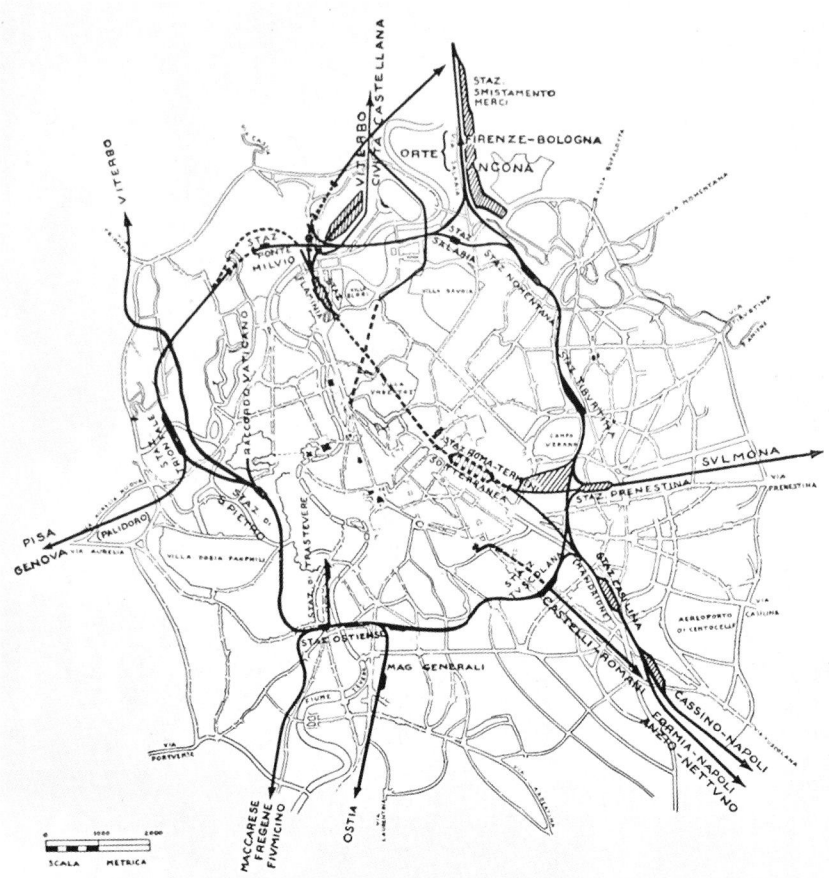

FIGURE 2.5 1931 Regulatory Plan for Rome (PR31), schematic plan showing rail systems. From *Planimetrie del Piano Regolatore 1931 IX. Riproduzione ridotta delle planimetrie allegate at R. decreto legge 6 luglio 1931, n. 981*. Courtesy of Library of British School at Rome.

1955 and changed its name to Metro B when the A line opened in 1980. This line now links Anagnina in the south-east to Battistini in the northwest from Ottaviano and *Cinecittà*. The two initial end stations of the Metro A connected St. Peter's to Anagnina and what later became a heavily populated part of the city built around the Fascist node of *Cinecittà* showing the continued impact of the Fascist legacy. Its extension to serve the ever more populous suburbs of Valle Aurelia and Battistini in the 1990s shows just how much residential development in the southwestern parts of the city was facilitated by the alliance between Vatican and conservative landholding interests who did all they could to conserve the *status quo* of the Fascist matrix.[29]

Land ownership and speculative development

The next threads are related to landownership, its relative value and its continued concentration among aristocrats, co-operatives and powerful real estate consortia such as the SGI. Founded in 1862 by Italian and foreign bankers it played an enormous role in building twentieth-century Rome. Ostensibly founded in the name of public utility, it has built everything from museums to metros, from roads to massive residential developments, from hospitals to hotels. Its list of main shareholders is a list of those with power and influence: in the 1920s it was Governor Cremonesi, in the 1940s the Pope's nephew Marcantonio Pacelli, in the 1960s mafia-connected businessman Michele Sindone.[30] In 1953 it owned 6,750,000 square metres of developable land and was, together with a handful of established families, one of Rome's biggest landowners. The War had brought about a hiatus in construction industry, and this, together with an urgent need for housing, meant that the land owned by these groups had risen exponentially in value.[31] This became the prime driver for development and was one of the contributing factors to the PR31 remaining in force beyond its original expiry date of 1951.

The reins of power

Despite the swift transition back to a democratic city council, mostly in the hands of Christian Democrat mayors, the real power lay with the aforementioned landowners, lobby groups and with individual figures like Virgilio Testa, a self-defined *urbanista* (urban planner/designer) who arguably had more impact on Rome's urban development both during and after the Fascist period than Mussolini, the governors, the planners and all the mayors put together. As the Governorate became increasingly bureaucratic, the power base shifted away from the governor towards its Secretary, Testa. He took charge of all the legal and technical aspects of urban planning and worked behind the scenes to convince then Governor Giuseppe Bottai to locate the site of E42/EUR to the south-west of the city. His vision to expand Rome towards the sea dates to 1929 and in 1951 he was given the opportunity to realize it as Commissioner of E42/EUR, a position he held until 1973, just five years before his death (see Chapter 2, pp. 21 & 45; Chapter 4, pp. 83–5).[32]

Funding models

Two more threads that determined Rome's post-war urban development were connected to pre-existing funding systems and post-war reconstruction policies that were key in shaping the residential nodes. Para-governmental bodies like the *Istituto Nazionale Assicurazioni* – INA (National Insurance Institute), the *Istituto di Case Popolari* (renamed the IACP by adding the word Autonomo) and semi-private housing co-operatives continued to be responsible for building housing stock. This was supplemented by international funding via the US Marshall Plan, the European Recovery Program (ERP) or the United Nations Relief and Rehabilitation Administration (UNRRA) in exchange for promises to keep the Italian Communist Party from taking hold of too much power. In another instance of continuity, the De Gasperi government used a national building programme to create employment.[33]

The third funding system, whose continuity we can trace back to the triumphal parades of the Caesars and Holy Year of 1300, is made up of international scale events requiring special services and infrastructure. This process was largely facilitated by the 1953 Pella Law which allowed Rome's ruling class to (once again) take advantage of extra funding under 'provisions in favour of the city of Rome' as long as it could be reasonably argued that the project they stood to profit from was of benefit to the city overall.[34] The 1950 Holy Year, the 1960 Olympics and the 1990 FIFA (*Fédération Internationale de Football Association*, International Federation of Football Association) World Cup were all events that for better or worse allowed Rome to make use of extraordinary funds and even more extraordinary planning frameworks to complete Fascist projects and realize new infrastructure to perpetuate its complex legacy.[35] As long-time editor of *Corriere della Sera*, Indro Montanelli put it so succinctly:

> Statistics show that Rome's demographic growth has never preceded urban development but followed it. This means that the city acts like a vacuum cleaner. It does not adjust housing offering to meet demand but actually solicits and stimulates the need for it through internal migration. And the ministries are the pretexts to both maintain and increase the flow. And the great exhibitions and International Expos. And the Holy Years. And now the Olympics. Switzerland, who were going to host the Olympics declined. They said that their budget did not allow them to spend billions upon billions on infrastructure that they would not know what to do with afterwards. Rome schemed to gain the Olympics. And I don't hesitate to believe the organisers when they say they will do the kinds of unprecedented things that will be, overall, worthy of the great name and prestige of the Eternal City.[36]

Unplanned or rogue development (abusivismo)

Another important and interwoven thread was the ongoing practice of *abusivismo,* unplanned (or rogue) development which began to impact Rome in the 1930s and 1940s with land being subdivided and sold outside

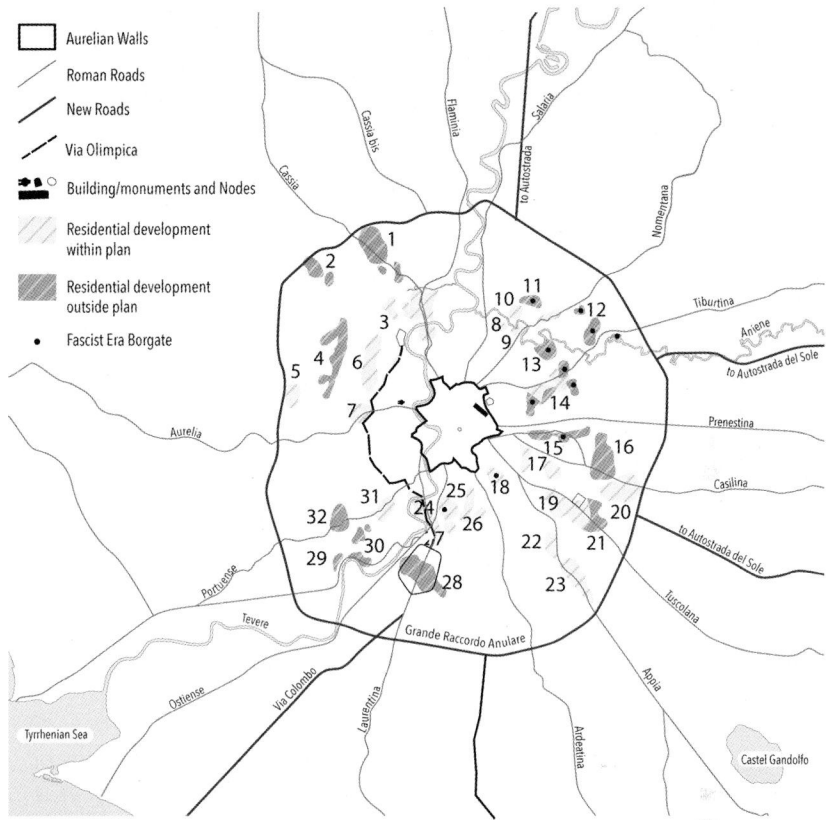

FIGURE 2.6 Map of unplanned or rogue development (*abusivismo*) in relation to Node 7 (*quartieri* and *borgate*) between 1952 and 1961 as reconstructed by Gigli Padellaro and Panizza. Drawing by Kylie Burns and author.

LEGEND

1 Tomba di Nerone
2 Ottavia
3 Vigna Clara
4 Primavalle
5 Boccea
6 Balduina
7 Gregorio VII
8 Quartiere Africano
9 Montesacro
10 Val Melaina
11 Tufello
12 San Basilio and Rebibbia
13 Pietralata
14 Tiburtino
15 Gordiani
16 Centocelle
17 Tuscolano
18 Appio Latino
19 Quadraro
20 Don Bosco
21 Cinecittà
22 Quarto Miglio
23 Statuario
24 San Paolo
25 Garbatella
26 Ostiense
27 Marconi
28 EUR
29 Magliana
30 Parrocchietta
31 Portuense
32 Corviale

the physical and legal limits of the 1931 plan. This went on to characterize the city's expansion in the 1950s and 1960s thanks, on the one hand, to the presence of what had by then become 'legal' housing development and, on the other, to continuing flows of internal migration caused by the war. Migration from rural to urban areas continued in the same pattern established in the Fascist era. Unskilled workers from the impoverished South and educated workers from the North continued to arrive in the capital to feed the ever-increasing need for manual labour in the construction industry and the growing public administration sector, respectively.[37] Public and private projects of varying sizes sprung up like mushrooms all over the city. All manner of housing from middle-class apartment blocks built by colleagues in the public service (like the one built by my grandfather) to makeshift hovels in the arches of the aqueducts were driven by this housing need (Figure 2.6).

Fascist construction of the past

Our contemporary experience of the city's Ancient, Renaissance and Baroque layers is one more thread of this matrix: the Fascist construction of the past. Tourists and citizens wander up and down the now pedestrianized Via dei Fori Imperiali little knowing that a century ago there was a maze of windy streets, a working-class neighbourhood full of shops, taverns and artisan's workshops. Under the soles of their sandals and walking shoes hundreds of black boots once marched in unison towards Piazza Venezia to salute the *Duce* in his balcony. When we walk along the Via dei Fori Imperiali to admire the (sometimes rather poorly reconstructed) ancient ruins we see them framed so as to act as backdrop to the theatre of consent. When we cross Corso Rinascimento from the Pantheon on our way to Piazza Navona, we see the Rome of Paul III or Alexander VII through a Fascist lens.

Nodes of Fascist Rome

As we saw earlier, Fascist Rome developed around seven nodes that carried out both practical and rhetorical functions. Mussolini's Rome had newly restored ruins, centralized church administration, new educational buildings and sports facilities, state-of-the-art cinema studios, a world expo site and new residential districts. These doubled as urban and architectural manifestations of *Romanità*, Militarism, Empire, Modernity/Fascist Achievement, Moral Behaviour/Social Control, National Unity, the Cult of the *Duce* and Catholic Power.

Node 1: The centro storico

The first node of Fascist Rome, the *centro storico* is bounded by the Aurelian walls and featured the centres of political power at Palazzo Madama, Palazzo Venezia and its piazza framed by the *Vittoriano* (Victor Emanuel monument) and surrounded by the resurrected grandeur of ancient Caesars and builder Popes lain bare through the *sventramenti*. Palazzo Venezia was more than a centre of political administration, it was the source from which the Cult of the *Duce* emanated. The *Vittoriano* was more than a monument to a Savoy King; together with the Tomb of the Unknown soldier it was Italy's solid and immoveable National Unity. The Via dell'Impero/Fori Imperiali did not just replace a supposed slum of dirt streets with a wide, straight avenue for parades and shiny motor cars alongside grand ruins it represented *Romanità* and Modernity/Fascist Achievement. Although there were numerous interventions within the ancient city fabric during the *ventennio*, the focus will be on the remodelling of Piazza Venezia as a representative case study.

Piazza Venezia

Piazza Venezia is the heart of Rome's historic centre, and its edges are defined by the looming neo-classicism of the *Vittoriano*, the early Renaissance Palazzo Venezia and its twentieth-century copy opposite which houses INA (*Istituto Nazionale Assicurazioni* – National Insurance Institute), another key player in Rome's urban development. The piazza was transformed during the Fascist era from setting for the *Vittoriano* to rally ground for Mussolini's rousing speeches that he delivered from the balcony of Palazzo Venezia after appropriating it for his headquarters in 1929 and renaming it the Palazzo del Governo (see Chapter 3, pp. 54–5). The *Vittoriano* was relegated to a backdrop with its steps merely becoming a good place to stand in order to get a better view of the *Duce* (see Chapter 5, pp.133–5).[38]

This transformation of Piazza Venezia from public space to rally ground was part of a national programme dominated by the presence of the *Duce* and by all the trappings of ritual that the propaganda machine could muster to reinforce the cult surrounding him. A piazza is a highly charged political space and depending on whether the crowds it gathers are angry or adoring, it can be a locus of both fear and control making it a key element of the consent-building process. As an ideology and in the person of its leader, Fascism brought together a plurality of different pasts and credos, it united industrialists, oligarchs and members of the working class alike. As an expression of National Unity the piazza was used to bring disparate aspects together, both physically and symbolically in public space using new forms of Fascist ritual that employed a parallel confluence of precedents and traditions. The piazza under Fascism became an urban theatre where the people became intrinsic to the State and, at the same time, the State intrinsic to its people. Pre-existing military parades, union rallies, political demonstrations, religious processions and assemblies with all their flags and medals, lapel pins and insignia, slogans and fanfares were all appropriated in a bid to both exalt and annihilate their original meanings and replace them with Fascist ones.[39]

Piazza Venezia was the most iconic stage for the theatre of consent, the one most often filled with the oceanic crowds like the one that looked up (some with patriotic spirit, some with resignation) towards the balcony of Palazzo Venezia when Mussolini declared Italy would enter the Second World War (Figure 2.7). It was the piazza conjured in the imaginations of those listening to Mussolini's speeches on their radios and the piazza featured in the hundreds and hundreds of newsreels that showed speech after speech, parade after parade, rally after rally. That is why when the regime fell in 1943 it became Rome's most eerily deserted public space. During the Nazi occupation it was like it had been deleted from the city's topography, you were not allowed to cycle across it, if you stopped anywhere you were immediately asked for your documents. Palazzo Venezia had become like a yew tree killing any plant trying to grow in its shadow – the Caffè Faraglia across the way had

FIGURE 2.7 The 'oceanic masses' gather in Piazza Venezia to hear Mussolini announce Italy's entry into the Second World War, January 1941. Scherl/Süddeutschezeitung Photo/Alamy. Used with permission.

closed down, the nearby hotels were empty and no one sat in the sun on the steps of the nearby churches.[40] And this atmosphere continued all the way through the 270 days of Nazi occupation until 4 June 1944 when the piazza was filled again with cheering Italians and masses in public space took on an entirely different meaning. The first newsreel produced by Nuova LUCE (the rebranded Istituto LUCE – *L'Unione Cinematografia Educativa* – Union of Educational Cinema) showed the arrival of the *Comitato di Liberazione Nazionale* (National Liberation Committee – CLN) from northern Italy on 26 July 1945 to form the new government. Prime Minister Ferruccio Parri chose a different balcony in Piazza Santi Apostoli where he and the other CLN leaders greeted the crowds holding hand-written placards with the words: 'New Government – New Men – New Direction' and 'Hooray for the Victorious Armies'.[41] Piazza Venezia had lost its magic.

Although the government of the First Republic was initially hesitant about continuing the overwrought celebratory practices of the previous regime, the public spaces of the *centro storico* created by Fascism for the theatre of consent were soon re-claimed for a new set of rituals. As an element of rhetoric, Militarism was still closely connected to National Identity with the First World War and the *Risorgimento* duly reclaimed and overlaid

FIGURE 2.8 The *Bersaglieri* run liltingly down Via dei Fori Imperiali. From *Italy Today*, Presidency of the Council of Ministers Information Service, 1962.

with martial aspects of armed Resistance and anti-Fascist struggle. Military parades went back to celebrating Italy's (not Fascist Italy's) victories, and 4 November is now both Armed Forces and National Unity Day when crowds line the Via dei Fori Imperiali to watch the *Bersaglieri* with their famous feather hats and gleaming trumpets perform their renowned running march (Figure 2.8). The 1 May was brought back as Worker's Day, two new national holidays were added to calendar: 25 April, the anniversary of Italy's liberation from Fascism, and 2 June, to celebrate the referendum that voted out the monarchy in favour of the Republic. Unlike 4 July for the US or 14 July for the French, 25 April as National holiday has always been contested and still does not belong to the nation as a whole.[42] It is more politically loaded than the 2 June holiday for the birth of the Republic, is directly identified with anti-Fascism and the Resistance and is centred more on Milan than Rome. Nevertheless, it was quickly codified in urban space, thus overlaying the avenues and piazzas created by the Fascists with a new set of meanings.[43]

To this Rome has added its own important dates: the city's liberation from Fascism on 4 June and the anniversary of the Fosse Ardeatine Massacre on 24 March where the president goes each year to hear the 335 names of the fallen. On the seventy-fifth anniversary of this day, Rome was awarded the Gold Medal for Military Valour for the role it played in the Resistance and the War for Liberation. The local branch of *Associazione Nazionale Partigiani d'Italia* (National Association of Partisans of Italy – ANPI) pulled out all the stops and staged eleven days of events throughout the city with everything from official speeches to parks teeming with flag-waving people, from seminars in schools to rock concerts, from commemorative rituals to flashmobs.[44]

Node 2: The Vatican City

Despite being strongly linked to papal identity, the Vatican City was still successfully orchestrated as a node of the Fascist city that restored the role of the Pope and represented Catholic Power as embedded in, rather than removed from, political life. The Vatican City's status as an independent state exempt from taxation and expropriation is part of the legacy of Fascism. It was an outcome of the 1929 Lateran Pacts which ended the severed relations between the Catholic Church and the Italian State in the wake of unification. As part of the terms of the agreement, the Fascist government carried out all the engineering and works necessary for the Vatican city to become a modern state.[45] The creation of an independent Vatican State became the most concrete manifestation of Catholic Power, and this was supplemented by numerous 'islands' of territorial concessions peppered throughout the *centro storico*.[46]

The regime celebrated this re-forged relationship with the Catholic Church in the best way they knew how: with a grand avenue called Via della Conciliazione to connect papal power in the Vatican to the lay power in the *centro storico*. The job was given to regime architect Marcello Piacentini who invited Attilio Spaccarelli, who was working on the restoration of the nearby Castel Sant'Angelo, to collaborate with him on the design. This visual connection between St. Peter's and the Tiber, and by extension with the rest of the city, was not part of the 1931 plan but was deemed important enough on a political level because in the words of Spaccarelli it brought 'St. Peter's closer to the city and corresponds to a return to its temporal power over Rome'.[47] The project was so ill-conceived that when urbanist Gustavo Giovannoni wrote to the *Duce* to warn against this kind of secretive, rushed brand of urbanism he risked being sent to prison.[48] Demolition began in 1937 but all work was interrupted when the men swinging the pick axes and pushing the wheel barrows were called up to carry rifles and throw grenades in the Second World War.

With the *Democrazia Cristiana* (Christian Democrats – DC) emerging triumphant from the 1948 election, what better way to celebrate continued Catholic Power than with the completion of Via della Conciliazione in time for the 1950 Holy Year. Piacentini, who had maintained many of his powerful connections in the post-war period, was invited back in 1948 to finish what he started this time with the crucial collaboration of the *Società Generale Immobiliare*.[49] Along with being dubbed the 'surgeon of Rome' he was, in the vitriolic words of Antonio Cederna, 'favoured by the Vatican, the curacy, the Christian Democrats, the big real estate development companies and the reactionary forces only out for profit that continue to re-organise themselves undisturbed so that things in Rome can continue to happen as before'.[50] Other works for the 1950 Holy Year included a new train station, two new buildings along Piazza San Pietro, the new home for the Academy of Saint Cecilia in the Auditorium and twenty-eight mini obelisks whose symbolic function was to continue the same narrative of power previously told by Augustus, Sixtus V and Mussolini and whose practical function was to act as lamp-posts.

The 1975 Holy Year came and went without much participation from Rome City Council but in 2000 there was a new brand of Mayor. Francesco Rutelli had a lot invested in Rome's international image so he restored gardens around Castel Sant'Angelo, pedestrianized the Lungotevere (avenue along the Tiber) around the Ponte Sant'Angelo and dug an enormous car park into the Janiculum Hill.[51]

The Via della Conciliazione is a glaring example of the Fascist legacy firstly, because it was the direct continuation of a Fascist project by the same architect to entrench the same ideology, secondly, and more importantly, all the decisions to complete it were made in the same way, with Pius XII and Mayor Rebecchini rushing approvals through in secret.[52] So thanks to the

FIGURE 2.9 Via della Conciliazione. Photograph by author.

convergence of forces that made Piacentini such a favourite, the project so desired by Mussolini and Pius IX was finally realized. The road itself was described as a surgical intervention of questionable aesthetic value but, as Piacentini said himself in a 1951 interview, it is justified because it renders homage to Michelangelo's *cupola*, the 'highest sculptural expression of Catholicism, like Monteverde's *Magnificat*, it is the most glorious exaltation of that same religion' (Figure 2.9).[53] With seamless continuity the Vatican City transitioned from a peripheral node of Fascist Rome to a central node of post-war Rome. It continued to act as a physical representation of Catholic Power further bolstered by the hegemony of the DC and the significant impact of its real estate arm, the SGI in the city's continued expansion in the northwest (Figure 2.6).

Node 3: The Foro Mussolini/Italico

Despite its change of name from *Foro Mussolini* to *Foro Italico* a month after the fall of the regime, this sporting complex to the north of the city remains one of the most blatant, and consequently most written about, examples of regime traces left in the country (Figure 2.10).[54] The architecture, monuments and inscriptions of what I will call the *Foro Mussolini/Italico*

FIGURE 2.10 Enrico Del Debbio, Academy of Sports 1929, proudly displaying its new name 'Foro Italico' in 1958. Luce Historical Archive.

are discussed in more detail in Chapters 3, 5 and 7, here the focus will be on how it impacted the urban development of the city in the post-war period. More specifically, within the matrix threads concentrated on landownership, real estate speculation and special events: the 1960 Rome Olympics and the 1990 FIFA World Cup.

Leaving aside its obvious political identification with the former regime, a city preparing for an Olympics bid would follow the laws of logic and locate all the necessary facilities in a single area. In the case of Rome this was within one of the Tiber's larger bends in a triangle formed by pre-existing sporting facilities: the *Foro Mussolini/Italico* on its Western bank, *Villa Glori* to the east and the Stadio Flaminio to the south thus expanding and consolidating this area into a full-scale City of Sport (Figure 2.11). Instead, it was decided to split the main events across two nodes of Fascist Rome: the *Foro Mussolini/Italico* and E42/EUR which was being resurrected and re-imagined as the *Città Parco della Roma Moderna* (Park-City of Modern Rome) by its original 'father', Virgilio Testa.

FIGURE 2.11 An aerial view of the *Foro Italico* for the 1960 Olympic Games in Rome, showing the main Olympic Stadium, with smaller stadiums and arenas and the new Ministry of Foreign Affairs on the left. 22 June 1959. Smith Archive/Alamy Stock.

The link between these two sites had a huge impact on Rome's postwar urban development thanks to the support infrastructure that a city worthy of hosting a major international event would require. Thanks to the Olympics, Rome now had public housing at the former Olympic village and a new international airport on the swampy lands near Fiumicino. To facilitate traffic flow between the two main Olympic sites a new artery called Via Olimpica was built along with multitude of underpasses along the northern section of the Aurelian walls along Corso d'Italia and on tracts of the *Lungotevere* which were also re-organized for one-way traffic along the Tiber. The 'Olimpica', as the Romans like to call it, was announced in 1955 and inaugurated on 6 August 1960. It is a concatenation of pre-existing and new roads that effectively sliced the Villa Pamphilj in two (Figure 2.6).[55] Built for the era of the motor car, it also did one other very important thing – it opened up all of the western part of Rome to expansion and development – a part of Rome where the SGI owned large swathes of land towards Monte Mario and Boccea driving its values, literally, to the heavens.[56] A connection between E42/EUR and upper middle-class suburbs was part of the VG41-2 and the

Olympics allowed for its realization. It also created the conditions for the SGI, with the support of the DC Mayors, to strike a special deal with the Hilton group and build a luxury hotel on the top of Monte Mario on land that was supposed to be set aside for a public park.[57] After seven years of battles the 400-room hotel was built in three years because the 'rivers of money' that would flow into the city as a result were worth more than public green space. New Olympics-related infrastructure like Pier Luigi Nervi's massive – though structurally elegant – Corso Francia viaduct, a railway bridge just north of Piazza Bologna and another across the Aniene north of the *Quartiere Africano* ensured that traffic from more swathes of new SGI developments at Vigna Clara, Pietralata and Tufello were now connected to the city centre (Figure 2.6).[58]

In a curious example of re-use the former 1911 Expo site between Viale Tiziano and Villa Glori had been renamed *Piazza d'Armi* in the Fascist period to use for rallies.[59] With Fascist rallies no longer a thing this flat open space offered an ideal opportunity for some bottom-up *abusivismo* and we saw the birth of the Campo Parioli shanty town. But, with the preparations for the 1932 tenth anniversary of the March on Rome, the city could not allow such an eyesore to remain and its inhabitants were cleared to make way for more permanent (and much more aesthetically pleasing) housing. As a result of a win-win deal between the *Comitato Olimpico Nazionale Italiano* (Italian National Olympic Committee – CONI) and the *Istituto Nazionale Case per Impiegati dello Stato* (National Housing Institute for Public Servants – INCIS), the shanty town was replaced by a village for athletes that could later be used to house 6,500 people. Designed by the former Rationalists Adalberto Libera and Luigi Moretti (alongside the younger Vittorio Cafiero, Amedeo Luccichenti and Vincenzo Monaco) it has been hailed as one of Rome's rare examples of modern housing within an organic and coherent urban planning strategy.[60] Needless to say its inhabitants are from the upper middle classes, and who knows what fate befell the original dwellers of the shanty town?

But the story of the *Foro Mussolini/Foro Italico*'s impact on the city does not end with the Olympics. In the late 1980s it was revived once again to prepare for the 1990 FIFA World Cup and, like with the Olympics, came with a series of disconnected and seemingly random public works. The opacity of how public monies were allocated and to whom was like the cork that popped out of the massive dam that was Italy's *Tangentopoli* (Kickback City) scandal which also inaugurated the era of the Second Republic. At the architectural level, the stadium itself was given a new roof (see Chapter 3, p. 63) and the city was endowed with three new train stations: two of them at Vigna Clara and Farneto allowed for better access to the stadium and a third, which inexplicably duplicated the existing Ostiense Station first built for the arrival of Hitler in 1938, finally created a much-needed rail link to Fiumicino airport.[61]

More renovations were carried out for the 2000 Holy Year, the 2009 World Swimming Championships and three failed bids to re-host the Olympics for 2004 and 2020 and 2024. In the first instance, Rome was outvoted by Athens but the next two bids did not even get government support. In answer to encouragement from then Prime Minister Matteo Renzi who said Italy should not let problems get into the way of dreams, then Mayor Raggi pointed out that how easily they turn into nightmares and that Rome was still paying the debts from the 1960 events.[62]

The post-war legacy of the *Foro Mussolini/Italico* shows Rome's continued dependence on extraordinary pots of money (and the laws that go with them) to drive urban development on both sides of the political fence demonstrating a continued lack of faith in the urban planning process.[63] As a node of post-Fascist Rome it provided important infrastructure for both extraordinary events and everyday life of football fans and foreign ministry employees. It also helped shore up the post-war rhetoric of Italy as an economically thriving, peace-loving, anti-Fascist nation.

Node 4: Città Universitaria *(University City)*

The central location of the *Città Universitaria* did little to drive post-war expansion but its presence arguably helped with the construction of another building slated in the PR31, the new *Biblioteca Nazionale* (National Library). In the PR31 the area around the first century Castro Pretorio military barracks was set aside as a cultural precinct influencing the Ministry of Public Works to announce a competition for a new national library in 1959. The winners had already had experience with a major public building – the new Termini station and finalized their design in 1965. The *Biblioteca Nazionale* was finally opened in 1970 due to delays in relocating military facilities and archaeological artefacts.[64]

Node 5: Cinecittà *(Cinema City)*

28 April 1937 was a busy day for Mussolini; he oversaw demolitions for the new Via della Conciliazione to connect St. Peter's to the Tiber, helped plant the first pine tree at the site of the future Rome Expo of 1942 and inaugurated *Cinecittà*, a massive studio complex on the Via Tuscolana, beyond the far-flung *borgata* of Quadraro.

During the economic boom of the 1950s and 1960s Federico Fellini was busy making movies in the studios while speculative developers were busy making houses and *Cinecittà* went from an isolated large-scale film studio to being surrounded by massive apartment blocks on either sides of the via Tuscolana – an area exemplifying Italy of the *miracolo economico* (Economic Miracle). In the 1980s and 1990s, with the construction of the Tor Vergata University (as per the 1962 Plan) and the Romanina Shopping Mall, it became a key directional centre for Rome's ever-growing population. *Cinecittà* remains Europe's largest and most important film studio.

Node 6: E42/EUR

Of all the single planning decisions made during the Fascist period, the one to build the 1941–42 World Expo as a permanent suburb cast a long shadow on the post-war development of the city, planned or otherwise. The architecture is discussed in detail in Chapter 4 and its monuments and epigraphy are dealt with in Chapters 5 and 6 but here we look at E42/EUR's role at an urban planning scale. E42/EUR as we know it today is an odd mix of the vestiges of Fascist grandeur, the indomitable energy of one individual (Virgilio Testa), the complex matrix of post-war urban development and the everyday reality of a contemporary Italian suburb. Its realization came about through a confluence of threads of the Fascist matrix: planning legislation, concentrated landownership, continuities of power, public-private funding models and extraordinary events. Testa began his career as Director of the Technical Office of Rome City Council in 1924 and worked his way up the bureaucratic ladder to the influential position of Secretary. He was also the founder of *Istituto Nazionale di Urbanistica* (National Institute of Urban Planning – INU), wrote the urban planning law n.1150 of 1942 that governed the majority of Rome's post-war urban development and was Professor of Urban Planning at La Sapienza University.[65]

The basic urban layout of E42/EUR that we see today dates back to 1939 when the original plan was modified to give the projected World Expo an air of solemn monumentality and to give urban and architectural form the Expo theme: the 'Olympics of Civilisation'. Prominent regime architect Marcello Piacentini emphasized and straightened the Fair's main axes in a bid to create a 'Third Rome' as a more modern (and more markedly Fascist) version of its Ancient and Renaissance-Baroque iterations. It was organized around a central north-south axis (or *cardo*) and four cross axes (or *decumani*) each dedicated to particular theme: Civilization, Empire, Society and Entertainment (Figure 2.12).[66] Unlike previous international expositions that were for the most part temporary, the main local exhibitions at the 1942 Expo were conceived as permanent: the Housing Expo would be lived in and the principal exhibitions would become museums to Italian Civilization, Autarky and Corporatism, Agriculture and Land Reclamation, even Racial Purity.

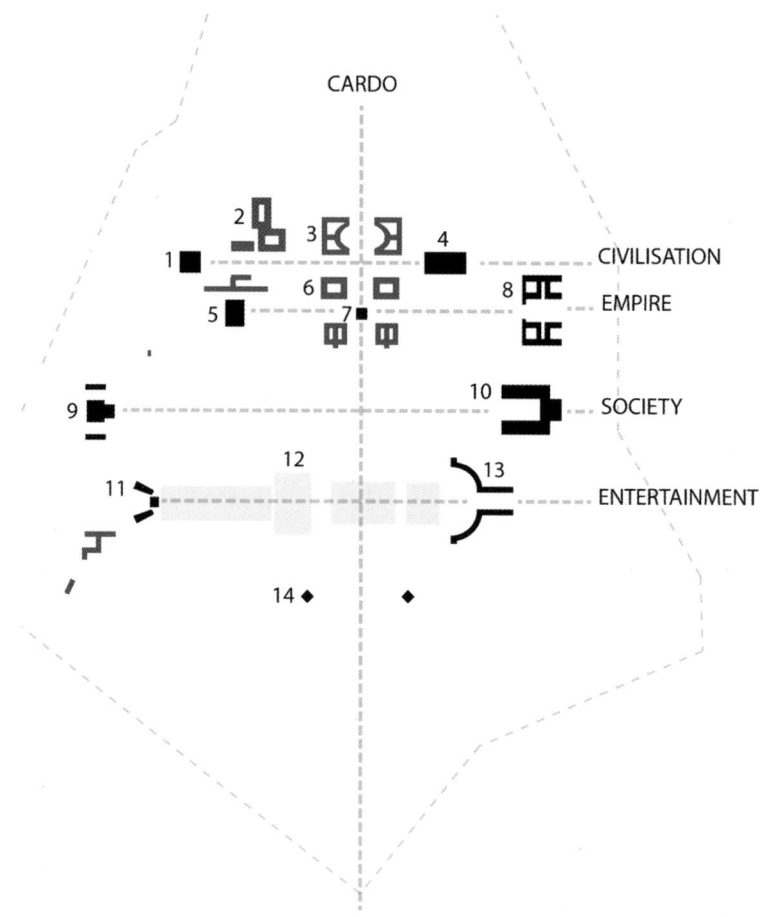

FIGURE 2.12 Schematic plan of *E42/EUR* showing principal buildings and four axes. Drawing by Brandon Gardiner and author.

LEGEND

1 Italian Civilisation Building
2 Office Building
3 INA and INPS Exedras
4 Conference and Receptions Building
5 Imperial Theatre (unbuilt)
6 Museums
7 Piazza Imperiale and Marconi Obelisk
8 Museum of Roman Civilisation
9 Basilica of Sts. Peter & Paul
10 Communications/ Autarky & Corporativism/Armed Forces Exhibition
11 Open Air Theatre (unbuilt)
12 Lake
13 Agriculture, Land Reclamation and Racial Purity Exhibition (partially built)
14 Monumental Arch and Palace of Water & Light (unbuilt)

E42/EUR in the 1950s was described in the local newspapers as a distant, unknown example of megalomania that was destroyed before it had even been conceived, crumbled to pieces before it was even built. By the early 1960s its commissioner Virgilio Testa had completely transformed it from a desolate collection of ruined buildings surrounded by barbed wire and populated by the odd flock of sheep to a thriving suburb of new homes and office buildings populated by 10,000 people with over 25,000 travelling there daily for work.[67]

Like the Wizard of Oz working the levers behind the curtains of the Governorate, Testa had well understood that Rome's urban and population growth was not sustainable without the creation of a new *centro direzionale* (development centre) leading to the decision to make the core infrastructure and a selection of buildings for the 1941–42 World Expo permanent. This in turn determined the Expo's location between the existing city and the Tyrrhenian coast which had been marked out in the 1930s as the main direction of urban expansion.[68] On his first day of work as commissioner of the very suburb he had dreamed up back in 1936, Testa saw something quite different. Not the splendid and majestic Third Rome of Mussolini's, Piacentini's and even his own imagination, but an E42/EUR that had been subject during the mid-1940s to early 1950s to what he himself described as 'fearsome degradation', a part of Rome over which 'a death-like dreariness still lingers'.[69] When President Luigi Einaudi went to visit the site in 1948 he declared that now he had experienced a three-dimensional image view of what ancient cities might have looked like as they slowly fell to ruin. This state of ruin had been accelerated by damage wrought to the structures during the war and Nazi occupation but it was largely due to the unfinished state of the buildings that exposed them to the detrimental effects of the weather.[70]

In 1951 Testa was appointed Commissioner of the EUR Corporation and he set the wheels turning once more to transform what he termed a 'modern Pompeii' into the 'greater urban centre extended towards the Sea that Rome's leaders of 1935 had solemnly proclaimed' (Figure 2.13).[71] Testa ran the state entity like a private company and set up partnerships with the *Campidoglio* to build housing and obtain funds through land sales.[72] Testa's genius, as he said himself, was the capacity to 'make public and private inseparable within a pleasing and attractive complex'.[73]

In 1952 Testa prophesied that E42/EUR would have a population of 70,000 and a year; later that projection went up to 100,000. The reality was far different with only 8,000 in 1961 and 14,000 ten years later.[74] It seems that the new Park City of Modern Rome was either too expensive or not attractive enough for people to go and live there.

In 1950 the Via Imperiale was completed and named in honour of the 'great' Genoese navigator Christopher Columbus. Together with improving connectivity for *borgate* like Garbatella and Tor Marancio, it opened opportunities for the SGI to build accommodation for pilgrims coming

FIGURE 2.13 'A little sovereign state for Prof. Virgilio Testa'. Testa archive, Box 8. Archivio Centrale di Stato, Rome.

to Rome for 1950 Holy Year and improved profitability for adjacent landowners, a number of whom were connected to Testa via the Rotary Club. The road's extension to the coast drove more development around Fascist *borgate* like Acilia and it also meant that Romans, could easily reach the beach. Driving through E42/EUR helped to turn what had been a phantasm of the Fascist past into a reality of everyday life. E42/EUR's growth was further facilitated by the construction of the Pontina Highway to Naples (which also connected Rome to the model Marsh towns Littoria/Latina and Sabaudia) and the Viale Marconi (a section of the Via Olimpica) which connected the growth areas around Valco San Paolo that had been funded by INA-Casa. In 1955 a completed Metro and a repaired Roma-Ostia train destroyed during the Nazi occupation were two more links in the chain between Rome and the coast.[75]

Helped along by the VG41-2 (that he had a large hand in) Testa also took advantage of funding connected to extraordinary events. As E42/EUR was built as a site for exhibitions, it makes sense that exhibitions would play a key role in its resurrection. As *Corriere della Sera* reported, they would: 'Bring a bit of life to that monumental appendix to Rome made up of exaggerated space, cold marble and frightening voids where even the resident statues seem besieged by agoraphobic angst.'[76]

The *Esposizione di Agricoltura* (Agriculture Exhibition 1953 – EA53), the installation of *Permindex* in the museum buildings around the Piazza Marconi (see Chapter 4, pp. 85 & 92–4) and the relocation of the Rome Trade Fair along the Via Imperiale/Cristoforo Colombo are three such examples. Just fourteen years after the *Bureau Internationale des Expositions* postponed the E42/EUR indefinitely, it was approving Rome's application to hold another kind of International Expo on the very same site: the EA53.[77] From an urban development perspective the EA53 further cemented E42/EUR as an important pole in Rome's growth towards the sea and a key node of post-Fascist Rome. From a funding perspective, Testa was able to appropriate all the improvements made from moneys given to the EA53 for the promotion and completion of his pet project. From a propaganda perspective, the modest and hard-working De Gasperi Government could put forth the image of a modest, hard-working and pacifist nation rewarded by unprecedented economic growth.[78]

Soon after the close of the EA53, Rome's Trade Fair moved from Piazzale Clodio in the north to E42/EUR attracting many more visitors to the area for the first time. The temporary pavilions looked incongruous among the half-built buildings and the trees planted there ten years earlier. At least water was flowing from the fountains, and Testa was able to use the Trade Fair as the impetus to complete the sewers and street lighting.[79] Like with the re-opening of the Museum of Roman Civilisation, the Fair's inauguration was timed to coincide with the opening of the first section of the Metro B from Termini to Piramide, the completion of another Fascist-era project that allowed visitors to reach E42/EUR directly from the city centre.

When Rome put itself forward as a candidate city for the 1960 Olympics many eyes turned to E42/EUR.[80] Only part-built and left to ruin, the site offered plenty of open space for large-scale sports facilities and the event was the perfect catalyst to complete its unfinished buildings and monuments. Ideas for a velodrome and a *Palazzo dello Sport* were put forward as early as 1953.[81] Bosworth argues that the choice of E42/EUR as an Olympic site was an attempt to purge it of its Fascist association by simply blotting it from memory and framing those two decades as a comparatively small blip in Rome's millennial history.[82] While for Carter the resurrection of E42/EUR is testimony to Italy's overall failure to 'de-fascistise' especially when compared to post-war Germany's efforts to 'de-nazify'.[83] But perhaps it is neither of these two. As we will see in Chapter 4, the realization of E42/EUR as an integral node of the post-war city had more to do with the confluence of matrix threads that have become a testimony of Italy's capacity to rebuild and express the rhetoric of a modern democratic nation.

Node 7: quartieri *and* borgate

The seventh node of Fascist Rome is actually a collection of peripheral nodes, the *quartieri* and *borgate*, that, together, form the regime's response to growing housing needs fuelled by the social revolution brought about by its own policies.[84] Firstly there was a national push for population increases through extra taxes on bachelors, extended loans to newlyweds and special prizes (given by the *Duce* himself at Palazzo Venezia) to families of seven children. Mussolini wanted Italy to virtually double its population to 60 million by the 1950s, and despite the massive war casualties, he was not far off. It took until 1961 but it had little to do with Fascist Party policies.[85] Rome was also being promoted as the nation's (if not the world's) greatest city, thus attracting a much higher proportion of the general trend of migration from the countryside. Between 1921 and 1936, its population increased by a phenomenal 74 per cent, roughly twice Milan's increase of 36 per cent and three times Turin's increase of 25 per cent.[86] This went against another key policy, *Sfollare le Città* (Clearing the Cities), that attempted to stop people leaving the countryside altogether and continue fighting the *Battaglia del Grano* (Battle for Grain). Rome's disproportionate growth shows both the failure of the Party's demographic campaigns and their consequent lack of initiatives to address the problem of inward migration that were felt for decades to come.[87] This, together with the aftermath of the war, meant that this thread of the Fascist matrix only thickened in a trend that continued unabated, creating a knock-on effect that had a massive impact on Rome's urban development.[88]

The locations for post-war housing development were determined by the existing nuclei built during the *ventennio*. For example, after only ten years the 1941 suburb of Primavalle was surrounded by new suburbs of Boccea, Val Canuta and Sant'Onofrio (for the most part on SGI-owned land) and by 1961 it had doubled in size. Outside of the plan boundaries, these suburbs eventually differed little from regular development thanks to the frequent *sanatorie* (amnesties) which made for ex post facto regularization of illegal development.[89] The *borgate* acted as satellites that favoured infill development along lines of major roads and, later, transport corridors. This paved the way for larger-scale *abusivismo* well into the early 1940s and entrenched a practice that would reach unprecedented levels in the post-war period (Figure 2.6).[90] The majority of Rome's twentieth-century urban development occurred outside of planning controls and is a legacy of the 1931 Plan and the VG41-2. This *abusivismo* was a national problem, an abuse of both the land as a resource and of those who, for one reason or another, ended up living in far-flung suburbs without proper civic and transport infrastructure. The pockets of *abusivismo* were either built-up areas being created inland not zoned for residential development or areas slated for development built at higher density and for greater private profit than the regulations allowed.[91]

Families who were not given homes by the State built their own shacks on the fringes of the *borgate* with found materials while illegal parcelling and sale of land by large-scale owners became rife. This happened particularly in areas that were not zoned residential development, had been zoned for lower densities and were less profitable or were located around the edges of official satellite settlements like Quadraro to take advantage of their very minimal existing infrastructure. This 'system' (if we want to call it that) established itself during the regime firstly through the realization of the Third Rome and secondly through complicit tolerance facilitated by the pure economics of a large-scale public housing programme.[92]

Conclusion

Rome's twentieth-century planning history shows what happens to even the best-laid plans of mice and dictators. Despite all the grand speeches and even grander plans, Mussolini did not succeed in transforming the existing city and Fascist Rome turned out quite differently from both the ancient Rome it wanted to resurrect and the existing Rome it tried to replace.[93] As Aristotle Kallis has pointed out, Italian Fascism aimed to appropriate Rome for its own political ends by presenting it as a sacred *locus* for its status as political religion.[94] The *Duce*'s 'prophecy' of a 'Rome [that] would expand along other hills, along the banks of the sacred river towards the beaches of Tyrrhenian Sea' did come true. A Third Rome was made flesh on the skeleton of the failed Exposition and Rome, thanks to the machinations of Virgilio Testa and big events like the 1950 Holy Year, the EA53, the Olympics and even the 1990 FIFA World Cup.

The PR31 had one client to satisfy (Mussolini), one interest group to look after (the Fascist regime and its associated businesses), a single vision for urban growth and social structure (the Fascist one), complete control of both the means to implement plans and legislation (a totalitarian regime and a Governor) and the means to promote itself (the Fascist press). The city's most significant transformations were less about actual monumental durability and more about 'the will to endure' and what Lefebvre has called 'the stamp of the will to power'.[95]

The post-war reality, instead of disinterring the PR31, actually helped it take root. Although the 1962 plan was able to successfully implement a smattering of progressive planning measures it was not able to undo a system that had enjoyed an extra thirty years to become entrenched. What eventually became the 1962 plan had to satisfy the needs and desires of an entire city not to mention a plethora of allied professional, business, political, religious and other interest groups like unions and conservation societies that gathered under their respective left- or right-wing banners. In the end, the right-wing groups outnumbered the left because they had business, aristocracy and the Vatican on their side.

Rome's post-war urban development was a kind of 'planning ping pong' with a Left and Centre-left alliance at one end of the table and a Right and Centre-right one with Vatican cheer squad at the other. 'Team Left' did all they could to undo the Fascist past, curb unmitigated speculative development and implement strategic activity centres and transport infrastructure towards the East: a direction that coincided (ironically or not) with Communist Russia. 'Team Right', in the interests of being seen to be democratic, did not openly support the Fascist past but adopted, instead, tergiversation tactics or a sort of filibustering approach that allowed them to continue to take advantage of the *laissez-faire* elements of its enduring planning law. They pushed for strategic development towards the West, the direction preferred by Mussolini and that also coincided (ironically or not) with the United States.[96] They advocated keeping the *status quo* because it served their economic interests, thereby indirectly supporting a key thread of the Fascist matrix.

Since the fall of Fascism, much was done to erase the traces of the past: organizations were disbanded, laws were annulled or re-drafted, ministries were re-configured, inscriptions were chiselled off, statues were taken down, streets were renamed. But how do you erase the actual fabric of the city? Any attempt to return the wide thoroughfares and open piazzas of Rome's city centre back to the winding (and possibly picturesque) alleys and disparate buildings we still enjoy in pockets of Monti, Trastevere and Campo Marzio is as impractical as restoring the ruins of the Forum back to the age of the Caesars. Like it or not, the Fascist-era transformations have become indispensable parts of Rome's contemporary urban topography.[97] Today these spaces encapsulate a horizon of meaning that embraces a multiplicity made up of subsequent layers of history and use. Via dei Fori Imperiali in particular is still important for military parades on 4 November, the parades for 2 June and marching towards the *Vittoriano* (partisans, etc.) and what is now the daily 'parade' of tourists who admire the ruins in the vision of Imperial glory that the fascists originally intended.

CHAPTER THREE

The architecture of Fascist Rome between politics and practicality

Roma ha già un aspetto diverso. Decine di quartieri sono sorti alla periferia della città che ha lanciato le sue avanguardie di case verso il monte salubre, verso il mare riconsacrato. I dati sintetici del vostro bilancio triennale eccoli: strade nuove, aumentati mezzi di comunicazione, miglioramento di tutti i servizi pubblici, scuole, parchi, giardini, assistenza sanitaria, organizzazione igienica in difesa della salute del popolo.

Rome already looks different. Many suburbs have risen on the outskirts of a the city which has launched a vanguard of houses towards the salubrious hill and the reconsecrated sea. Here are the results of the last three years: new roads, more public transport, better infrastructure, schools, parks, gardens, medical and hygienic services to defend the health of the population.

MUSSOLINI – AL POPOLO DI ROMA, 19 APRIL 1924.[1]

Introduction

Many of Rome's citizens today would pop into a post office, take their children to swimming lessons or sort out their War Veteran's pension without thinking they just walked into building built by Mussolini. They appreciate and probably take for granted a swathe of public buildings and services unaware of how modern they were, how they were touted as jewels of Rationalist architecture and how important they were in building consent. The Fascist era created high-quality architectural and urban experiences now appreciated by generations with no experience of the repression that went with it.

A lot of Rome's Fascist-era architecture does not scream out 'Fascist Architecture', nor does it look remarkably different to what was being built in Europe in the 1920s and 1930s. This applies particularly to the everyday buildings built in Fascist Rome's residential nodes like apartments, schools or post offices whose political message was communicated through simple provision without the need for bombastic styling. As such, they continued to serve their original functions. Other building types, like independent war veterans' associations, co-opted under the militarist banner of Fascist propaganda, simply switched back to their prime role of looking after returned soldiers. Once they had been cleansed of propaganda elements (which was usually as simple as chipping off inscriptions, covering frescoes and changing the name) bespoke buildings for Fascist ministries and organizations such as Fascist Youth tended to continue their main function or, in the case of *Case del Fascio*, were repurposed to serve other manifestations of civic order: police stations or *carabinieri* (Military Police) barracks.

This chapter will focus on the post-war histories of selected buildings of the *ventennio* as a complex interplay of disruptions and continuities that, if anything, shows there is no easy way to deal with the heritage of a past regime. Italy's post-war period is not a solid block of history and each government dealt with the legacy of Fascist architecture in different ways to build an ever-evolving image of a democratic nation. This shifted according to the socio-political circumstances they were confronted with: the Reconstruction period of the 1950s, the Economic rebirth of the 1960s, the Civil violence of the 1970s and 1980s, the scandals of the 1990s or the new Italy of the 2000s. Each chose a different path as a function of their particular time and in each case they made the most of what Mussolini had left behind placing a different degree of focus on rhetorics of National Unity, Militarism, Modernity and Catholic Power (Figure 1.2).

Rome's largely State-funded architecture of the Fascist period is concentrated within its Fascist nodes (see Chapter 2, p.18) where each assemblage of buildings represented aspects of the new society and reinforced one or more elements of Fascist rhetoric. As we will see these nodes continued to impact Rome's post-war development and were repurposed both for their pragmatic use and for how they could convey repurposed meanings for post-war Italian society. The *centro storico* (Node 1) and the Vatican (Node 2) have kept their original identities as First and Second Romes but this is also largely due to the transformations wrought during the *ventennio* and in the post-war period they continued to represent political power.

The new 'Cities' of Sport, Education, Cinema and Civilization hosted the most politically charged buildings making their re-use and adaptation more fraught than, say, an elementary school. The *Foro Mussolini/Italico* sporting complex (Node 3) became, thanks to the continued presence of mosaics and monuments celebrating Fascism, a highly contested site for the 1960 Olympics that was successfully turned around to communicate Modernity, Democracy and Economic Rebirth. The new university campus, the *Città Universitaria* (Node 4), was able, with some minor modifications to its frescoes and inscriptions, to continue educating the next generation of anti-Fascists. *Cinecittà* (Node 5), after a brief period as a refugee camp, also continued in its function as Rome's Hollywood while the site of the incomplete World Expo of 1942 (Node 6) had a far more varied fate. After its resurrection in the mid-1950s, a number of its buildings had to be completely repurposed while others easily adapted. Finally, in the peripheral nodes, or new residential areas, the inter-war apartments have almost blended into the background of the high volume of post-war housing that now surrounds them while other everyday buildings such as post offices, schools or sports centres have often been modified to an extent that has them little resembling their original state. These last three nodes were also key to bolstering the *miracolo economico* (Economic Miracle) rhetoric.

Node 1: *centro storico*

Fascism created a presence within the dense urban fabric of the *centro storico* by appropriating existing buildings and demolishing others. The building most closely connected to Fascist Rome, Palazzo Venezia, dates back to the fifteenth century and was once the home of the Venetian cardinal Pietro Barbo, whose balcony on the *piano nobile* has achieved worldwide fame as the platform for the *Duce*'s rousing speeches. New buildings were concentrated around the new street alignments required by the *sventramenti* (see Chapter 2 pp. 21–2). The Via del Mare/Petroselli has the former offices of the Governatorate which were easily converted into Rome's Civil Registry Office, the Corso Rinascimento and Via Bissolati are defined by non-descript office buildings for INA (*Istituto Nazionale Assicurazioni* – National Insurance Institute) and the piazza around the Augustan Mausoleum is shaped by a set of sombre-looking yet anonymous building distinguished only by mosaics and grandiose inscriptions (see Chapter 6 pp. 145–6).

The *centro storico* has three new government buildings of the Fascist era built in the severe *Stile littorio*: the Ministry of Aeronautics, located near the new *Città Universitaria*; the Ministry of Corporations on the Via Veneto and the Ministry of African Colonies just opposite the Circus Maximus. Given the continued importance of the Defence Forces for Italy's post-war Italian identity, the Ministry of Aeronautics continues its original function as an arm of Italy's Ministry of Defence complete with untouched fasces on its door frames; the Ministry of Corporations continues to look after Economic Development while the building for Ministry of Italian Africa, suppressed in 1953, is now occupied by the Food and Agriculture Organisation. To befit a modern democracy, other Ministries distributed across historic buildings of the *centro storico* were centralized and relocated to brand new modern skyscrapers at E42/EUR which, under the single-minded leadership of its new Commissioner Virgilio Testa, was being transformed from a tragic collection of ruins to a burgeoning modern suburb and business centre (see Chapter 4, pp. 83–5). This allowed E42/EUR to have a dual representative function as a node of political and economic power.

Fascism's biggest ongoing contribution to the urban life of the city centre was the construction of the new Termini station which started its life as a metaphysical expression of Roman arches, was completed in the best post-war organic style and has been transformed into a default shopping mall in the same vein as many other European railway stations.

Palazzo del Governo *(Government Building)* *(now Palazzo Venezia Museum) and National Archaeology and Art History Library*

Here we will look at two examples personally appropriated by Mussolini to convey a dual image of powerful leader and *pater familias*: Palazzo Venezia and Villa Torlonia to feed Fascist rhetoric's Cult of the *Duce*. Despite its century-old history, Palazzo Venezia's place in the popular imagination remains linked to the decades of its time as the *Palazzo del Governo* (Government Palace) or Mussolini's personal headquarters. Chosen for its central location it also had high symbolic value as the former Austrian embassy. To take the Palazzo as the seat of Government was to treat it as war booty from Italy's 'Victory' against the Austro-Hungarian empire in the First World War. Having his own *palazzo* also put Mussolini on par with the king in *Palazzo Quirinale* that had become the Royal Residence in 1870 and is now home to the president.

Mussolini set up his office in the *Sala del Mappamondo* after the world map known to be there in the Renaissance. This representation of dominion was added to by a new Roman-style mosaic replete with Fascist symbols (still there today) and a representation of the Rape of Europa as if to presage Fascism's future dominion over the Mediterranean as it had been in the heyday of the Venetian Republic.[2] The room was big enough to seat all members of the Grand Council and its balcony was perfectly positioned to command a view to the *Vittoriano* (see Chapter 5, pp. 133–5) on the left, Trajan's Column to the right and the Colosseum in the centre. This hulking symbol of Roman greatness was obscured by a higgledy-piggledy array of medieval streets and houses lived in by the urban poor. Mussolini had giant fasces mounted onto the door frame and turned it into pulpit and *arengario* (speaker's platform) rolled into one from whence he could hold vast crowds in his sway. The physical masses who gathered in the purposely enlarged Piazza below were joined by what we would know call his 'virtual' audience who listened in on their government-subsidized radios or watched newsreels on movie screens. Recent excavations have revealed the concrete-lined rooms of a personal air-raid shelter under the fifteenth-century towers.[3] As the sirens sounded out across the city on 20 July 1943 Mussolini supposedly declared: 'They have built me a shelter here but do not let anyone think I have any intention of going down there ... If the Angloamericans reach Rome they will find me here, in my place of work'.[4] But Mussolini was nowhere near Palazzo Venezia during the heaviest waves of Allied bombing – he was on the shores of Lake Garda trying to rebuild power in the puppet state of Salò.

On the morning of 25 July 1943, once the news that the *Duce* had been deposed was broadcast on the very same radios he put in everyone's home, the fasces on either side of the balcony door were chiselled away. But their eerie outline remained like the imprint of a strange fossil and it was not until the preparations for the 2000 Jubilee Year that any trace of them was wiped away. The principal scholar of civil religion, Emilio Gentile was quick to point out the irony of this gesture. The Italian Republic only thought to remove this vestige whilst celebrating the international Catholic ritual of hosting Holy Year but in doing so removed the ultimate symbol of a Nationalist political religion which, without the incorporation of Catholicism, could never even have properly existed.[5] In 2013 Mayor Veltroni declared those parts of Rome connected to Fascism are 'no longer taboo' and during a visit to Palazzo Venezia could not understand why the balcony was blocked off by a black room divider. 'It's not a fetish', he noted, 'it is a square metre of space where history, a tragic history, was made'. For Veltroni the balcony should be opened up so that the former domain of a tyrant could become 'everyone's balcony, the balcony of democracy'.[6]

Palazzo Venezia is now a museum and home to the National Archaeology and Art History Library. The balcony, now divested of its fasces, offers a sliver of shade against the sun or a modicum of shelter from the rain for the odd tourist or citizen waiting for the bus. The Palazzo has reverted to its cultural importance as there was no place in post-Fascist rhetoric for the Cult of the *Duce*, and although nearly a century has passed since he stood on it to face the crowds in the piazza it remains Mussolini's balcony.

Villa Torlonia

Like many of Rome's patrician villas, the former home of the Torlonia princes (descended from Marino Tourlonias who had converted from Judaism to become the Pope's Banker) on the Via Nomentana is now a public park.⁷ Most people wandering about holding hands with their lover or kicking a ball around would have little or no idea that the house standing within it was once inhabited by the Italian dictator's family. Prince Torlonia, who 'scarcely throbbed with Fascist purpose', agreed in 1929 to move into the nearby *Casina delle Civette* (Owls' House) and charged his *Duce* the nominal rent of 1 lira.⁸ Up until July 1943, the Mussolinis projected an ideal image of family life: Benito played tennis and drove sports cars, Dame Rachele modernized the kitchen, grew vegetables and raised chickens, together they celebrated the wedding of their daughter Edda to the future foreign minister Galeazzo Ciano (Figure 3.1). The neo-Classical nineteenth-century villa whose expansive gardens were decorated with more exotic elements like a Moorish tower and fake Egyptian obelisks remained largely unchanged except for a modern annexe built as a ballroom and reception area (Mahatma Gandhi visited in 1931) but was mostly used for watching Laurel and Hardy films.⁹

While Mussolini was inciting what was left of the Italians' patriotic spirit to enter the Second World War he was secretly building an underground refuge to protect himself and his family under the villa's small artificial lake. Undeterred by the known presence of Jewish catacombs, the excavators began their work and built a state-of-the-art shelter equipped with 'all mod cons': battery-operated lighting, anti-gas and air purifiers, double security doors and a personal telephone. It was soon deemed inadequate and a new one was built in the cellars of the Casino by adding an air filtration system and a 120 centimetre layer of reinforced concrete to the walls. At the end of 1942 a new and larger bunker was begun 6 metres under the piazzale in front of the Casino. This cruciform structure had a 4-metre-thick ceiling and was left incomplete in July 1943 when the need to protect Mussolini vanished together with his hold on power. It later came in handy for the inhabitants of the area who were able to take refuge there during the Nazi occupation.¹⁰

After liberation in 1944, the Villa was used as Allied military headquarters and then returned to the Torlonias who basically left it abandoned until it passed into City hands. It seems the Mussolinis had left quite a taint on the place: the Allied soldiers 'disgracefully misused' it, the Torlonias ignored it and the City left it to rot lest it should incite Fascist nostalgia. In 1993, after a suitable amount of historic distance, restorers were finally able to begin work and the debate about what it should be used for began. A (critical) Museum of Fascism? A Museum of the Holocaust? In 2013 the air-raid shelter was discovered, and former mayor Veltroni spoke out about the importance of restoring it. In an interview with *La Stampa* he said:

> Villa Torlonia is no longer a myth. Children ride their bicycles on the same paths where Mussolini rode his horse. You can go and eat pizza in the lemon house. But if you are passionate about it you can go and look at

FIGURE 3.1 Just another day at Villa Torlonia for Mussolini at the wheel of an Alfa Romeo hobnobbing with famous racing car driver Tazio Nuvolari. Prospero Gianferrari Archive owned by his son Vincenzo. Public domain.

it with a historian's eye. The villa was decrepit. We put back some of the original furniture, including Mussolini's bed and [restored] the drawings by the American soldiers who occupied it. And now the Villa is back to what it was, you can feel the disgust at the idea that the *Duce* enjoyed lunch on the garden while our soldiers were dying of cold in Russia.[11]

Overshadowed by the iconic status of the Palazzo Venezia balcony, it remains a politically neutral venue hosting temporary exhibitions of modern and contemporary art. Its website keeps the focus on the Torlonia family and their love of art, with only a couple of lines mentioning the fact that it housed the Mussolini family for fourteen years.

Ministero dell'Africa Italiana *(Ministry of Italian Africa)* *(now Food and Agriculture Organisation)*

Commuters coming out of the Metro onto Viale Aventino are greeted with a parade of flags to signal the headquarters of the Food and Agriculture Organisation (FAO). Known to Romans as *Palazzo FAO*, its stern presence recalls the stripped neo-Classicism of the *Stile littorio,* a particular style of monumental architecture used to invoke admiration and respect for the great achievements of the Fascist era and in particular the rhetoric of Empire as befitting its original destination as the Ministry of Italian Africa. Following the addition of Ethiopia to its existing colonial possessions in Libya, Eritrea and Somaliland in 1936 the government announced a design competition for a new ministry building on a large tract of land along the newly named Viale Africa (now Aventino) just across from the Palatine Hill and Circus Maximus. The competition attracted twelve projects, six were chosen to proceed, and the committee decided that the final design proposal should incorporate the recently erected Aksum Stele (see Chapter 5, pp. 122–4; Figure 5.5). Although largely incomplete, the building was officially inaugurated by Mussolini in September 1938 and not finished until 1965.[12]

In the interim, the Second World War brought an end to Italy's colonial era and the suspension of the ministry, leaving the nascent government of the Republic with the question of what to do with this half-built complex of four buildings. Appeals were made to the Ministry of Post-war Assistance to convert them into apartments for those left homeless by Allied bombs but the young Giulio Andreotti had to contend with imploring letters from the Minister for Post and Communications who claimed cramped conditions at the former headquarters Via del Seminario.[13] In 1947 construction resumed to accommodate them in Building D but in the meantime, a new body of the United Nations, the Food and Agriculture Organisation, was also looking for a home. New York did not seem like the right city for an organization concerned with food, fisheries and forestry so in 1949 it voted to accept Italy's offer of a site for its new headquarters. In his history of the FAO, Ralph Phillips glossed over the fact that the UN was moving into what was formerly a Fascist structure mentioning only that it had been designed by 'an earlier Italian government for use as a Ministry for Italian Territories in Africa'.[14]

Keen to return to the fold of the United Nations and be accepted into the democratic community the Italian government offered generous terms to the FAO giving them impetus to complete construction and overlay new meanings onto the former colonial ministry.[15] In 1951, with 76 families on their way from Washington to begin work in Rome, Cafiero was brought back to complete the designs and contend with a complex of buildings in various states of completion to adapt them for their new uses. Building A already had foundations and was promptly completed that year; Building B was ready for occupancy; Building C, comprising a single stairway and elevator tower, was finished by October 1964; Building E was completed in October 1965 and Building D was newly refurbished in 1980.[16] The FAO and the Ministry of Post and Communications shared digs until 1977 when a new building was provided for the latter at E42/EUR. Completed in 1976 by Paniconi and Pediconi, the bronze-clad tower extends its four wings to define the corner between the Viale Cristoforo Colombo and Viale America (see Chapter 4, p. 108).

The story of the FAO building shows us how the post-war Italian government was able to 'make the best of a bad lot' and take a half-built building of both questionable and defunct political intent and re-adapt it to serve a set of multiple needs. It gave a temporary home to an expanding ministry while its new and more official headquarters were being built in the growing business district of E42/EUR and helped cement Italy's new image as an international player on the democracy world stage. The building that began its life to symbolize its dominion over Africa and brought League of Nations sanctions on Italy now stands for a United Nations organization which dedicates its efforts to achieving food security in Africa. While this is all noble and good one can only ask whether this is tantamount to another form of imperialism that is tied up with privileged forms of subjectivity that also marginalizes the recipients of Western progress. Arguably the FAO building represents an integral component of institutionalized power relations between Europe and the Global South that perpetuates the image of Africa as a starving child and forgets to celebrate, instead, its rich and multiple cultural identities.[17]

Stazione Termini *(Termini Railway Station)*

Passengers getting off the train at Rome's Termini Station will walk through a building that is partly of the Fascist era. Its repetitions of arches and giant columns were there to reinforce the rhetoric of *Romanità* and communicate the great Fascist achievement of a nationally networked railway system with the 'trains running on time'. Like many other nineteenth-century European capitals, Rome ushered in the 'modern' age of steam and the beginnings of mass transport with a grand railway station. Although not as monumental as its counterparts, St. Lazare in Paris or St. Pancras in London, it slipped in well among the new ministerial buildings that cropped up on the northern edge of the city centre after Rome took on the mantle as capital of a united nation in 1870. Progressive electrification and a four-fold increase in the number of platforms meant that Salvatore Bianchi's 1869 design was, from a practical point of view, out of date. Although it retained a sort of naïve charm, for Mussolini it stood for a bygone era: inefficient, staid and backward like the Liberal State he did away with. In 1936 he called on Angiolo Mazzoni – the former Futurist who had become the chief architect of the State Railways – to come up with designs for a new central station that would also symbolize Fascist achievement. Mazzoni's first, rather Miesian, effort was a long glass prism of calibrated proportion suspended on *piloti*, but this solution did not fit into Rome's imperial image so he came up with a collage of Classical motifs: the interiors had coffered ceilings veneered with 'autarkic' marble from Carrara, rows of De Chirico-esque arches ran along the platforms and the main entry portico was to be held up by double order giant Corinthian columns that would have had Sant'Elia spinning in his grave. The new design called for the demolition of an entire city block so when war interrupted construction it was far from complete.

If the nineteenth-century design was too old-fashioned for Mussolini then the monumental design was too Fascist for President De Gasperi. Besides, the capital of a democratic nation needed a properly functioning central railway station and to do things democratically they held a national competition. Prospective entrants had to contend with the stylistically appropriate (yet inherently practical) portions of the Fascist-era project and a section of fourth-century city walls that had come to light after the demolition of the old station. At the same time they were to update the design with more staff offices, ticket booths, cafés and restaurants, a day hotel, subway connections and an extra 50 m of platforms. Two entries stood out: 'Servius Tullius catches a Train' by architect-engineer team of Eugenio Montuori and Leo Calini and '$y = 0.005x^2$' by the architect trio Massimo Castellazzi, Vasco Fadigati and Annibale Vitellozzi in collaboration with the engineer Achille Pintontello. The teams were given equal first prize and asked to work together on a design that would combine the best aspects of each project.

The new building was built between March 1948 and November 1950 whilst the rest of the nineteenth-century structure was demolished, in stages, around it.[18] The giant Corinthian capitals in Apuan marble destined for the portico were sent off and repurposed as civic fountains and the only decoration is an abstract *bas relief* by Amerigo Tot along the overhang of the main entry.[19] Tafuri saw the new design as a liberation on two levels. It showed architects were now free of the *Stile littorio* and structure was now free from the materiality of form.[20]

For fifty years the 'Dinosaur' (as it was nicknamed for the curved profile of the entry hall) served the needs of the capital but the 2000 Holy Year highlighted the need for a facelift. This included the Leonardo Express train to Fiumicino Airport and the transformation of the transport hub into a veritable shopping mall with the addition of 12,000 square metres of shops. In a repeat of the eviction of the urban poor from the area around Piazza Venezia in preparation for the 10th Anniversary of the March on Rome, the papers spoke of an 'ethnic cleansing' of Termini to remove those taking refuge at the station (and compromising the respectability) to the new pilgrims' reception centre.[21] The refurbishment, which took 14 months and cost 325 billion lire (220,000,000 euro), has destroyed the unique sense of space of the entry hall (Figure 3.2) and the flow of the internal street connecting Via Marsala and Via Giolitti is obstructed by franchise kiosks that you can find in many other railways stations across Europe. Today it is testimony of Italy's capacity to rebuild and teems with tourists trying to work out the ticket machines while busy workers dodge the ticket machines that now fill the main entrance as they rush to get the high-speed train to Milan.

FIGURE 3.2 Angiolo Mazzoni and later Leo Calini, Massimo Castellazzi, Vasco Fadigati, Eugenio Montuori, Achille Pintonello, Annibale Vitellozzi, Rome Termini Railway Station, the ticket hall and internal street in the 1950s. Images by kind permission of Archivio Fotografico Fondazione FS Italiane.

Node 2: The Vatican

Fascist interventions in the area of the Vatican were more about demolishing the old than building the new. The creation of Via della Conciliazione (see Chapter 2, pp. 37–8) called for a number of new buildings to create the new street alignment but their architectural individuality was subservient to the need to create an homogeneous space that clearly expressed enduring Catholic Power.

Casa Madre dei Mutilati (Headquarters of the National Association of War Wounded)

Unlike the buildings along the Via della Conciliazione, the *Casa Madre dei Mutilati* stands out within the Vatican node as a recognizably Fascist building, an expression of architecture as a crucial element of civic monumentality in a bid to have a transformative effect on the image of Rome as a Fascist City.[22] It keys into two elements of Fascist rhetoric: Militarism and National Unity and still operates as headquarters of the *Associazione Nazionale Mutilati e Invalidi in Guerra* (National Association of War Wounded – ANMIG). The association, and the architecture that went with it, was temporarily co-opted by the Fascist Party in a bid to gain consent from war veterans. Each regional area had its *Casa dei Mutilati* as they formed part of the national civic building programme but the Roman one was known, in imitation of religious institutions, as the *Casa Madre* (the Mother House). Taking advantage of the irregular site Piacentini designed a three-sided brick building whose form echoes the nude monumentality of the (then) recently restored Castel Sant'Angelo on one side with decorative elements in travertine that tie it to the ornately classical *Palazzo della Giustizia* (tribunal) or *Palazzaccio* on the other (Figure 3.3). Solid and stately, it exemplifies late

FIGURE 3.3 Marcello Piacentini, National Association of War Wounded. Photograph by Ian Woodcock.

1920s architecture in the Roman tradition and is not immediately identifiable as a Fascist-era building and now does the job of symbolizing the Militarism and National Unity of post-war times.

Node 3: *Foro Mussolini/Italico*

The *Foro Mussolini/Italico* was one of the key nodes of the Fascist City that celebrated the importance of a military-style physical education for Italy's youth with a view to training a new generation of Fascist to ensure the regime's perpetuity (see Chapter 2, pp.38–42). Although no longer militarized, physical education and sport remained important to post-war society, particularly for youth with the *Gioventù Italiana del Littorio* (Italian Youth of the Lictors) simply dropping the 'L' to become *Gioventù Italiana*. Despite the highly charged political symbolism of its art, architecture and monuments, the *Foro Mussolini/Italico* has been used continuously throughout the post-war period and because it was essentially a sporting facility, the majority of its buildings continued in their original use. From the mid-1940s it served as a US Army rest centre, in 1950 it provided accommodation for Holy Year pilgrims and hosted hundreds of young women from the Catholic Action Group, in 1960 it held the Olympics and in 1990 the FIFA World Cup.[23] In this way its appropriation in the post-war period has, aside from fulfilling practical needs, been harnessed to bolster numerous elements of post-war rhetoric: the reborn democracy built on the dual pillar of Marshall Plan intervention and the dominance of the DC, enduring Catholic Power, Modernity/Democratic Achievement and economic rebirth (Figure 1.2).

Buildings that were straightforward sporting infrastructure like the tennis centre, the swimming pools and two stadiums only needed some upgrading to continue their former use. The Academy of Physical Education by Del Debbio was adopted by the *Comitato Nazionale Olimpico* (National Olympic Committee – CONI) but also made room for Italy's national broadcaster, *Radiotelevisione Italiana* (RAI). Mussolini's personal gymnasium simply shut its doors and the gargantuan *Palazzo Littorio* (National Fascist Party headquarters) that lay half-finished nearby was re-purposed to house the Ministry of Foreign Affairs. The *Casa delle Armi* (Fencing Academy) by Moretti also fell into disuse until 1980 and after a stint as the *Aula bunker* (fortified court room) it has since risen like a Rationalist phoenix from the ashes. Despite being the most powerfully symbolic space, the Piazzale dell'Impero/Foro Italico has undergone the least change (see Chapter 3, pp. 66–8). In 1989 the Ministry of Cultural and Environmental Heritage declared the *Foro Italico* a site of 'artistic and historical interest' thanks (rather ironically) to a 1939 law.[24]

Palazzo Littorio/Ministero degli Affari Esteri (now La Farnesina, *Ministry of Foreign Affairs and International Co-operation*)

If the monumental and severe façade of the *Farnesina*, the semi-official name of the Ministry of Foreign Affairs and International Co-operation, seems a little overblown for its function that is because its original design was the outcome of a two-round national competition for the *Palazzo Littorio* (National Fascist Party Headquarters) meant to also bolster the Cult of the *Duce*, Fascist achievement and National Unity. The 1933 round offered a prestigious site between Piazza Venezia and the Colosseum while in the 1937 round the location was moved near the Pyramid of Caius Cestius. It was moved again to land set aside for a shooting range just north of the *Foro Mussolini* because, in the meantime, the complex had grown from an Academy with allied sporting facilities into a large-scale 'Gymnasium' for Italy's youth to temper their minds and bodies for the glory of the Fatherland.[25] It was presumed that the young creatures doing their gymnastics and military drills on the vast mosaicked Piazzale dell'Impero or in the stadium ringed by colossal representations of Fascist virility would look towards the grand, stately building and see the 'spirit of the Fascist idea' radiating from it (Figure 3.4).[26] With more than one grumble of protest

FIGURE 3.4 Enrico Del Debbio, Arnaldo Foschini, Vittorio Morpurgo, Ministry of Foreign Affairs (formerly *Palazzo Littorio*) with Arnaldo Pomodoro's *Sfera grande* in the foreground. Photo by Gianni, Wikimedia Commons.

the competition winners: Foschini, Morpurgo and Del Debbio headed back to the drawing board and modified their design to address the Tiber and suit the backdrop of the Monte Mario – a distinctly un-urban context for a *palazzo*. In front, there was to be a vast piazza to hold 400,000 people (12 times bigger than Piazza San Marco and twice the size of Piazza San Pietro) overshadowed by a colossal statue of the *Duce*, an enormous *Torre littoria* and a requisite supply of monumental mosaics and statuary.[27]

In 1939 Ettore Muti took over as secretary of the PNF and decided to 'gift' the former Party Headquarters to his friend the Foreign Minister Galeazzo Ciano who was incidentally Mussolini's son-in-law.[28] This, compounded with a failed competition for a new Ministry of Foreign Affairs at Porta Ardeatina, led to the Party's decision to re-assign the building's use. Rome was also poised to expand towards the sea which would be rendering the northern location too remote so it was decided to halt the construction of the *Torre littoria* and *Sacrario* and consider moving the *Palazzo Littorio* to E42/EUR.[29] The three architects were called back yet again to make changes to their design and accommodate the building's new use as a ministry. From then work proceeded slowly, partly due to the difficulties surrounding reinforced concrete construction, and when it was finally interrupted in August 1943 (2 weeks after the Fall of Fascism) only the building's exterior and structure were complete. The ample space and piles of unused building material made the surroundings ideal for war refugees to grow food and build themselves shelters turning the area into a small informal village.[30]

In the immediate post-war period the ministry was largely re-organized and merged some of the responsibilities of the defunct Ministry of Italian Africa. But what to do with this half-built and abandoned mastodon? In 1951 they crunched the numbers, and when they saw it was more expensive to demolish than to complete, the trio of architects were brought back to resolve urgent questions with the roof to prevent further erosion and adapt it to host a helicopter pad. Three years later the interiors were partially redesigned to suit a democratic rather than totalitarian ministry. The architects also designed new fountains to replace the original proposal that was based, unsurprisingly, on a giant fasces and the interior decorative programme was completely rethought.[31] As for the enormous piazza destined for ever-more oceanic Fascist rallies in 1942 it was being used to grow wheat and in 1960 it served as a car park for Olympic events being held nearby.

Construction was sped up in early 1958 because the prime minister was keen to move out of the Viminale and into Palazzo Chigi where the Ministry of Foreign Affairs had been during the Fascist period. In September 1959, Minister Pella officially moved in to the *Farnesina* bringing together thirteen disparate offices under a single roof.[32] Diplomats were perplexed, to say the least. Was it right to associate the Ministry of Foreign Affairs of a new democratic Republic with a building that represented all the overblown grandeur of a former Fascist regime? A building that Mussolini left half built and that the Italian state was spending billions of lire to complete? They would lose the benefits of having their office in the heart of the city but at least they would not have lived with the ghosts of Ciano and Mussolini and, besides, there was plenty of space to park their cars.[33] One journalist joked that it should be called la *Farnesona* given that it was larger than the Colosseum, and he questioned the appropriateness of welcoming important diplomats in what he called a depressing place among the cheers of the football fans, the beeping of car horns or the antics of the 'bozos' attending the Roma-Lazio Derby games.[34] Another welcomed the idea of re-using buildings of the Fascist era without falling prey to Fascist rhetoric but why there? So close to the *Foro Italico/Mussolini*, such a glaring example of *megalomania mussoliniana*? Would it ever divest itself of its Fascist associations?

The ministry took a dual approach. Foreign affairs during the *ventennio* were tied to Palazzo Chigi, so by moving to new headquarters they were essentially leaving that association behind and, yes, the new building they moved into retained its severe *Littorio*-style exterior but this was redeemed by commissioning an entirely new decorative programme that celebrated new, more abstract, directions in Italian art. In this way, the building could retain its function as an element of National Unity but its reappropriation and completion came across as the achievement of a strong democratic nation based on honest labour.

Casa delle Armi *(Arms House) (now* Casa delle Armi *Edoardo Mangiarotti)*

The story of the architecture of Fascism after the fall of the regime has many episodes but the one with the most plot twists stars the *Casa delle Armi* built to house a new Fencing Academy. This icon of Rationalist architecture by the solidly Fascist but much venerated Luigi Moretti was officially inaugurated in 1936 but masked fencers never had the opportunity to dance their way across its linoleum floor. Instead, US troops stayed there immediately after the war and aside from basketball games and providing the setting for a funeral scene in Mario Monicelli's 1958 film starring Totò, *I soliti ignoti (Persons Unknown/Big Deal on Madonna Street)* – the building sat empty for many years. Despite his post-war rehabilitation, Moretti's status did not save the building from being repurposed as a *carabinieri* barracks and courtroom for high-security trials. In 1976, in the midst of the darkness of the *anni di piombo* (Lead/Bullet Years), one of Italian architecture's most innovative and poetic spaces was taken over by the Ministry of Grace and Justice. Under anti-terrorism legislation it expropriated the building from CONI (just for couple of years, they said) to use as Italy's highest criminal court. They filled in the reflective pool,

FIGURE 3.5 Luigi Moretti, Fencing Academy. The cages for the accused fitted into the main hall while being used as the *Aula Bunker* for high-security trials. Roberto Koch Agenzia Contrasto, Immagini del Novecento dall'Archivio fotografico del PCI.

put up a high-security fence, installed bullet-proof glass in the windows and vertically barred cells for the accused in the courtroom space. Its impenetrability earned it a new name: the *Aula Bunker*. In 1981 the terrorist group *Brigate rosse* (Red Brigades) was brought to trial for one of the highest profile cases of the century: the assassination of former Italian Prime Minister Aldo Moro (Figure 3.5).[35] It was also used for other hotly debated and controversial trials connected to the violence of the *anni di piombo* for terrorists at both extremes of the political spectrum. Left-wing groups *Autonomia operaia* and *Lotta continua* as well as 164 members of neo-Fascist groups like *Ordine Nero, Avanguardia Nazionale, Terza Posizione* and the *Nuclei armati rivoluzionari* were tried for a long list of crimes that included shootings and bomb attacks. Less debated but equally high-profile trials were also held there: Mehmet Ali Ağca for the attempted murder of Pope John Paul II in 1981, the 1994 trial against the 'devil lovers' Silvana Agresta and Massimo Pisano who brutally murdered his wife Cinzia Bruno and the organized crime syndicate known as the Banda della Magliana in 1995.[36]

Its period as a bunker ended once the ministry was able to make use of other high-security courtrooms at Piazzale Clodio or within the Rebibbia jail, and the space was documented by artist Rossella Biscotti whose audio installation *Il Processo (The Trial)* 2010–11 included negative castings she made of the courtroom's interior details before it was demolished.[37] Campaigns to free the building from the clutches of the Ministry of Grace and Justice began in earnest in 1990 but eight years later they were still having to call former mayor Veltroni – who by that time had become minister for Cultural Heritage – to step in. Unlike other cases of re-use and adaptation when it came to the *Casa delle Armi* it was considered a real contradiction that the ministry be allowed to 'monopolise' a space destined for sport, a building of such high artistic value, with activities that are so different to what it was designed for. Even the president of the Tribunal, Luigi Scotti, spoke of the discomfort and embarrassment he felt each time he walked through the heavily armoured gates, feeling offence that the 'needs of justice prevailed over architectural beauty'.[38] The national heritage organization *Italia Nostra,* the Order of Architects as well as intellectuals of every political stripe were not about to give up the fight, and with pressure from the Minister for Culture and Sport Giovanna Melandri, the Minister for Grace and Justice finally gave the building 'back to the people' in 2000.[39] But in April 2005, still nothing. Money had been set aside but, as is often the case with other examples of important cultural heritage in Rome – like the Galleria Borghese, for example – it became enmeshed in disagreements about management and use between local and national entities.[40] The final agreement to return the *Casa delle Armi* to the people of Rome was signed between Mayor Veltroni and Justice Minister Roberto Castelli but they – and Moretti fans around the world – would have to wait another eight years to have their desire fulfilled. In 2013 CONI (which now owns the building) had the spaces restored to their former purity and in 2020 still intended to turn it into a Museum of Sports.[41]

And that would seem to be that, excepting for one final contradiction pointed out for us by historian Giuseppe Strappa who said that the *Casa delle Armi*:

> does not simply give back that classical order that governs the modern universe of pure volumes. It also represents a vital moment in the artistic development of Luigi Moretti. Moretti who, in reality, dedicated himself to celebrating another Italy, the one belonging to the cynical, business-minded Italy of real estate speculation.[42]

In 2019 the building was named after the legendary 'King of the Sabres', Edoardo Mangiarotti, who also holds the record for most Olympic medals won by an Italian, six of which were won at the 1936 Berlin games in the name of Fascist Italy. The legacy of the *Casa delle Armi* as a fencing academy (that was never actually a fencing academy) lives on, but in the memories of the generation who remember the *anni di piombo* it will always stand for that brand of militarism born of the unresolved tensions of the Fascist legacy.

Node 4: *Città Universitaria* (University City Campus of Rome La Sapienza University)

On the day of its inauguration in 1935, the new campus of Rome's 'La Sapienza' University, the *Città Universitaria*, was presented as a modern, unitary expression of Mediterranean civilization, a perfect congruence of militarism and education in a climate of reborn Empire.[43] Though its intent was to train the next generation of Fascists it also educated some of the more prominent members of the *Gruppi Azione Patriottica* (Patriotic Action Groups – GAP) who fought against Nazi occupation. Thirty years on, during the student protests of the late 1960s, it came to symbolize the confluence of militancy and education ushering in the violent decades of the *anni di piombo* (Lead/Bullet Years).

Once they had repaired the damage from Allied bombs and re-instated its Jewish professors it was a swift and easy matter to remove any portraits or busts of Mussolini and the King and the buildings of the campus so that an ever-expanding and more motley cohort of students could continue its use as before.

Node 5: City of Cinema – *Cinecittà* (1937)

Cinema was a key element of propaganda to represent the splendours of the Fascist era and important enough to build what is still Europe's largest and most important film studio: *Cinecittà* (City of Cinema). Located beyond the far-flung *borgata* of Quadraro on the Via Tuscolana, it was inaugurated in 1937 and comprised of studios where many films are still made; the headquarters of the Istituto LUCE (*L'Unione Cinematografia Educativa* – Union of Educational Cinema) which now hosts a senior citizens centre, a pre-school and a library to meet the needs of the locals; and the national film school: the *Centro Sperimentale* where future directors still go to learn their craft.[44] *Cinecittà* halted production in late 1943 and was abandoned soon after. Allied bombs destroyed three of the soundstages and the Istituto Luce headquarters.[45] From the Second World War to the early 1950s *Cinecittà* was a refugee camp, in the 1950s and 1960s it was made famous by Federico Fellini and historical blockbusters like *Ben Hur* (1959) and in the 1980s and 1990s the surrounding area became a key directional centre for Rome's ever-growing population with the construction of the *Cinecittà2* shopping centre.

In 1943 local inhabitants scoured the deserted sets and offices of *Cinecittà* in search of food and fuel but were soon driven out by occupying Nazi soldiers who set up one of their military command centres there and saw it as an ideal site to store ammunition and set up a transit camp for prisoners on their way to concentration camps.[46] As tram conductor Pietro de Angelis recalls: 'Lined up with the others I was taken to *Cinecittà*: my companions of misfortune, many of whom had been taken by surprise in the middle of the street, were hurriedly writing notes for their families to let them know what had happened to them'.[47]

The *Wehrmacht* drove tanks and cannons across the soundstages, slept in dressing rooms and passed the time smashing sets and equipment. They uprooted trees and amassed horses, and just before the Allied Control commission took over in June 1944 they ran off taking anything they could get their hands on from pots and pans to bricks and nails, even fake beards.[48]

Allied bombing across the peninsula left thousands of Italians homeless, prompting a veritable refugee crisis which 'set the stage' for the next episode in the *Cinecittà* story. The United Nations Relief and Rehabilitation Administration (UNRRA) partnered with the American government to provide food and shelter relief. This humanitarian gesture had the underlying political motive of keeping Communism (or threat of 'a new totalitarianism') at bay.[49] The Italian government was dealing with numerous requests for half-built buildings such as the former Ministry of African Colonies to be used, at least temporarily, as housing for refugees and agreed they were better concentrated in sites far away from urban centres to maintain greater control.[50] Enter *Cinecittà*, a perfect location to confine refugees, as if on an actual film set: disconnected from reality.[51] As many as 3000 foreign and 1900 Italian refugees were brought there transforming what was once the heart of the Fascist film industry into an entirely different environment. No longer the realm of 'white telephones' or swords and sandals sagas but one where children played, food was cooked on makeshift stoves (or by Chinese chefs), washing was hung to dry. Lucky families had basic furniture but a lot of these 'homes' were entirely makeshift enclosures of curtains or straw bales supplemented at times by what remained of décor, sets or studio equipment. So the opulence of a gilded door once used to film a scene in a patrician palace for a princess was used to give a shred of privacy to a filthy mattress covered in rags for a whole family to sleep on.[52] Whilst refugees slept on the sound stages, the Ministry of Post and Communications took advantage of the garage to park mail delivery trucks.[53]

The first refugees were moved out in September 1947 but the process was not effectively completed until the international camp was officially de-requisitioned three years later. The Italians were relocated to barracks in Centocelle, the former Worker's Village of E42/EUR and in the *borgata* of Acilia and some may well have gone to live in the makeshift housing under the nearby aqueducts of the Acqua Felice.[54] *Cinecittà* soundstages went back to their original function with the filming of MGM's blockbuster *Quo Vadis?* (1951) with colossal sets being built in the backlots while

FIGURE 3.6 Sets under construction at *Cinecittà* for the swords and sandals blockbuster *Quo Vadis* with 700 refugees still on site. Luce Historical Archive, Rome.

700 refugees (who you may well spot in the crowd scenes as some of the extras) were still on site (Figure 3.6). Who knows if Federico Fellini and Giulietta Masina ever knew that soundstage Number 5 (reportedly Fellini's favourite) that created the context for some of the iconic scenes of Italian cinema was once the place that thousands of Italians only a few years earlier had called their miserable home.

Node 7: *quartieri* and *borgate*

The nodes we have previously discussed were clearly identifiable complexes of large-scale public and representational buildings concentrated in strategic areas of the city but a large part of the Fascist city and its legacy can be found in the many smaller residential nodes distributed between them. Made up of middle-class apartment blocks, worker housing, factories, services as well as sports and leisure facilities, these nodes transformed the outskirts of the city into a setting for the new life and social order provided by the Party (see Chapter 2, pp.48–9).

The types of housing, where they were located, who financed them, who built them and, ultimately, who came to live in them are all directly or indirectly influenced by the policies and politics of the *ventennio*. The mission of the *Istituto di Case Popolari* (Worker Housing Institute – ICP) was to provide apartments for workers that would, in the words of its president Antonio Calza Bini, 'call them towards a higher level of civic life'. Planned according to rational and hygienic principles, decorated with just the right amount of Classical elements and enriched with inscriptions they would 'educate and elevate the masses by providing recreation for the spirit, rendering their existence more comfortable and reinforcing family cohesion' (see Chapter 6, pp.165–6).[55] They contributed to the rhetorics of Moral Behaviour/Social Control and Fascist achievement.

Broadly speaking villas, town-houses and boutique apartments for the middle classes were built by private developers or housing co-operatives in the *quartieri* next to parks and infrastructure. The *borgate* consisted of one-room shacks, 4–6 storey apartments and tower blocks of up to 12 storeys and were located on the city fringes. This is where most of the population evicted by the *sventramenti* were sent and provided with shared services, no public transport and a very basic church.[56] The 1950s saw little improvement to these areas, and in 1959 many Romans still lived in shanty towns of the urban periphery at times just a stone's throw from the *Foro Mussolini/Italico* where the government was intent on completing a resplendent palazzo bigger than the Colosseum to house the Ministry of Foreign Affairs (see pp.64–6 above).

After the war, the ICP was re-organized, de-fascistized and renamed as the *Istituto Autonomo di Case Popolari* (Autonomous Worker Housing Institute – IACP). It continued to provide housing for major influxes of internal migration to cities compounded by the effects of the war. Enter the INA-Casa plan of 1949 whose dual aim (like many civic building initiatives of the Fascist era) was to provide jobs for the working class and homes for them to live in.[57] The construction sector was a major economic driver (and engine of consent) for Mussolini and, likewise, for Amintore Fanfani, Minister of Labour and Social Security under the De Gasperi government, who defined it as 'fly-wheel' of the post-war economic system.[58] Like the ICP and other State-funded Housing of the Fascist period, INA-Casa saw the value of good design and engaged experienced architects many of whom had, in some cases begrudgingly, cut their teeth on regime architecture. The INA-Casa programme was national and provided homes along the length of the peninsula but Rome was naturally the epicentre with a total of six major estates built over thirty years.[59]

As we saw in Chapter 2, these residential areas were all provided with the para-governmental organizations at the root of the new Fascist society: local Party headquarters (*Case del Fascio*), local Fascist Youth headquarters (*Case*

THE ARCHITECTURE OF FASCIST ROME

FIGURE 3.7 Ettore Rossi, Nanni Moretti's *Nuovo Sacher* cinema (formerly After-work circle for employees of the State Monopolies). Photograph by Ian Woodcock.

GIL), Maternal and Child Health Centres (ONMI) and after-work circles (*Dopolavoro*). Because this last type often included a theatre, these were most often converted to cinemas and in the case of the After-Work circle for employees of the State Monopolies by Ettore Rossi (1936) it has become the flagship cinema for the openly left-wing director Nanni Moretti, thereby flipping the building's political meaning (Figure 3.7).[60] These new building types reinforced Moral Behaviour/Social Control and while at the same time standing as gleaming examples of Fascist Modernity and Achievement with their sleek new forms and modern technologies. Here we will look at two of these building types: the *Case del Fascio* and the *Case GIL*.

Case del Fascio *(House of the Fasces, or local National Fascist Party Headquarters)*

Starting out as local initiatives, the *Case del Fascio* (sometimes called *Casa del Littorio* or *Casa Littoria*) were often housed in existing buildings and, once the Party machine became more established, purpose-built *Case del Fascio* were built all over Italy in a relatively brief period of time. They were heralded as a new building type that acted as a both beacon and representation of Fascism. Although there were no national directives for how they should be designed, they shared a set of essential features. These included formal elements such as the *Torre littoria* (Lictory tower), an *arengario* (speaker's platform), a range of decorative elements on their otherwise stripped facades ranging from stylized fasces to imperial eagles and an inscription – usually a pithy quote by Mussolini (see Chapter 6 pp. 148–9).[61] On the inside they were mainly offices but often included a section for the *Fasci femminili* (Women's groups), gymnasiums, meeting rooms, libraries, cinemas and a *sacrario* or shrine for Fascist martyrs. Depending on their size, each town had one or more *Casa del Fascio* and in the case of big cities *Case rionali* were provided in each suburb. Rome had thirty *Case del Fascio* often named after a local First World War hero or Fascist martyr, three were built from scratch, with another five left incomplete or unrealized because of the war.[62] As capital city it was also home to the biggest and most important *Casa del Fascio*, the *Palazzo Littorio*, which eventually became – as we saw above – the Ministry of Foreign Affairs.

After their use became obsolete *Case del Fascio* in loaned or rented spaces of existing apartment buildings simply went back to how they were and walking past them today you would never know that local Fascist Party meetings were ever held there. Similarly, the purpose-built ones were soon stripped of their Fascist trappings: quotes and fasces removed and, because their interior layout was essentially office spaces, they were easily adapted to new uses. In the case of the *Casa del Fascio* della Marcigliana the *Torre littoria* was knocked down while the one in Tor di Quinto stands out as a Fascist-era building. The discerning eye will easily pick out the *Torre littoria* with its tripartite window echoing a stylized fasces, the eagle *bas relief* above the *arengario* and the large section of blank wall that would, once upon a time, have boasted a long inscription. But most are almost entirely unrecognizable and have been converted to police stations, *carabinieri* barracks, schools, church-based charities and, in the case of the Enrico Maggi section of Montesacro, a Japanese restaurant.[63] For the inhabitants of Primavalle the mere presence of a *Casa del Fascio* was simply untenable and the Rino Daus Section was entirely demolished. The mythology of this Fascist martyr lives on with a new headquarters of *Forza Nuova* dedicated to him in Siena, once a heartland of the Resistance.[64]

Case Balilla/GIL *(Fascist Youth Association Headquarters)*

Case Balilla (later *Case GIL*) were another new Fascist building type that communicated the rhetorics of Modernity/Achievement and Moral Behaviour/Social Control (with a dash of Militarism thrown in). Writing in *Casabella* in 1933 Giuseppe Pagano stated:

> If you see the letters ONB lording it over a building, you can cheerfully assume it to be the most modern in town, the most up-to-date, the one which, at least in international terms, would be seen to represent a real step on the road to progress. And, in 80 per cent of cases, you would be right.[65]

Again, Rome was home to the national headquarters of the *Balilla/GIL*: the *Foro Mussolini/Italico* discussed earlier in this chapter, and local branches were built in many new areas of residential development. The two best-known examples are the one in Montesacro by Gaetano Minnucci (1934–7) and the one in Trastevere (1933–6) by the much-venerated Luigi Moretti. In the immediate post-war period *GIL* buildings continued to be managed by the barely restructured *Gioventù Italiana* and after it was disbanded in 1975 its properties were given over to regional administrations.

The Montesacro GIL served the *Città Giardino* Aniene and included a theatre, swimming pool, playing fields, gymnasium with solarium, School for Home Economics and experimental kindergarten.[66] Minnucci used a series of inter-connected volumes to define the edge of the site, protect the outdoor playing areas from the street and create a series of small courtyards. A suspended volume straddling two of the smaller buildings strongly reminiscent of Gropius's Bauhaus gave the building a sense of entry. It was an important local hub that served both the core of Giovannoni's buildings around Piazza Sempione from the 1920s and the more peripheral *borgate* of Tufello and Val Melaina.

When the Lazio Regional administration took over the building they tampered significantly with its form and layout splitting it into three separate civic functions needed for the fast-growing Montesacro area: their own administrative offices, a middle school and a post office. The theatre was demolished, the sports fields were built on and new regulations fire stairs were added with no regard for the original architectural form. From then parts of the complex have been slowly restored to their original functions. First in 1982 and then in 1985 (when it was dedicated to Ferdinando Agnini, a young local partisan leader killed at the Fosse Ardeatine) but in 2014 the building had once again fallen into disrepair. At this time the gym was refurbished with the financial contribution of the Col family whose daughter Valentina played volleyball there. In 2018 it was further revived as a cultural hub and began to host a number of events in the community hall from movies to music to Marxist seminars.[67] With its bright red Madonna shrine on the corner and coloured mural on the side this example of Rationalist architecture in Rome is barely recognizable. Although in continued use the complex, in particular the swimming pool, remains in a general state of disrepair. Only the cubic forms and use of marble indicate that it was once a Fascist building and it is difficult to imagine that the phrase *Credere Obbedire Combattere* once lorded it over the now defunct diving tower (Figure 3.8).

On the other side of town, the *Casa GIL* in Trastevere is in a much better state. This would be partly due to less post-war interference, its more central location and the relative fame of Moretti. Located on the Viale del Re (now Viale Trastevere) it defined the corner of the road leading through to Testaccio opposite the Ministry of National Education. With an indoor swimming pool, gymnasiums, library, administrative offices, meeting spaces,

FIGURE 3.8 Gaetano Minnucci, Montesacro Post Office, Middle School, Regional Offices Sport and Community Centre (formerly *Casa GIL* Montesacro). Photograph by Ian Woodcock.

classrooms, a 650-seat theatre and a *Dopolavoro* just opposite, it too was an important hub that also served the Testaccio area. The interior was decorated with encaustic paintings by Orfeo Tamburi, 'graffiti' decorations by Achille Capizzano in the theatre, frescoes of Empire in the Hall of Honour by Mario Mafai and they even uncovered late empire mosaics of a Roman bath while digging for foundations.[68] Keeping a blank facade along Via Induno, Moretti marked the entry with a 30-metre high *Torre littoria* that included an *arengario* looking onto a small piazza still named Largo Ascianghi, after the lake in Ethiopia where Italian troops had defeated the 'Abyssinians'. More experimental than Minnucci's effort, the building featured innovative reinforced concrete construction, a helicoidal stair, open-air gymnasiums and, in a more traditional vein, interiors richly decorated with the best of Italian marbles (Figure 3.9).

In 1975 the sports facilities became property of the *Regione Lazio* who kept up its original function to serve the local community while the theatre passed into the hands of Rome City Council who leased it to a private cinema. Named after the famous Neapolitan actor comedian Massimo Troisi it was restored in 2019 after a closure of eight years. Over the decades the building facing Largo Aschiangi was used by charities and trade unions for professional development and despite the Region announcing an accurate restoration respecting Moretti's original design in 2007, eight years later it was still in a sad state of disrepair[69]. As with the *Casa delle Armi*, ideas for what to do with the spaces had been batted about for twenty years: a *Casa dell'Architettura*, the public face of Regione Lazio, a 'cultural hub'.[70] After being re-launched in 2020 as an exhibition, culture and events centre

FIGURE 3.9 Luigi Moretti, WeGIL and Sports Centre (formerly *Casa GIL* Trastevere). Photograph by Ian Woodcock.

the hub is now in full swing. The classrooms no longer teach allegiance to the *Duce* but run courses in cinema, cooking and cybersecurity. It has been given the name WeGIL which, far some hiding its former use, actually celebrates it.[71]

Ostiense Station

This chapter on the examples of everyday Roman life that came as a result of Fascism concludes with Ostiense Station. Once a mere stop on the goods line servicing Rome's industrial areas, it was transformed in 1938 to greet the arrival of Mussolini's new ally and emulator, Adolf Hitler. Termini station was too antiquated and too big to be rebuilt in time and Ostiense was in a strategic location for the Führer to be brought into Piazza Venezia in a Fascist interpretation of the triumphal route of the ancient emperors. Once he stepped off the train he was treated to an exciting display of neon swastikas and fasces (in the patriotic shades of red, white and green) and artworks celebrating the cultural might of the two nations, with a strong emphasis on ancient Rome. Outside a motorcade awaited to take him to the heart of the Fascist empire, Piazza Venezia (Figure 3.10).

FIGURE 3.10 Roberto Narducci, Ostiense Station as decorated for Adolf Hitler's state visit to Italy, May 1938. From *Architettura*, 16 August 1938, 490. Courtesy of American Academy Library.

After Hitler's visit Ostiense reverted to its function as a goods station and was used during the occupation by the *Wehrmacht* for transporting goods and deporting prisoners to concentration camps.[72] As a result it was targeted by Allied bombs on 7 March 1944 that destroyed the tracks and much of the surrounds whilst leaving the building undamaged.[73] In what could be a blithe or purely pragmatic reversal of Hitler's visit, President Giovanni Gronchi set off from the station on the anniversary of Italy's liberation from Fascism in 1956 to set off for his state visit to France and in December of the same year was on his way to Germany (Figure 3.11). Throughout the 1950s it became the official station for presidential trains and welcomed a string of dignitaries and VIPs to Rome. In yet another instance of appropriation that balanced pragmatics and politics President Coty, the German Chancellor Heuss, the King and Queen of Greece, Elizabeth II and Prince Philip, even Sophia Loren and Clark Gable all walked through the very same halls designed for the world's most infamous man.[74] Thanks also to its proximity to public transport, the large piazza outside the station was also used by trade unions to rally workers before marching towards Piazza del Popolo with a tense atmosphere of potential skirmishes between neo-fascists and their Maoist, Trotskyist and anarchist adversaries.[75]

FIGURE 3.11 President Gronchi leans out of the window of the Presidential train at Ostiense Station on his way to Germany in December 1956. Luce Historical Archive.

Romans travelling in and out of the city continued to share Ostiense Station with freight trains until 1987 when it was adapted for a new airport train in preparation for the 1990 World Cup when tens of thousands of fans came through to watch the tournament's first kick-off between Italy and Austria. The transformation of Ostiense was part of a large programme of works designed to get as many fans as possible from the airport into the city and further north to the *Foro Mussolini/Italico* to enjoy the matches in the recently renewed *Stadio Olimpico* with the added advantage of additional commuter services for those living in the south of the city.[76] After three years the station and the shopping centre built next to it, nicknamed the Beaubourg of the World Cup, was declared a failure. The main station of the airport train shifted to Tiburtina and the new terminal stood abandoned and empty until 2010 when Oscar Farinetti decided to invest 10,000,000 euros to resurrect it into the now ubiquitous Eataly chain of restaurants and food stores.[77]

Conclusion

These architectures of continuities and disruptions, demolitions and adaptations have inspired every emotion from admiration to abhorrence and most Romans will gloss over their Fascist origin, express gratitude or sit somewhere in between. Much has been written about this twenty-year period of Italy's architectural history with a historical distance that allows us to divest buildings of political meaning and focus on their formal, aesthetic and architectonic merits. No matter which party they vote for or how many *Balilla* membership cards are sitting in shoe boxes of family photographs the fact remains that the everyday lives of Roman citizens still feel the impact of Fascist-era architecture and its waning or re-worked political message. Practicality can soon triumph over politics when there is a social and cultural need for post offices, railway stations, housing, sports facilities, open spaces and museums. Removing the political layer of these Fascist-era buildings in order to continue using them was particularly important in the period immediately after the fall of the regime when the memory of Nazi occupation was still a raw part of living memory. The need to continue using buildings was compounded by processes of post-war reconstruction. As the post-war period wore on the political resonance of these buildings gradually faded or was overlaid with new ones. In recent years these Fascist-era buildings, preserved to varying degrees thanks to their continued use, have been restored and rehabilitated to become a key part of Rome's overlooked but increasingly appreciated twentieth-century architectural heritage. Moreover, these buildings were given new layers of meaning connected to Italy's own post-war rhetoric of Modernity and achievement, of Democracy and economic rebirth.

CHAPTER FOUR

The Fascist phoenix

Virgilio Testa and the resurrection of EUR

Di una cosa sono orgoglioso, di avere ricondotto i romani al mare.
I am proud of one thing, that I have brought
Romans back to the Sea.

MUSSOLINI – LA ROMA DI MUSSOLINI, 19 MARCH 1932.[1]

Introduction

The *Esposizione 42* or E42 is the fourth node of Fascist Rome. Once destined to be the site of the 1942 Rome Expo, under the theme of the Olympics of Civilisation, Rome's EUR quarter is often considered the lost fantasy of an ideal Fascist city. It is the ultimate node of Fascist Rome that brought all the elements of Fascist rhetoric together. *Romanità* is present in the overall layout and architectural style, Militarism is built into the depictions and expressions of *Romanità*, Empire in bas reliefs and the collection of the Museum of Civilisations, Modernity in the Post Office, National Unity in the Autarchy and Corporativism complex, the Cult of the *Duce* in his quotes on the buildings, Catholic Power in the imposing form of the Basilica of Sts. Peter and Paul. Its principal avenue, the Via Imperiale (renamed to honour the now contested but then hero navigator Christopher Columbus), and its four principal cross streets retain a pompous and monumental air reinforced by symbol-buildings towering over the surrounding space. But most of this identifiably Fascist part of Rome was actually built after the war and, as we saw in Chapter 2, it was largely due to the influence of Virgilio Testa and the various threads of the Fascist matrix that impacted on Rome's post-war urban development. This chapter tells the architectural part of that story.

The expo was run by a self-managed legally independent body set up in 1936: the Ente EUR. Similar to Milan's Triennale, it received government funds and ultimately answered to the head of government.[2] Without this *Ente* the resurrection of EUR would not have been possible. Many of its buildings are still there today because, unlike other international Expos, Rome's national exhibits were to become permanent museums enshrining Fascism's perpetuity within the nucleus of a new, Third Rome. Italy's entry into the Second World War in June 1940 did not immediately halt construction at E42/EUR but it certainly slowed it down. By December 1942, the head of Ente EUR, Commissioner Cini, had to admit to his *Duce* that it was not possible to continue with construction and the site was virtually abandoned.

After the Fall

On the eve of Nazi occupation in September 1943 E42/EUR was the site of the first violent battles between the Italian army's *Granatieri* and *Montebello* divisions who, alongside Resistance fighters, did their best to fend off the Nazi troops coming in from the coast some of whom had climbed onto the cupola of the partly finished church to fire from above.[3] In this way, that part of Rome intended to best represent Fascism became the bastion of the fight against it. Once the *Wehrmacht* had taken over the city, visitors to E42/EUR were not eager fairgoers from all parts of the world but Nazi or Allied Troops, gangs of youths stealing building material, women collecting wild chicory to feed their families and the occasional shepherd guiding flocks around the piles of bricks, slabs of marble and reinforcing bars waiting to be put in place. This isolated complex of solidly built and now forlorn buildings in various states of completion made it an ideal place for refugees to take cover or Nazi troops to barrack because they provided protection from Allied artillery.[4] During the war there was such scarcity of fuel, household items and building materials that this building site in a state of suspended animation became a free-for-all supply centre. Romans and refugees, Nazi and Allied troops alike appropriated, raided or 'officially requisitioned' unused building material as well as everything from desks to typewriters from the site offices belonging to the various building firms. Whatever was not nailed down simply disappeared; Nazi troops marched into the incomplete church and walked out with sinks and toilet bowls and the restaurant was completely cleared of all its tables, crockery and refrigerators (even its gelato-making equipment) to furnish their mess halls.⁵ The building companies were left out of pocket for building materials they had supplied in faith before the war and, to make matters worse, were now bereft of valuable office furniture. But not everything was stolen, there is evidence of the Todt Construction Company paying for materials they gave to the many prisoners of war they exploited with forced labour. After the Allied command took over in June, forty-four others were given vouchers by the military in exchange for the sections of asphalt destined for EUR's roads so they could be installed at the Cecchignola military base.⁶

The administration of the *Ente* was reduced to skeleton staff who moved offices to Via della Conciliazione, meaning there was little they could do in the second half of the 1940s to repair damages and prevent further ruin. EUR's temporary commissioner Leonardo Severi spent his first period in office trying to find ways to keep 'delinquents' out of the area and placating exasperated building supply companies who wanted their office furniture back or needed to be paid for slabs of marble or pallets of bricks that had since disappeared leaving him with no choice but to pay the overdue invoices of a dead regime.⁷

The resurrection begins

Once the war was over and Italy had transitioned to a peaceful, democratic republic, the question arose: what do we do with this half-built thing (Figure 4.1)? How can it have some kind of public utility? What about reviving the exposition as a City of Progress in time for the upcoming 1950 Holy Year? This last idea, which came from the Vatican and its *Società Generale Immobiliare* (General Real Estate Company – SGI) together with big business partners like FIAT, Montecatini and SNIA Viscosa, was quashed amidst fears that it would attract rampant land speculation. As history played out these fears turned out to be a reality: FIAT completed the Museum of Roman Civilisation, Montecatini eventually became part of Ente Nazionale Idrocarburi (ENI) and built a flagship skyscraper right by the lake and the SGI profited greatly from both the sale of local land and the eventual connection to the *Foro Mussolini/Italico* for the Olympics (see Chapter 2, pp.38–42).⁸

After some debate about whether E42/EUR should come under the auspices of Rome City Council, (re)-enter Virgilio Testa (Figure 2.12) who, like some kind of urban Doctor Frankenstein, was nominated Commissioner of EUR. In his autobiography (which he wrote, like Julius Caesar, in the third person) he described his feelings when first returning to the site:

> Looking over the grounds covered in weeds, strewn with the fragments of vandalised artworks and torsos of abandoned statues, looking over

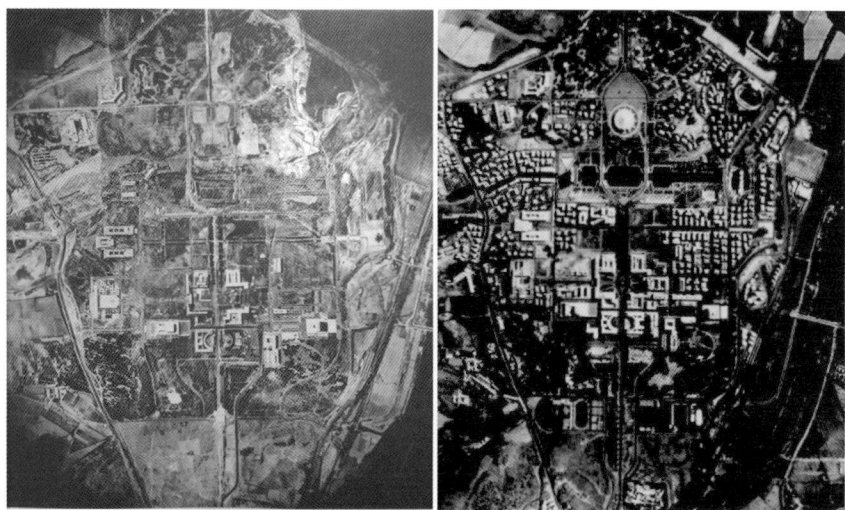

FIGURE 4.1 Aerial views of EUR in 1951 and 1961. From Virgilio Testa, *Relazione sull'attività svolta nel decennio 1951–1961*. Testa Archive Box 31. Archivio Centrale di Stato, Rome.

the hovels inhabited by miserable people with no means of support and shifting his attention to the buildings that had either been dismantled or whose half-built state merited demolition, Testa was overcome by a moment of total discouragement and murmured to his driver 'What on earth possessed me!'[9]

In the meantime, his friend and colleague Marcello Piacentini was enthusiastic and declared that 'Grand gestures, new things can be done using what is already a *fait accompli*, what was going to be the "E42" and pushing [the city] in a previously dared direction: towards the sea'.[10]

Testa ran his operations from the Ente EUR's original headquarters in the *Palazzo Uffici* (Office Building) while other nearly complete buildings like the post office and the church were able to serve its early residents. It was time to give these ghostly, sometimes half-built structures a new lease of life but to do so Testa needed money. Government coffers had been devastated by an over-spending regime and a disastrous war on three fronts and both the United States' Marshall plan funding and the United Nations' Refugee Relief Fund (UNRRA) were being poured for the most part into housing so Testa had to look elsewhere. He found the solution within the threads of the Fascist matrix: extraordinary events, concentrated land ownership, public–private partnerships and land speculation. Because E42/EUR was too far from the Vatican to be of much use for 1950 Holy Year events Testa's first opportunities came in the shape of the *Esposizione d'Agricoltura* (World Agriculture Expo of 1953 – EA53) and the 1960 Olympics (see Chapter 2, pp. 43–8).

Of the principal buildings, the Museum of Roman Civilisation was one of the first to be completed, thanks to its original sponsors FIAT. Next came the Conference and Receptions Building that was put to good use as Rome's only large-scale conference centre. Other buildings like the Exedras, the Autarky and Corporatism Exhibitions and the four museums around the vast piazza dominated by the Marconi obelisk could, with a few tweaks, house extra offices or cultural institutes.[11] Structures yet to be commenced like the grand Porta Imperiale, a giant aluminium arch to rival that of St. Louis or the spectacular *Palazzo dell'Acqua e della Luce* (Palace of Water and Light), remained on paper. Other semi-completed buildings like the Race and Land Reclamation Buildings were used as foundations for the ENI Skyscraper and the bizarre ruins of the massive Forestry Institute were not cleared away until the end of the 1950s despite architect Armando Brasini's best efforts to come up with new projects for its re-use.[12] E42/EUR's most iconic building – the Italian Civilisation Building – tells the most intriguing story in the lead up to its incarnation as the headquarters of Fendi fashion label.

After the Olympics, E42/EUR ensured its continuity thanks to the *miracolo economico* (Economic Miracle) of the 1960s by becoming a new suburb, administrative hub and business district in one.[13] When it came to industrial development, Rome could not compete with Turin or Milan where FIAT, Pirelli and Olivetti drove post-war resurrection. However, as the country's capital it could house the administrative and bureaucratic engine behind the nation's economic development and that is where E42/ EUR came to the fore by becoming home to reconfigured versions of pre-existing Fascist institutions alongside new ministries and institutes as well as partially state-owned companies like ENI. Mixed in between the re-used vestiges of the past, these new buildings – together with infrastructure for the 1960 Olympics – represented Italy's new identity as a modern, anti-Fascist and peace-loving democracy ready to rejoin the ranks of economically successful European nations.

Post-war building stock makes up the majority of E42/EUR (Figure 4.2), but we still identify it as a Fascist city because structures like the Italian Civilisation Building with its severe cubic form, cartoon cut-out arches and quote from Mussolini have become an easily reproducible caricature of Fascist architectural iconography. E42/EUR is far from the anti-romantic vision of some critics who like to dismiss it as the 'slow and sombre agony of the Fascist regime'[14]; it is more like a living example of how an unpopular and unpalatable vision of a crumbled regime can be completed with a complex interweaving of previous ideals and new socio-political contexts to become a thriving, sought-after and begrudgingly loved part of the Eternal City. It's time now to take a walk through E42/EUR and discover, building by building, how this realization came about.

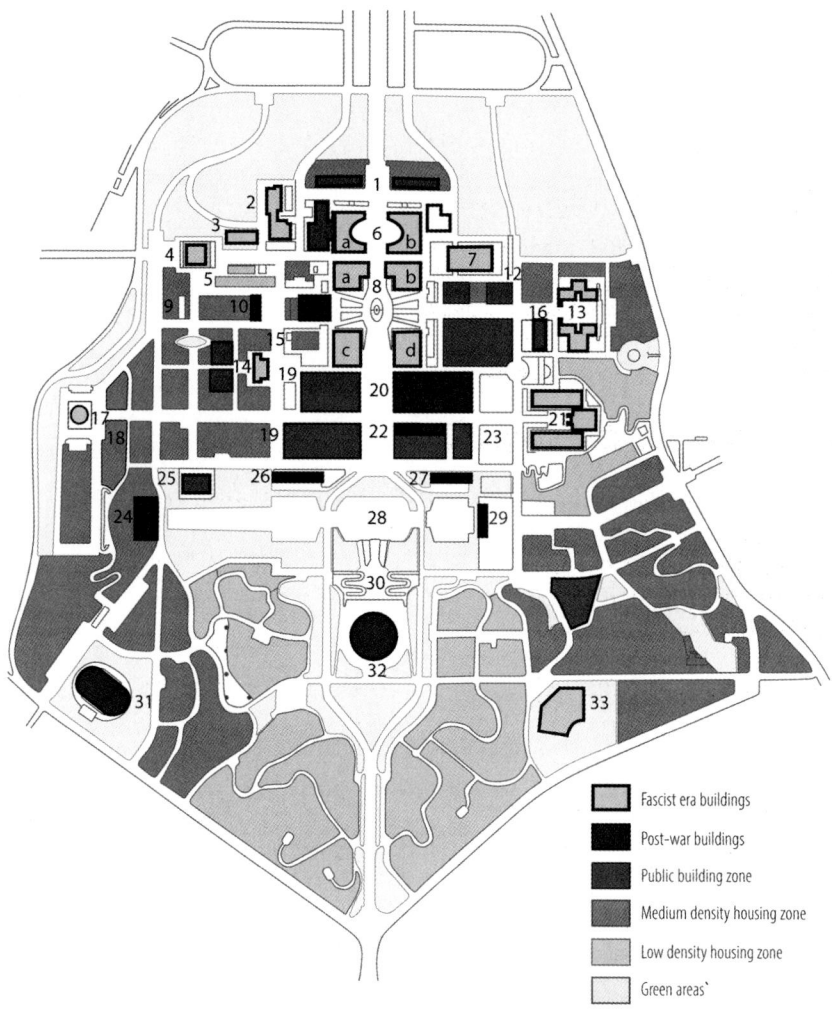

FIGURE 4.2 Map of EUR showing pre- and post-Fascist-era buildings. Drawing by Kylie Burns and author.

LEGEND

1 Esso/Credito Italiano/ SGI HQ
2 EUR Office Building
3 Restaurant
4 Italian Civilization Building/*Palazzo Fendi*
5 Governorate of Rome Building/Urban Planning Institute/School
6 Exedras: a)INPS and b) INA/Agency for the Development of Southern Italy
7 Conference and Receptions Building
8 Piazza Imperiale/Marconi and Former Museums: a) Ancient Art, b) Modern Art, c) Science, d) Popular

Arts and Traditions/ Ethnography
9 National Association of Service and Manufacturing companies
10 Former Christian Democrat Party HQ/*Palazzo Sturzo*
11 Site of Imperial Theatre/*Grattacielo Italia*
12 Italian Authors and Publishers' society
13 Museum of Roman Civilization
14 Post Office
15 Institute of Foreign Trade
16 Alitalia Building/ National Institute for Insurance against Accidents at Work
17 Basilica of Sts. Peter and Paul
18 Site of Housing Exhibition
19 Post and Communications Ministries of Post and Communications and of Economic Development
20 'La Nuvola' Congress Centre
21 State Central Archives
22 Former Ministry of Finance Towers
23 Ministry of Foreign Trade
24 Open Air Theatre/ former Hotel du Lac/ Palazzo Unicredit
25 'The Roses' Olympic Swimming Pool
26 Eur Fermi Metro Station
27 Eur Marconi Metro Station
28 Park and Lake
29 ENI Skyscraper
30 Site of Palace of Water and Light/ Fountain
31 Site of Imperial Arch/*Palazzo dello Sport*/ Palalottomatica
32 Velodrome
33 Former Orthogenesis Institute/Sant'Eugenio Hospital
34 Site of Forestry Institute
35 Italian Real Estate Institute
36 Site of Arch/Palace of Water and Light

Esedre dell'INA e dell'INPS (Headquarters of the National Insurance Institute and the National Social Security Institute)

Our narrative walk through E42/EUR starts with two seemingly identical buildings that act as the Expo's 'urban vestibule' and were designed by the Roman duo of Paniconi and Pediconi (under the guidance of Giovanni Muzio of *Ca' Brutta* fame). These two exedra-shaped buildings were modelled on Trajan's markets and are prime examples of *Romanità* and Fascist Achievement (Figure 4.3). One was to house displays on the benefits of social security while the other was set aside for unspecified exhibitions.[15] Partially funded by the *Istituto Nazionale Fascista della Previdenza Sociale* (National Fascist Institute of Social Security – INFPS) and the *Istituto Nazionale Assicurazioni* (National Insurance Institute – INA) they were easily converted to offices for INPS (with an excised F) and INA who continued to play an important role in post-war development through their housing arm INA-Casa. As work place for hundreds of State employees, their presence was key to E42/EUR's post-war Renaissance as a major activity centre.

FIGURE 4.3 Mario Paniconi, Giulio Pediconi and Giovanni Muzio, INPS Exedra showing 1950s extension in background. Photograph by author.

INA and INPS hired Paniconi and Pediconi to modify the interiors and add a substantial extension to the INPS building on the western side of the *cardo* (main axis, now Viale Cristoforo Colombo). In an attempt to contend with the heavily Classical style they were obliged to use as young graduates, they came up with a purposely asymmetrical tribute to Nervi in glass and steel. Raised on *pilotis* to create an arcade linking it to the more solid colonnade leading towards the Via Colombo, it acts as a transition between the original exedra and the *Palazzo Uffici* behind.[16] Both buildings continue to be used as government offices and the piazza between – bisected by a constant flow of traffic – has been renamed in honour of the United Nations. It is now used as a car park with a principal bus stop that is either windswept or sun-baked, depending on the season.

Palazzo dei Ricevimenti e Congressi (Conference and Receptions Building)

Looking towards the east along E42/EUR's first principal *decumanus* (cross axis) or Axis of Civilisation is the *Palazzo dei Ricevimenti e Congressi* (Conference and Receptions Building – PRC) by Adalberto Libera

FIGURE 4.4 Adalberto Libera, Conference and Receptions Building. Photograph by Ian Woodcock.

(Figure 4.4). Its innovative cross-vaulted hall rises above a stark colonnade in a supposed re-interpretation of the Pantheon and feeds into the rhetoric of *Romanità*. After winning a second round of competition, Libera's final scheme featured a large central space with atriums on either side connected by wide open corridors recalling the aisles of a basilica. Although adamant to be the author of a modern building he reluctantly agreed to add a row of stripped Doric columns on the front façade to match the monumentality of the nearby Piazza Imperiale.[17]

With construction beginning in 1939, it was one of the last building sites to be shut down in December 1943 and one of the first to pick up again in 1951. Although it suffered much damage during the war, its post-war vicissitudes are far from complex. Libera was brought back to complete the building according to its original plan so that it could play the starring role in the EA53 as well as host exhibitions on textiles, folklore and cinema.[18] At the time Rome had no adequate large-scale conference venue making a building of this size a huge drawcard for E42/EUR. Testa spent over 210 million lire on it – compared to only 18 million on the *Palazzo della Civiltà Italiana* – of which 8 million was just on linoleum.[19] By 1954 his investment had already paid off with the International Radiology Convention. The PRC then took centre stage during the Olympics Opening Ceremony and its central hall offered a unique space for fencing and pentathlon events.[20] By 1961 Testa was able to promote it as 'tourist attraction in its own right'.[21]

Palazzo della Civiltà Italiana (Italian Civilisation Building/Palazzo Fendi)

E42/EUR's most iconic piece of architecture: the *Palazzo della Civiltà Italiana* (Italian Civilisation Building) sits at the other end of the first *decumanus*, opposite the PRC, as the ultimate encapsulation of *Romanità* dedicated to Fascist Achievement (Figure 4.5). Visible from great distances, its iconic cubic shape pierced by arches has been nicknamed the Square Colosseum and has become the headquarters of the Roman luxury brand Fendi. Designed to house the Exhibition (and later permanent museum) of Italian Civilisation, it was one of the few buildings of E42/EUR to be inaugurated before the descent into war. Its architects – Giovanni Guerrini, Ernesto La Padula and Mario Romano – designed an edifice of 'grand solemnity, that clearly expresses a Roman form of Italian-ness' but, according to Gio Ponti, they succeeded only in creating 'an architectural ghost, a flashback, a stage set of stone and concrete – not a work of architecture'.[22]

Under occupation, Nazi troops found the large hall of the ground floor convenient for repairing military vehicles (though one does wonder how they got them up the stairs) and it was later used by UNRRA as a shoe factory offering employment for refugees. From the end of the war to the early 1950s it lay in a state of abandon with Testa at one point considering its re-use as the new National Library.[23] Instead he decided to harness the

FIGURE 4.5 Giovanni Guerrini, Bruno La Padula, Mario Romano, Italian Civilisation Building. Photograph by Ian Woodcock.

PDCI's iconic power for the EA53 by putting it on posters and promotional medals. The lower floors were completed to host exhibits on agricultural production, land reclamation, irrigation and transformation as well as rural housing and credit initiatives.[24] These themes were not dissimilar to what had been planned for the Land Reclamation and Agriculture Exhibitions of the original Expo.

After the close of the EA53 there were ideas to turn the PDCI into a Technology Museum but instead it was given over to the National Federation of the *Cavalieri del Lavoro* (Italy's version of the knighthoods). In a typical Testa deal, the Federation undertook to pay for the necessary repairs and re-modelling in return for twenty-nine years' worth of free rent and gave the building a new name: the *Palazzo della Civiltà del Lavoro* (Civilisation of Labour Building).[25] What had been once built to honour *Romanità* and Fascist achievement now stood for the glory of Labour, defined by Social-Democrat President Saragat as 'the greatest civil virtue, that supports the nation'.[26]

The PDCI has been rehabilitated by Italy's architects and critics who were happy to divest it of its ideological function and celebrate its pop aesthetic, making it one of the few twentieth-century examples on Italy's list of culturally significant buildings. Although this meant the Ente EUR could access 40 million euros for its restoration, the building's actual use continued to be debated. Would it house a new museum of multi-media, a permanent 'Made in Italy' Exhibition or would it just continue to be a dramatic backdrop for Armani's fashion shows and discerning film directors? In a deal worthy of Testa Fendi signed a fifteen-year lease in 2012 to pay rock-bottom rents in exchange for an act of patronage to safeguard Italy's heritage.[27]

Its iconic character has inspired numerous filmmakers who have used it as a ready-made set to symbolize totalitarian appropriations of the past, metaphysical forms, rigidity, militarism, vacuous grandeur and a monumental disregard for human scale – all qualities shared by signature Fascist architecture.[28] But the Palazzo's meaning goes beyond its architectural form: for Federico Fellini it was a device for caustic satire, Peter Greenaway used it to muse on the human condition, Julie Taymor played up its temporal connections to the Roman past thus stripping E42/EUR of its modernity and Kurt Wimmer had it project a future of resistance.[29] As the majority of Romans and tourists only ever perceive its empty architecture and imposing forms, Ponti was more prophetic than he could have known.

Palazzo Uffici (Office Building)

Just next to the PDCI the *Palazzo Uffici*, with its clean travertine facade, functionalist forms and spacious colonnade, is a typical example of *Stile littorio* architecture that keyed into Fascism's own take on Modernity

FIGURE 4.6 Gaetano Minnucci, Office Building showing quote by Mussolini and statue of the 'Genius of Sport'. Photograph by author.

(Figure 4.6). The first building to be completed, it was the headquarters of the *Ente* EUR and during the fair would double as a ticket office. Its furniture and interiors were also discreetly modern and would act, both during the Expo and afterwards, as a kind of retrospective of the best of Italian furniture and interior design with a markedly traditional bent.[30] A 500-square metre air-raid shelter furnished with special exercise bikes that could also generate electricity, air filters and signs iterating the importance of 'Calm' and 'Silence' was built underneath for the exclusive use of Fascist gerarchs but even when EUR came under fire from the *Wehrmacht* there was no evidence it was ever used.[31]

In November 1944 the Ente decamped from E42/EUR and the few remaining staff members moved to Via della Conciliazione but not in time to avoid hand grenade damage during 9 September 1943 battles and soon after all its furniture and office equipment was cleared out by the *Wehrmacht*.[32] After the war, parts of the building were rented out while others were shared by a number of public organizations such as *Difesa Aerea Territoriale* (Air Defense Department) and the *Centro Internazionale del Calcolo* (International Calculation Centre) where some of the world's first computers were born.[33]

Testa and the staff of Ente EUR moved back into their offices in 1952, giving the building a solid air of continuity, and it now houses the headquarters of EUR Spa, the private company formed in 1999 to manage EUR's physical assets. While the original Ente EUR was about glorifying the achievements of Fascist Italy, Testa's reign was about building on the past infrastructure to glorify the achievements of Italy's Economic Miracle and the current Ente EUR still aims to make a profit while at the same time looking after its artistic and architectural heritage.[34]

Most of the building continues its original function as offices while its most elegant space, the *Salone delle Fontane* (Hall of the Fountains), where the original architects built models and drew up many of the plans for the Expo, is used for exhibitions and can be hired out for events. It is presented as a fine example of Rationalist architecture with the vaguely apologetic slogan 'Where history become the future'.[35]

Musei della Piazza Imperiale/Marconi (Four Museums of the Piazza Imperiale/Marconi)

The Piazza Imperiale (now Piazza Marconi) was to be an enormous colonnaded urban space. Girded by the square colonnades of four museums with the *Teatro Imperiale* (Imperial Theatre) closing it at one end, an obelisk in the centre and the Via Imperiale running underneath, it stood to rival even the piazza of St. Peter's (Figure 4.7). The museums were to represent four cornerstones of Italian achievement: Modern Art, Ancient Art, Universal Science while the fourth changed from Ethnography to Popular Arts and Traditions and back again according to political whim. Proceeding along E42/EUR's next grand axis – the Axis of Empire one would come upon a fifth museum solely dedicated to Roman Civilisation. Like the majority of E42/EUR's permanent buildings the museums were built in the monumental

FIGURE 4.7 Aerial view of Piazza Marconi looking towards Museum of Roman Civilisation. Arrows by author indicate (left to right) Conference and Receptions Building, Piazza of Museum of Roman Civilisation, Alitalia/INAIL Skyscraper and 'Nuvola' Conference Centre. Photo by Andrea Ricci.

(and seemingly timeless) classical style that was more than a nod to the rhetoric of *Romanità*. Piacentini designed the overall piazza and hired architects whose projects had come in second in design competitions as a sort of consolation prize. Like most of E42/EUR's buildings, these were largely unfinished when work was interrupted in September 1943 and in 1959 they still looked like there was a long way to go.

When faced with the partial existence of four massive museum buildings but only two viable collections Testa started a game of 'musical exhibitions'. It appears that up until 1958 he still intended to complete three of the museums according to their original use and the same went for the fourth whose destination had, sometime between 1956 and 1958, shifted once again from Popular Traditions to Ethnography. While he was deciding on more permanent tenants, Testa secured an income stream by renting all four to a multinational company called Permindex (a contraction of Permanent International Exhibition) for nine years. Permindex thus partially revived the Expo's original function by using the combined 40,000 square metres of space for a semi-permanent trade fair.[36] The aim was to boost the Italian economy by capitalizing both on the Olympic events and Rome's tourist trade with the idea that visitors may want to take a day off from looking at the Colosseum or St. Peter's and pop down to E42/EUR and talk business with Italian companies eager for international clients.[37] During the Olympics, the Science Museum held an exhibition on Sport in Art sponsored by the Olympic Committee and the Ministry of Education. With a slightly troubling exultation of the Roman past reminiscent of the Augustan Exhibition, it brought together material from eighty museums and thirty libraries over three years to celebrate 'the moral and spiritual significance that sport has always held for humanity'.[38]

By 1961 the idea for the two art museums had been abandoned and up until the mid-1960s they were used for a succession of temporary commercial and industrial expositions combined with office space. From 1967 the building originally destined for the Museum of Ancient Art became the home for the newly established *Istituto Italo-Latino Americano* now *Organizzazione Internazionale Italo-Latino Americana* (Latin American-Italian Institute/ Organisation) set up in 1967 to promote cultural, scientific, economic and social links between Italy and the twenty republics of Latin America.[39] Testa also used proceeds from selling development land to ensure public safety by inserting a police station in the Science building and building a *carabinieri* barracks next to what was going to be the Modern Art Museum.[40]

The other two museum buildings destined for Science and Popular Arts and Traditions/Ethnography have hosted a number of collections over the years: Prehistoric Art, High Medieval Art, Aerial Photography, Oriental Art and the Luigi Pigorini ethnographic collection that had, until the early 1960s, been squeezed into inadequate accommodation at the Palazzo del Collegio Romano.[41] In 2015 an idea was floated to sell the buildings to private companies to help fund the completion of the beleaguered *Nuvola Congress Centre* by Massimiliano Fuksas but EUR Spa managed to keep the buildings in public hands thanks to the intervention of INAIL, Italy's National Institute for Insurance against Accidents at Work.[42] In 2016 the collections were brought together and rebranded as the *Museo delle Civiltà* or MuCiv (Museum of Civilisations – plural) to bring it in line with post-colonialist practices.

The Museum of Civilisations includes over 10,000 artefacts collected from the Colonial Museum set up by Mussolini in 1923 in the city centre and much of it remains unreturned war booty. The Colonial Museum was then moved to via Aldrovandi which is, given the consideration given to the culture and civilizations of African peoples at the time, disturbingly close to the Zoo. It was closed in 1972 to become the headquarters of *Istituto Italo-Africano* (Italo-African Institute – IIA) but it now appears to no longer exist. Its displays, which took up eighteen rooms over three floors, were less about African culture and more about an Italian imaginary of Africa. Parts of the collection were moved to the Pigorini museum while others lay forgotten in the basements of Via Aldrovandi and the Museum of Roman Civilisation.[43]

The museum's overall aim is to treat its collections of cultural artefacts from Europe, Asia, Oceania, America and Africa in a way that removes the distinction between Western civilizations and the 'others' but Fascist politics still haunt its halls. Archaeologists and curators are still figuring out how to display and, more importantly, how to frame a collection that includes jewels, statues and plaster casts of Ethiopians' faces. Before his untimely death its director, Filippo Maria Gambara had limited his remit to representing the

FIGURE 4.8 Luigi Brusa, Gino Cancellotti, Eugenio Muntuori and Alfredo Scalpelli, Museum of Civilisations (formerly Science Museum). Photograph by author.

'complexities' of Italy's colonialist project and left the interpretation up to the visitors.[44] Part of its re-invention includes participatory processes that also involve immigrant communities but it remained one step back from a museum that places Italy's colonialist project under proper scrutiny.[45] In 2022 its new director Andrea Villani committed to a more pro-active approach that shifts away from the positivist, Euro-centric and colonialist ideas of the nineteenth and twentieth centuries to transform the role of a twenty-first-century museum from reassuring institutional custodian to active critic of civilization.[46] In 2022 trial installations of artefacts had banners asking: 'How to exhibit the exploitation?', 'How to exhibit the violence?', 'How to avoid the removal of the colonial experience?', 'How to display the theft?' (Figure 4.8).

Museo della Civiltà Romana (Museum of Roman Civilisation)

The Museum of Roman Civilisation is, in both content and expression, the most direct expression of the rhetoric of *Romanità* and was built as a permanent home for the 1938 *Mostra Augustea della Romanità* (Augustan Exhibition of *Romanità*). Held in the *Palazzo delle Esposizioni*, it was the main event of the year-long festivities for the bimillenial of the emperor Augustus. A highly effective propaganda exercise in the guise of the largest collection of plaster casts of Roman antiquities in the world, it gave a complete picture of Roman life curated and organized so as to highlight parallels between the Augustan and Fascist eras.[47] Financing for the museum was secured from the FIAT car company who gave Piacentini *carte blanche* to hire architects, draw up a budget and present an appropriate design. The set designer Pietro Aschieri led a team who designed two symmetrical buildings connected by an open colonnade to enclose a monumental piazza to be presided over by an enormous equestrian statue of Mussolini.[48] Four bronze statues of emperors and two *quadrighe* (victory chariots) completed what could have easily served as a set for Carmine Gallone's 1937 swords and sandals epic *Scipione l'Africano* (Scipio the African), for which Aschieri had actually designed the sets. Construction began in 1939 and, like many of its counterparts, was interrupted with the onset of the war while Giglioli's collection was ceded to the City of Rome in 1946 who kept it in storage as it waited for its new home.[49]

In one of his many panegyrics of the Renaissance of E42/EUR, Virgilio Testa refers to the museum as a 'grandiose building' with a floridity of language to challenge the best Fascist propagandists: 'With its solemn structure and airy porticoes it hosts a most excellent collection of high scientific and cultural worth.'[50] FIAT, a major player in the forthcoming *miracolo economico* (Economic Miracle), was one of the first companies to respond to Testa's call to complete the major buildings that would allow E42/EUR to fulfil its destiny as a modern Rome and the museum was one of the first building sites to start up again in 1952. In another instance of continuity, the museum was inaugurated on 21 April 1952 (considered a neutral date of the foundation of Rome), a date made to coincide with the completion of the Metro link so that the Agnelli family and FIAT CEO Vittorio Valletta could travel out on a special train that would 'help bring the monumental "dead city" of EUR back to life'[51] (see Chapter 2, pp. 43–8). The building was completed in record time but it took curators another three years to reorganize Giglioli's vast collection to play down the propaganda and present Roman civilization more objectively.[52]

In 1995 it was agreed that the museum should share spaces with Rome's Planetarium and Astronomy Museum (previously housed in the Baths of Diocletian) with the somewhat tenuous reasoning that the Romans were interested in astronomy.[53] The structure closed in 2014 because it leaked and did not comply with new building regulations. At the beginning of 2022 the date of its reopening was still up in the air despite the efforts of local committees, change.org petitions and the promises of Rome City Council's cultural commissioner. Thanks to 1.2 million euros from Rome City Council

FIGURE 4.9 Pietro Aschieri, Domenico Bernardini, Cesare Pascoletti, Gino Peressutti. Museum of Roman Civilisation. Photograph by Ian Woodcock.

together with an all-too-familiar 18 million of extraordinary funds from the government's *Piano Nazionale di Ripresa e Resilienza* (National Recovery and Resilience Plan) it is predicted that its doors will re-open in early 2023.[54] Today the empty piazza is used primarily as a car park and occasional cans of beer on the step indicate that it is a favourite spot for night-time gatherings (Figure 4.9). It smacks only of an overblown sense of scale that appealed to contemporary film director Julie Taymor who thought it a great spot to film scenes from her 1999 adaptation of *Titus Andronicus*.

Piazza ed Edifici delle Forze Armate (Armed Forces Exhibition, now State Central Archives)

From the exaltation of an ancient society along the Axis of Civilisation, the next axis of E42/EUR celebrated contemporary Fascist society. With the Basilica of Sts. Peter and Paul at one end and a 'solemn temple to Italy's warlike glory' at the other' the Society Axis captured two core elements of Fascist Rhetoric: Catholic Power and Militarism. Armed Forces Exhibitions were to be in a complex of three buildings with a pavilion each for Army, Navy and Air Force. But in between competition rounds it was decided that Modernity/Fascist Achievement would be more appropriate rhetoric and it was decided that the exhibitions would centre around the topic of Telecommunications. Then in the early 1940s, with levels of consent ever slipping, it was decided to shift away from armed forces and technology towards Fascism's most solid success stories: Autarky and Corporatism to give an impression of strength and self-sufficiency both to Italians and to the rest of the world.[55]

By the time Regime had fallen not only was the building complex left unfinished, its destined use had become obsolete (Figure 4.10). At the beginning of 1952, the three largely incomplete buildings, were already earmarked for the newly created *Archivio Centrale di Stato* (State Central Archives) for material pertaining to the institutions, authorities and entities of the Italian state (i.e. from 1861 onwards). This came about through a curious combination of defunct use, a size guaranteeing a 'capacity' of 100 years' worth of material, a state of semi-completion that allowed for adaptability and the need to house new or rapidly expanding government institutions.[56] This played well with Testa's vision to enliven E42/EUR with important government institutions to both draw employees and build prestige.

Many a scholar of modern Italy like myself have woven their way past the many parked cars that occupy the plaza between the buildings to consult archival material (for this book!) and in particular all the documentation of the design and construction of E42/EUR itself.

FIGURE 4.10 Luigi Figini and Gino Pollini with Mario De Renzi, Piazzale degli Archivi. Photographs taken from the central building along the Society Axis in 1951 and 1961. From Virgilio Testa, *Relazione sull'attività svolta nel decennio*. Testa Archive Box 31. Archivio Centrale di Stato, Rome.

Basilica dei Santi Pietro e Paolo (Basilica of Saints Peter and Paul)

Looking a bit like a giant LEGO construction, the Basilica of Sts. Peter and Paul exemplifies the former regime's relationship with the Catholic Church (Figure 4.11). Located at the other end of the Society Axis it represented religion as a linchpin of society counterposed with the Autarky and Corporatism Complex (now the State Archives). Construction began in December 1938 and finishing touches were still being put on the dome in May 1943, making it one of the last building sites to stop work.[57] The dome of this fairly standard Greek Cross plan church was to act as an important reference point and like its counterpart, St. Peter's in the Vatican, is E42/EUR's tallest building. Thanks also to its location on the highest hill, the church is visible from the main approaches to the city from the south-west whether it be the via del Mare highway, the metro or the train from Fiumicino airport.

Around the church's feet like an adoring flock, a Housing Exhibition was to become the nucleus of the residential area once the Expo was converted to a permanent suburb. The Housing Exhibition, loosely modelled on the Weissenhof Siedlung built for the Stockholm Exposition 1929, was to present 'a complete solution to the problems of modern housing in its most advanced forms'.[58] The exhibition was funded by a co-operative of upper middle-class citizens who would trade the opportunity for profit with the privilege of living in a noble and luxurious modern house designed by Italy's best architects like Luigi Piccinato, Adalberto Libera, Mario Ridolfi and Enrico Del Debbio.[59] In the original plan, the housing was primarily single-family villas but also included town houses, terraced houses (to account for the existing slope) and medium-scale apartment buildings (Figure 4.12).

In 1952 the church was given over to a convent of friars who, in exchange for the property, agreed to complete the interiors while the Ente EUR looked after the roads, exterior paving, grand staircase and the two towering statues of Sts. Peter and Paul standing on either side.[60] The church was inaugurated in 1955 and in 1965 Pope Paul VI conferred it a new status by including a trip to E42/EUR in his calendar of events for the *Corpus Domini* rituals.[61] As its tallest building the stark cupola of the Basilica lords it over EUR in same way as its Vatican counterpart symbolizing enduring Catholic Power in post-war Italian society.

The exhibition was never realized but the areas around the Basilica stayed zoned for housing. Apartments were built, like so much of Rome's post-war housing, by co-operatives who played a key role in E42/EUR's financial plan. Having evaluated the value of land for residential development based on similar middle-class suburbs Testa sold the land with a healthy profit of 200 per cent.[62] Both these areas are now inhabited by the same class of people although there are very few villas, instead the area is occupied by large light-filled apartments surrounded by greenery just as the initial plan intended.

FIGURE 4.11 Basilica of Saints Peter and Paul with statues of the Saints by Domenico Ponzi and Francesco Nagni. Photograph by Ian Woodcock.

FIGURE 4.12 Final model of the Housing Exhibition/residential area around the Basilica of Saints Peter and Paul, 1943. From: ASFE42 0683 – Archivio Storico Fotografico di EUR SpA.

Ufficio Poste e Telegrafi (Post and Telegraph Office, now Poste Italiane)

E42/EUR's post office was slated to play an important role during the Expo itself. Exemplifying the Fascist rhetoric of modernity, it would be a building visited by practically every Fair-goer wanting to send a postcard home to show the rest of Italy and the world the wonders of the Olympics of Civilisation. It is the only Roman example by the Milanese firm BBPR and in the words of Bruno Zevi the only building at EUR that 'proves the existence of the modern movement in Italy amongst the thoughtless drunken-ness of fake arches and false columns'.[63] It acts as the end point of Viale Asia, one of E42/EUR's minor axes, and is nestled into the suburb's more intensely commercial district. A long, thin marble-clad plane is seemingly sliced into three separate elements with a wide gap to signal the main entry and a narrow one to the left for staff. Behind it an open grid of windows of the four-storey block signals the busy work that happens behind the scenes.

It was one of the few buildings to be completed by August 1942 so that when E42/EUR was kickstarted ten years later it had a fully functioning Post Office.[64] As with other buildings of this type the Ente gave the building over to the Ministry of Post and Communications who completed a series of minor repairs and promised Testa a 'modest payment' for utilities.[65] A series of skylights in the main hall, painted over during the post-war period, were restored in 2004 by Filippo Murcia who had recently worked at the Aventino post office. Murcia also restored the external façade and reconnected some of the interior circulation that had been compromised by a 1990 extension.[66]

Parco e Laghetto (Park and Lake)

The lake and its surrounding park, watched over by the hulking rotundity of the *Palazzo dello Sport* (Palace of Sport), mark the backdrop of E42/EUR. Piacentini handed over the responsibility for the Expo's primary site of rest and recreation between exhibits to Rome's premier landscape architect Raffaele de Vico and his collaborator Maria Teresa Parpagliolo.[67] The area was organized around an entertainment Axis and included an amusement park, naturalistic planting, picnic tables and four structures that were never built: a monumental arch nearly 100 metres high, a Palace of Water and Light, an open-air theatre and an exhibition on Agriculture and Land Reclamation.

When Testa took over the helm of E42/EUR the lake was still a large misshapen hole surrounded by weeds and thus it remained until 1955 when the first bulldozers began to reshape its banks and De Vico returned to realize a modified version of the original designs (Figure 4.1). Parks and gardens were an integral part of the Expo from its inception with up to 25 per cent of its total area dedicated to green space. Getting vegetation established in what was essentially a bare plain was of the highest priority if the Expo site was to fulfil its aims as the regime's greatest showpiece so in 1938 nearly 8,000 mature trees were planted along the future road network with another 13,000 in areas destined for parks. Upwards of 3,500 trees of suitable Mediterranean species (oaks, pines, magnolias and basewood) were planted at E42/EUR between January 1941 and March 1942 alone. When the Nazi troops marched into Rome many of the trees were damaged by bullets or set on fire while hedges and shrubs were simply trampled or crushed by the soldiers and their vehicles.[68]

Testa understood the relationship between aesthetics and economics and was happy to spend more than 3.5 billion lire on adequate green space for his new suburb but despite this much of the planned green space was compromised by the need to subdivide and sell land for houses. But it was not all dire, the poplars, pines, cypresses and laurels around the lake were added to with 3,000 cherry trees donated by the Japanese emperor, a gesture of peace that also saved Testa a lot of money. The lake was filled with 220,000 cubic metres of water which, in addition to adding beauty to the surroundings, provided recreation in the form of boat hire (even water skiing!) and doubled as a water reservoir for fire fighters (Figure 4.13).[69]

FIGURE 4.13 Park and Lake showing a collection of post-war buildings. From left to right: Telecom Italia Tower, *Grattacielo Italia*, Ministry of Finance, INAIL and ENI Skyscraper. Author: Dueduezerosettesettequattro. Wikimedia Commons.

For Testa it was imperative that the lake be completed in time for the Olympics and so it was that he was able to inaugurate it, with a pomp and circumstance befitting the preceding regime, on the Feast Day of Sts. Peter and Paul, the patron saints of Rome. The grand plans for the monumental arch and the palace of Water and Light were replaced by the *Palazzo dello Sport*, and de Vico redesigned the landscaping to better frame its circular form. A new terraced layout, more modest fountain and play of coloured lights accompanied by music was inaugurated exactly one year later in 1961, complete with a blessing from Cardinal Traglia.[70]

The new buildings

Hotel du Lac *(Lakeside Hotel)*

Up until 1956 it appears there was still an intention to build the open-air theatre until it was replaced by a lakeside hotel to help bring the Ente's accounts back into the black. But it was never to be because, during construction, it mysteriously became the National Headquarters of the Banco di Roma. Together with the ENI Skyscraper which now looks over the eastern end of the lake, the *Hotel au Lac* was at the centre of one of the many *Tangentopoli* (Kickback City) scandals erupting across Italy in the early 1990s. The cast of characters reads like the plot of a James Bond film: a mysterious multinational company, Permindex, a Hungarian former prime minister and Nazi sympathizer, CIA agents involved in the plot to assassinate Kennedy, a Prince from Palermo, the *Organisation armée secrète* (Secret Armed Organisation – OAS), a paramilitary organization against Algerian Independence, the president of the Fascist Militia, the son of Rome's former mayor, the Rothschilds. Add scenes involving Swiss banks and African trading corporations with their headquarters in Monrovia and all that was missing were Blofeld and his white cat.[71] The Grassetti construction company, ex-Assessors of Rome City Council and executives of Ente EUR were hauled over the coals for what was termed *illeciti urbanistici* (urban planning crimes) that allowed the land to be sold for upwards of 400 billion lire (roughly 5.5 billion euros).[72] It was later revealed that Ente EUR executives falsified zoning plans to bring 2 billion lire (2.7 billion euros) into their coffers.[73] This was only the tip of the iceberg: the Ente EUR was enmeshed in a number of other *tangenti* (bribes and kickbacks) involving contracts with cleaning firms, the management of sporting clubs and first dibs on nearby luxury apartments by none other than Grassetti.[74] The building itself is now known as the Palazzo Unicredit, the European banking group that absorbed the Banco di Roma in the early 1990s (Figure 4.13).

The ENI Skyscraper

For the Fair it was intended that the eastern end of the lake would be framed by two identical Agriculture and Land Reclamation buildings composed of a rectilinear block and quadrant connected by a portico to form a hemicycle. In 1940 Plinio Marconi, Giuseppe Samonà and Guido Viola were still putting the finishing touches to the drawings and construction had barely begun when work was suspended in July 1941. Photographs of the site show both the rectangular sections and half of the exedra in an advanced stage of construction.[75] The two rectangular buildings were completed in the early 1950s and re-purposed to house offices and a police station. With E42/EUR progressively defining itself as a business district and embodiment of the *miracolo economico* (Economic Miracle), the idea of completing the exedras

FIGURE 4.14 Marco Bacigalupo and Ugo Ratti, ENI Skyscraper. Cover of *Il gatto selvatico*, 7, 9 (1962).

for an Agriculture Museum was finally abandoned and the semi-complete exedra was demolished between 1956 and 1958.[76]

Instead, a flagship skyscraper for ENI, Italy's largest energy company, was built over its remains and, like the *Hotel du Lac*, was enmeshed in similar scandals.[77] The ENI skyscraper began construction after the Olympics and brought all its employees together in a single, flagship building that was 'practical, powerful, elegant and harmonious' (Figure 4.14) and despite having a Metro station literally at its door the skyscraper was equipped with a large car park befitting an oil company.[78] Bacigalupo and Ratti's slender form and elegant glass curtain wall matching the green water of the lake also reflected the late work of Mies van der Rohe.[79] The architectural language of the building was all about putting forth an image of Italy at the forefront of technological change with aspects of modernity such as light, air and hygiene. Like much of the Rationalist architecture of the Fascist period, it demonstrated a technical synthesis of functions and services that together serve the 'single vital principle of modern life and the needs of industrial progress'.[80] In 1999 French 'starchitect' Jean Nouvel won a competition to refurbish the building but his vision to 'to make use of the original positive features and "inject" new genes so as to create this twenty-first-century mutant' has yet not come to fruition.[81]

The Olympics

E42/EUR's biggest transformation came thanks to Rome's biggest post-war event: the 1960 Olympics. Plans dating from 1952 already show an area to the south-west destined for a velodrome and a *Palazzo dello Sport* on the axis of the Via Colombo above the yet–to-be-completed lake. Despite the extensive facilities already built at the *Foro Mussolini/Italico* an Olympic size swimming pool, the *Piscina delle Rose*, was also added after 1958.[82] Ever the dealmaker, Testa gave the Olympic Committee exclusive use of the three structures for eighteen years in exchange for a percentage on proceedings from ticket sales after which time the buildings would be owned and managed by Ente EUR.[83]

Palazzo dello Sport *(Sports Building)*

The *Palazzo dello Sport* saw E42/EUR's master architect, Marcello Piacentini, return to the scene to design one of its most visible buildings. Testa and Piacentini were university colleagues and Testa had provided much-needed support within the Governorate to ensure that Via della Conciliazione would swiftly come to fruition.[84] Together with the engineer Pier Luigi Nervi, who was also busy designing other Olympic facilities around the *Foro Mussolini/Italico*: the *Palazzetto dello Sport,* the Flaminio stadium

FIGURE 4.15 Former Mayor Umberto Tupini, President Giovanni Gronchi, Public Works Minister Giuseppe Togni, Defense Minister Giulio Andreotti, Mayor Urbano Cioccetti and others in front of the model of the Palace of Sport, May 1959. Luce Historical Archive.

district and the Corso Francia Viaduct, Piacentini conceived of a 100-metre diameter structure to host a range of sports, from basketball to boxing. It was roofed with an 'audacious' dome 'bigger than St. Peter's' and, featuring Nervi's characteristic reinforced concrete ribs, it impressed the dignitaries who stood admiring the model during an official visit to inspect the works underway for the Olympics (Figure 4.15). Throughout the 1960s it was used for concerts and even *Holiday on Ice*.[85] In 1999, a large terrace was added to the front to give views over the lake after which time Mayor Rutelli had it closed for maintenance and repairs, mainly to improve acoustics for concerts. These lasted until 2003, and after the requisite blessing by the Monsignor and an inaugural concert by Santana it was renamed the *Palalottomatica* in honour of its new owners: Italy's lottery company.[86] A neat continuation of the sorts of co-funding arrangements used by Testa to kickstart E42/EUR fifty years earlier.

Velodromo Olimpico (Olympic Velodrome)

The Velodrome was built on a site in the southwestern corner of E42/EUR in an area originally destined for an artificial lake. Though the structural system was innovative for its time it had to be shut down by CONI in 1968 due to instability.[87] Here, Italy won four of its fourteen gold medals at the 1960 games and the last main event held there was a Bruce Springsteen Concert in 1987 when the grass hockey pitch was destroyed by the dancing crowds, who did not forget to take away bits of the precious parquet flooring with them as a souvenir of their night with the Boss. In 2007 there were grand plans to rehabilitate it into a wellness centre inclusive of a library, kindergarten, saunas and new swimming pool, surrounded by new apartments some of which was reserved for social housing. But roughly one year later 50 kilograms of dynamite reduced it to rubble.[88] In 2021 Romans were still asking what would become of this open space and whether the A.S. Roma football club would have the opportunity to build a new stadium on the site.[89]

Ministries, government buildings and other flagships

Ministry headquarters and flagship buildings were key to the rebirth of E42/EUR and an integral part of Testa's financial plan. In exchange for free land he could secure a regular income stream through a series of rent-to-buy schemes which allowed the cash-strapped national government to eventually own the land over the course of the succeeding decades. In the case of the Finance Ministry, Testa was willing to foot the bill for the building's construction with the long view that, by helping the State, Ente EUR could only help itself as the presence of significant branches of the public service would drive the suburb's further development.[90]

After the Olympics, E42/EUR continued to grow with the construction of flagship skyscrapers for state-owned companies like the Alitalia airline and ministries for Post and Telecommunications, Foreign Trade and Finance. With a bit of imagination it would be possible to imagine that the vision of E42/EUR by Pagano and co. with their Hilberseimer-inspired skyscrapers had actually come true.[91] Post and Telecommunications (Paniconi and Pediconi, 1963–65) takes up two blocks along the Via Colombo next to the lake and is a complex articulation of volumes and sculptural staircases clad in copper. It now shares spaces with the Ministry of Economic Development whose headquarters in Piacentini's building on Via Veneto had become too small (see Chapter 3 pp. 53–4). Foreign Trade (Antonelli and Greco, 1959–62) with its aluminium cladding has now become the Italian Trade Agency. The Ministry of Finance (Ligini, Marinucci and

Venturi, 1958–62) a.k.a. *Torri delle finanze* (Finance Towers) were once praised for a Miesian splendour that helped cement the image of E42/EUR as a modern business district. They were slated in 2001 to become luxury hotels thanks to their proximity to the new Congress Centre.[92] In 2005 they were bought up by a business consortium with plans to demolish them and replace them with a project by Renzo Piano for an office, hotel and apartment complex[93]. Local residents have nicknamed them 'Beirut' or 'Sarajevo' because in 2021 they remain skeletal, their facades stripped, awaiting their fate.[94]

Luigi Moretti, author of the never-realized Imperial Theatre, was another architect of the Fascist period who returned to E42/EUR to make his contribution to its post-war existence with twin office buildings: one for the Esso oil company (later the Credito Italiano, one of Italy's oldest and most important banks) and the other for the SGI, whose unmitigated success clearly needed new, more luxurious digs in the suburb that had indirectly contributed to much of its success.[95] In collaboration with Vittorio Ballio Morpurgo, he devised two T-shaped buildings to act as the area's new entry gate and whose pronounced horizontality is tempered by vertical sun shading of a pronounced elegance.

The presence of numerous important national bodies is further testimony to Testa's indefatigable drive to make E42/EUR the jewel in the crown of Italy's post-war social and economic recovery. These include Confindustria (Italian Industrial Federation), the *Istituto Nazionale Assistenza Infortuni sul Lavoro* (National Institute for Insurance against Accidents at Work – INAIL), the *Istituto Immobiliare Italiano* (Italian Real Estate Institute – IMI) and the *Agenzia per la Promozione dello Sviluppo del Mezzogiorno* (Agency for the Development of Southern Italy).

Palazzo della DC *(the new Christian Democrat Party Headquarters)*

Signs that E42/EUR was 'the place to be' came with the *Democrazia Cristiana* (Christian Democrat – DC) Party's decision to build its new headquarters there. The results of a 1956 architectural competition placed Adalberto Libera and Saverio Muratori equal first but attempts to fuse their two very different designs into a third solution failed. The DC had to choose between two very different designs: a pure, modernist volume raised on slender Y-shaped pillars or a brick and travertine re-interpretation of a Renaissance Palazzo.[96] Were they a modern Party driving a new society or were they steeped in tradition? The answer is in Muratori's conservative composition, a *palazzo pubblico* in the tradition of Renaissance civic centre complete with *piano nobile* but with hints of modernity expressed in its set back ground floor portico (Figure 4.16). In a precursor of the violent *anni di piombo* (Lead/Bullet Years) to come, the DC Headquarters were subject

FIGURE 4.16 Saverio Muratori, Former Christian Democrat Party Headquarters. Photograph by Ian Woodcock.

to a bomb attack in 1964 which, if successful, would have brought it to the ground.[97] Now known as Palazzo Sturzo, named after Don Luigi Sturzo the anti-Fascist priest and founder of the *Partito Popolare d'Italia* (Italian Popular Party), was given over Italease, a banking consortium, in exchange for unpaid debts.[98]

Centro Congressi la 'Nuvola' (the 'Cloud' Congress Centre)

As part of Mayor Rutelli's programme to relaunch E42/EUR the suburb got its 'starchitect' building with the construction of a new congress centre by Massimiliano Fuksas, nicknamed the 'Cloud' for the ethereal form floating through the massive transparent volume that acts as its main foyer. The site, originally destined for the international pavilions, lay empty for decades and was largely ignored save for the time Fellini used it to film scenes from *Boccaccio 70*.[99] A project launched by Rutelli, championed by his successor Veltroni and alternatively damned and supported by the right-wing mayor Alemanno was finally inaugurated by Raggi in October 2016.

The 1998 competition called for a new congress centre on a 27,000-square-metre site, and the scheme by Fuksas was chosen by a jury presided over by Sir Norman Foster from a total of 286 entries, 50 of which were from international architects. Continuing with Testa's tradition of public-private partnerships the building costs for what was touted as Europe's biggest congress facility were split fifty-fifty with a private firm that would manage it (and Libera's original Congress Building) for the next thirty years. The building includes conference halls for up to 6,000 people along with a hotel, bars, restaurants and ample underground parking.

By the initial completion date of 2003, the contracts had not even been signed and the cost had doubled to 400,000,000 euros; in 2009 the building site was still an accidental lake.[100] Construction proceeded with fits and starts with completion dates announced for 2011, 2012, 2013, 2014 and 2016. The project was plagued with all manner of problems: beginning with issues with the soil and the underground car parks, to tiffs between Fuksas and Alemanno, from laying the blame on 'snake charmer' architects to a patent lack of funds which in 2014 risked leaving the building forever incomplete.[101] In 2015, the idea to sell E42/EUR's Fascist-era buildings in order to fund the completion of the *Nuvola* was met with outrage on the part of right-wing *Fratelli d'Italia* (Brothers of Italy) Party and the perplexities of the left who questioned the undemocratic decision-making process. Construction resumed with a further injection of state funding, and the ribbon was finally cut in October 2016 by Raggi with Veltroni, Rutelli and Prime Minister Renzi standing by.[102] In 2021 the *Nuvola* had become important enough to host the G20 putting the building on the international stage but not even a star like Fuksas can beat the twenty world leaders throwing their specially minted one euro coin into the Trevi fountain (Figure 4.17).[103]

FIGURE 4.17 Massimiliano Fuksas, The 'Cloud' Congress Centre. During the 2021 G20 meeting in Rome, Italy. LSF Photo/Alamy Stock.

Conclusion

Of the many nodes of the Fascist city, E42/EUR is the most representative as it expresses, in one form or another, all the aspects of Fascist rhetoric dealt with in this book. As we saw in Chapter 2 this node was one of the strongest forces driving Rome's continued urban expansion towards the sea, and this was almost entirely due to the continuous presence of Virgilio Testa, the former Secretary of the Governorate of Rome who was firstly one of E42/EUR's main instigators and then became its Doctor Frankenstein. Through a combination of land deals, public–private partnerships, financing arrangements and special events like the 1960 Olympics he wove together many strands of the Fascist matrix to transform the ruined vestiges of a lost regime into a splendid incarnation of post-war economic recovery and all in a park-like setting well connected with the city centre!

E42/EUR is an assemblage of iconic buildings whose architectural style is more often than not brought forth to signify the ultimate in Italian Fascist architecture. But the unfinished buildings of the defunct 1942 Expo that were completed, refurbished and sometimes repurposed after the war are a minority compared to the many new buildings that filled the monumental gaps between them from the mid-1950s all the way up to the inauguration of the *Nuvola* conference centre by Fuksas in 2016.

In reality E42/EUR, with its complex history of stops and starts, layers of styles and financial scandals, is much more indicative of Italy's post-war history than its Fascist one yet the 'Square Colosseum', a building that still bears a quote by Mussolini on its parapet, remains one of the most recognizable examples of Italian twentieth-century architecture.

CHAPTER FIVE

Mothers, martyrs and military men

The changing meanings of Rome's Fascist monuments

Quando ... sentiamo echeggiare nel nostro orecchio il grido fatale di Garibaldi: 'O Roma o Morte', ciò significa che per gli italiani di quell'epoca, ed anche della nostra, quell'antitesi stessa viene a significare che Roma è fonte di vita, senza della quale non vale la pena di vivere.

When we hear Garibaldi's fatal cry 'Rome or Death' echo in our ears it means, both for the Italians of those times and for us today, the very antithesis: that Rome is the source of life and it is not worth living without it.

MUSSOLINI – LA ROMA DI MUSSOLINI, 19 MARCH 1932[1]

Introduction

Every city has its share of monuments but Rome, thanks to its continued status as a capital city and for its millennial history, is simply replete. Some may appear to belong to ancient Rome, the *Risorgimento*, the nineteenth-century colonial enterprise or the First World War but were actually erected in the Fascist period. That is because alongside a range of new monuments dedicated to the heroes, anniversaries and important events of the Fascist regime they also capitalized on the pre-existing waves of national monument-building in Italy.

In 1943, the same year the Grand Council of Fascism deposed Mussolini, the architect Josep Lluís Sert, the artist Ferdinand Léger and the historian Sigfried Giedion defined the most vital monuments as those that 'express the feeling and thinking of [the people's] collective force'.[2] So what happens when the collective force changes but the monument stays the same? Do we then call it obsolete? And if so, how do the monuments retain their power as objects forming links between past and present?[3]

The monuments of this complex legacy belong to three main groups each woven into key aspects of Fascist rhetoric like Militarism and *Romanità* and contested in different ways. The first group were existing historical monuments of ancient Rome, the *Risorgimento*, the nineteenth-century colonial enterprise and the First World War that were stretched to fit Fascist propaganda ends and then easily snapped back once the regime had fallen to suit the rhetorical needs of the democratic republic. Militarism and *Romanità*, after all, were not unique to Fascism and because the empire was essentially no more it did not need to be reckoned with. The second group were new monuments built for heroes and (a!) heroine from these selected pasts and, again, because they belonged to a pre-Fascist era their rhetorical function during the *ventennio* could be sloughed off like an old skin or simply translated to stand for the less strident and more honorific Militarism of the post-war period. The third group of monuments was dedicated to the achievements and heroes of Fascism's own mythologies and these have met with a range of disparate and dissonant fates that, like their architectural, artistic and epigraphic counterparts, has depended on their level of political content, their location and their potential for re-interpreted meanings. Like many other aspects of the Fascist legacy we encounter in this book, there was no coordinated national campaign to remove monuments of the Fascist period after the Second World War. The Republic simply re-claimed what had been appropriated, dismantled the most offensive or prominent Fascist ones, ignored others and then built a whole new group of monuments to honour and glorify the anti-Fascist Resistance.[4] The monuments are many and a full discussion merits its own book. Here I will focus on some key case studies under the three groups that best represent the key elements of Fascist rhetoric: *Romanità*, Militarism, Empire, Modernity/ Fascist Achievement, Moral Behaviour/Social Control, National Unity and the Cult of the *Duce*. Catholic Power was left out of the equation and, if anything, there was a glorification of its temporary losses during the period of the Roman Republic and the *Risorgimento*.

Appropriated monuments

It was all well and good to usher in an era of modernity but the regime believed this was better done with legitimacy from the idealized pasts of Imperial Rome, the *Risorgimento*, the nineteenth-century colonial enterprise and the First World War.[5] Monuments were a key medium for making these temporal connections in the everyday urban spaces of the city so the Fascist regime capitalized on pre-existing waves of national monument-building that coincided with the eras marked by Militarism, National Unity and Empire. These epic sword-wielding and flag-waving heroes populating the piazzas and avenues of Italian towns and cities now belonged to the Fascist State.[6] Rome also had a veritable treasure trove of monuments from the ancient world to be discovered, excavated, reconstructed and appropriated to serve those same elements of Fascist rhetoric to which they added *Romanità*. For example, the Augustan Mausoleum and adjacent *Ara Pacis* Museum were used to make teleological links between the ancient Roman past and the Fascist present. Myths of honour and glory connected to Italy's (somewhat disastrous) efforts in the First World War and the (arguably even more disastrous) colonialist campaigns of the 1890s were harnessed to gain consent from war veterans, keep flames of Nationalism alive and provide a foundation for renewed expansionism in East Africa.

As capital of a new, united nation Rome has more than the usual share of monuments connected to the *Risorgimento* period that was appropriated by Fascist propaganda to promote National Unity. Despite the unification's democratic basis, the concept of a single people led by military-style heroes such as Giuseppe Garibaldi became useful fodder to feed the Nationalist aspect of Fascism and give prominence to the King, whose heir had given Mussolini the reins of government, and at the same time keep the monarchists on side. The *Vittoriano* (Victor Emanuel II Monument) was dedicated to the first King of United Italy in a bid to inspire the everyday citizen to feel part of a new national Fatherland. Along with Giuseppe Mazzini, Camillo Cavour and Giuseppe Garibaldi, he was presented as a key protagonist of the *Risorgimento*.

Garibaldi's monument on the Janiculum hill was given a companion statue of his wife Anita and an Ossuary for the many other soldiers whose motto was *Roma o Morte* (Rome or Death). They are joined by the *Bersaglieri*, a branch of the Army's infantry corps famous for storming the Porta Pia and whose 1932 monument still bears a quote by Mussolini. Italy's short-lived status as a colonial power has left its own legacy that will be explored through the monument to the Battle of Dogali near Termini station and the Aksum Stele which, after many vicissitudes, was returned to Ethiopia.

Alongside the heroes and martyrs of the *Risorgimento*, there is the curious case of the fifteenth-century Albanian hero Giorgio Castriota Scanderbeg and statues of ancient Roman leaders erected alongside a related archaeological site. Along the Via dei Fori Imperiali you can still see bronze reproductions of famous statues of Julius Caesar, Augustus, Trajan and Nerva standing proudly in front of their respective forums. Their thorough excavation and hasty reconstruction was carried out in time for the inauguration of the Via dell'Impero on the tenth anniversary of the March on Rome in 1932 (see Chapter 2, p. 33) and the pedestals still bear the date of the Fascist calendar: *Anno X*.

Fascist-era monuments

Because Fascism placed much importance on public memory as a means of creating consent it was important to populate the monumental landscape with the heroes and martyrs of the Fascist era.[7] Along with muscly allegorical figures representing Fascism as a virile ideal, like the many statues around the *Stadio dei Marmi*, a multitude of effigies of Mussolini kept up the Cult of the *Duce*. He was accompanied by individual heroes like the aviator Italo Balbo, the inventor Guglielmo Marconi, Mussolini's brother Arnaldo, and a bridge doubling as monument to Empire dedicated to Amedeo of Savoy, the Duke of Aosta. Alongside heroes, there were also the martyrs of the Fascist Revolution. This new kind of civic religion merged Christian concepts of martyrdom and mourning with militarist ideas of sacrifice for a greater, patriotic cause drawn from both *Risorgimento* and the First World War.

Romanità

Mausoleo d'Augusto *and* Ara Pacis Augustae *(Augustan Mausoleum and Altar of Peace)*

What better case study to illustrate *Romanità* than the urban assemblage of the Augustan Mausoleum and the *Ara Pacis Augustae* in their own brand-new piazza in the heart of the *centro storico*. The specific connection between Mussolini and Augustus also bolstered the Cult of the *Duce* and was a key facet of the rhetoric of *Romanità* which reached a culmination during the year-long celebrations for the Bimillenial of the Emperor's birth in 1937. The figure of Augustus was brought to the fore with a swathe of events, an exhibition dedicated to the Augustan age at the *Palazzo delle Esposizioni* on Via Nazionale, the excavation of his forum, the reconstruction of the *Ara Pacis* and the 'restoration' of his mausoleum, as part of a broader programme to resurrect the ancient ruins of imperial Rome.[8] But the mausoleum fed more than the rhetoric of *Romanità*; plans to bury members of the Mussolini family in there also promoted the Cult of the *Duce*.[9]

The reclaiming of the Mausoleum began on a fine autumn day in 1934 when Mussolini, his beret at a jaunty angle and wearing a jumper that looks like it was knitted by his mother, struck the first blow of a pickaxe.[10] However, excavations near the mausoleum site had begun as far back as 1926 during which time substantial remains of another key Augustan monument, the *Ara Pacis*, were found. To reconstruct it as a holy site of empire had enormous propaganda potential: a monument built by an emperor of the past after his victories in Spain and Gaul was recreated and by extension appropriated for all to admire, courtesy of the *Duce* after his 'conquest' of Africa and his victories alongside Franco in Spain. Further fragments were recovered and a campaign began to bring others held in museums around the world to Rome. But neither Giglioli nor Mussolini could convince the Louvre or the Vatican to give them back so it had to be hastily put together using plaster casts of known pieces along with wild guesses for pieces that remained missing.[11] The reconstruction was housed in a pavilion by Vittorio Ballio Morpurgo next to the Mausoleum separating it from the traffic a long the Tiber.

And there the Mausoleum sat for decades like a decaying tooth (Antonio Cederna, in one of his many scathing invectives on the urbanism of the Fascist period called it the *dente cariato*) in a traffic-ridden piazza defined on one edge by the non-descript and leaking *Ara Pacis* pavilion and on the three others by stylistically bland and mysteriously occupied buildings that no amount of fancy mosaics or Latin inscriptions could redeem (see Chapters 5, pp. 116–18 and 6, pp. 145–6). But *Romanità* is a continuing myth that has belonged to Italians for much longer than the two decades of Fascism and connections to the Cult of the *Duce* are there only for the aficionados. Under centre-left mayor Francesco Rutelli (1993–2001) the time came to claim these ancient Roman monuments back for the people and the area around the Mausoleum of Augustus felt the reverberations of the Fascist era once more. Rutelli wanted to divest the *Ara Pacis* of its Fascist associations with a brand new museum as one of his Miterrand-style *Grands projets* so he personally invited American 'star-chitect' Richard Meier to design a new *Ara Pacis* pavilion (Figure 5.1).

FIGURE 5.1 Richard Meier, *Ara Pacis* Museum 2006. Photograph by Palickap. Wikimedia commons.

Rutelli attracted criticism from the Right that he was behaving like a Renaissance lord (not a dictator) and Meier was attacked by the local architectural profession who claimed that they 'knew Tibet better than Meier knew ancient Rome'.[12] The art critic Vittorio Sgarbi, who had served as Undersecretary of Arts and Culture for the Berlusconi government, called it 'an indecent cesspit by a useless architect'.[13] The project went ahead regardless and when the right-wing mayor Giovanni Alemanno (2008–2013) was elected he swore to tear it down or at least move it to the outskirts somewhere, who knows where, perhaps near one of Mussolini's *borgate*? But the state of conservation of the *Ara Pacis* made this an impossible promise to keep and his comments were dismissed as 'seeping with the culture of extremism'.[14] Alemanno's supporters were less lofty and more practical either shouting protests about wasted money and waving black flags, going about at night spattering its walls with red, white and green paint or installing a porcelain toilet next to it to make their opinion of modern architecture known.[15] Whether they were crypto-fascists or disgruntled Roman architects sick of foreign architects 'tampering' with their city, we will never know.[16]

Despite the continuing criticism from Berlusconi calling it a 'monstrosity' to local residents proclaiming it a *transatlantico* and the architect Massimiliano Fuksas calling it 'a mistake from the beginning' it has had great success. Like all new things that cause furore, citizens are growing used to it and even learning to like it. In 2006 it was Rome's third most visited museum and it continues to attract tens of thousands of visitors a day thanks to the clever ruse of juxtaposing the ancient first-century BCE monument to exhibitions about everything from Hokusai prints to Cleopatra's cosmetics.[17]

The Mausoleum has had its own resurgence after a new phase of excavation between 2007 and 2009 and extensive restoration work carried out between 2016 and 2021. Archaeologists found that only half of its wall structures were original while the rest were 1930s reconstructions which are being considered, along with other remains of the Medieval and Renaissance periods as intrinsic parts of the monument's history. Plans are also afoot to completely redesign the Fascist-era piazza and create pedestrian areas so that 'the piazza and the monument can go back to being what they have always been: that meeting between past and present that makes Rome one of the most beautiful cities in the world'.[18]

Militarism

Ossario del Gianicolo *(Janiculum Ossuary)*

Monuments honouring military glory in Rome can mostly be found within the walls of the Verano cemetery but on the Janiculum Hill, which looks over the city from the western bank of the Tiber, statues large and small commemorate its time as a key site during the 1848–9 battles for the Roman Republic when Garibaldi took on the French armies defending the Pope. The regime took the existing monumental assemblage and overlaid it with Fascist meanings by first appropriating the existing statues of Garibaldi and the many busts of impressively moustached heroes and then adding two new monuments to give physical form to the rhetorical links between the *Risorgimento* and Fascism. The fiftieth anniversary of Garibaldi's death in 1932 just happened to coincide with the tenth anniversary of the advent of Fascism. The Garibaldi celebrations included a major exhibition in Rome's *Palazzo delle Esposizioni*, a national edition of Garibaldi's writings, commemorative stamps, celebrations in schools, universities and the major *piazze* of Italian cities in a bid to reframe the national history of the *Risorgimento* as Fascist.[19] Much of the impetus for this came from Ezio Garibaldi, son of Ricciotti and Constance who had fought in the First World War and had theorized a (somewhat colour-blind) historic continuity between the *Risorgimento* and Fascism that linked the redshirts of the *Garibaldini* to the blackshirts of the fascists.[20]

Halfway up the hill and surrounded by lawn, between the Acqua Paola Fountain and Bramante's *Tempietto* is a small, square monument that looks like a scaled-down version of E42/EUR's Square Colosseum. Across its parapet, the battle cry *Roma o Morte* (Rome or Death) indicates it is an ossuary for soldiers who died in the battles for the Roman Republic (Figure 5.2). Ossuaries were used by the regime to 'manipulate the memory

FIGURE 5.2 Giovanni Jacobucci, Janiculum Ossuary. Photograph by Ian Woodcock.

of the First World War, to shape Italian culture and identity, and to promote ideals of sacrifice, heroism and martyrdom'.[21]

It was funded by the Governorate and its committee, presided over by Ezio Garibaldi, who hired architect Giovanni Jacobucci from the ranks of the Garibaldi Society to design it. In order to leverage the monument for National Unity, the remains of the *Risorgimento* poet and patriot Gofredo Mameli who wrote the national anthem were also transferred from the *Vittoriano* to a special shrine under the monument. By celebrating the *Risorgimento* fascism was completing what the previous revolutionary movement for National Unity had left undone. Today it continues to stand for just that.

Empire

Monumento a Dogali *(Dogali monument)*

Although a relatively short-lived colonial empire compared to those of France and Britain, for example, Italy's colonial past still bears numerous traces in the contemporary city. In terms of stand-alone monuments, the two examples here show two distinct approaches. The Dogali monument is an example of how pre-existing Colonial monuments were appropriated for the Fascist cause. In February 1887 the news reached Rome that 548 Italian soldiers had been killed at Dogali, Eritrea, by the forces of the ras Alula Egida. By 5 June of the same year, the piazza in front of Termini station was named after them and Rome City Council declared that a monument be built in their honour. It included an obelisk (brought to Rome by the Egypto-phile emperor Domitian and rediscovered by Lanciani in 1883 near the church of Santa Maria Sopra Minerva) atop a cruciform base adorned on four sides with shallow aedicules to frame bronze plaques listing their names. The papers called the monument itself an 'artistic prank', 'a poor effort' and an insult to the soldiers. They were also very critical of the location in front of the station that made Rome feel like a cemetery.[22] An octagonal pedestal was added later to give it a more 'military' aspect and for the 1925 Holy Year the monument was moved from its prominent position in front of the station ostensibly to allow for better traffic flow but possibly also because of the sentiments above. Its new spot in via Principe di Piemonte was also lamented, military honour now kept company with public toilets and drink kiosks.[23] The story may well have ended there had Fascist Italy not decided to expand its African colonies.

In emulation of British and French (not to mention ancient Roman) imperialism, Italian troops looted many valuables whilst invading the Ethiopian capital in 1936. They took books from the emperor's library, paintings from museums, money from the Bank of Abyssinia, entire monuments like the Axum Stele and the highly symbolic statue of the Lion of Judah (given to the emperor by a French railway company) which represented the noble lineage of the Ethiopian emperor. The smaller objects went on display alongside other 'ethnographic' artefacts in the African Museum built near the Villa Borghese (see Chapter 4, p. 94). The Lion, on the other hand, was placed in a politically strategic position at the feet of [Italy's] avenged heroes 'on the base of the Dogali monument'.[24] This was meant to connect the (final) defeat of the Ethiopians (thanks to plenty of Geneva-convention-banned tear gas) with vengeance for the deaths of the 500 killed at Dogali. It was graced with a new inscription that read: This statue of the Lion of judas / was brought here from Addis Abeba / after the imperial conquest / O glorious Dead of Dogali / Fascist Italy has avenged you (Figure 5.3). In case the locals rushing past the monument on the way

FIGURE 5.3 Postcard of the Dogali monument with the lion of Judas in place, 1936. Author's collection.

to catch a train did not get the message, popular songs played to them on the radio about Adowa now being 'free', 'conquered' and 'avenged' drove it home.[25] The sight of the national symbol of the Ethiopian Emperor at the foot of a monument honouring Italian soldiers was too much for young Eritrean interpreter, Zerrai Deress, whose protest in front of the monument had him arrested and interned in a psychiatric asylum. He later became a hero of Ethiopian independence.[26]

In 1944 the Lion was removed from the Dogali monument by Allied troops put safely in storage and returned to Ethiopia in 1969 thanks to the efforts of then Minister of Foreign Affairs, Aldo Moro, whose visit to Ethiopia was more than standard diplomacy – it was an important step towards reconciliation between the two countries.[27] The monument itself still stands, largely ignored, surrounded by discarded beer cans, fast-food wrappers and even condoms. There is an air of shame about it but, as Igiaba Scego asks, is it the shame of yet another monument fallen into oblivion? Or is it the shame of Italy's colonial past that Italy still finds hard to face?[28]

Stele di Axum *(The Aksum Stele)*

The Aksum Stele was Italy's largest and most significant item of war booty but it had to wait another thirty-six years after the Lion of Judah to be returned to its homeland. Brought to Italy under direct orders from the *Duce*, it was originally destined for E42/EUR but instead it was decided to link it more closely to the rhetoric of Empire and appropriating as a beacon of Fascist imperialism by locating it near the soon to be erected Ministry of African Colonies (now Food and Agriculture Organisation building) (see Chapter 3, pp. 57–9).[29] This location right near the Circus Maximus, which once displayed obelisks from ancient Egypt, also made symbolic links to the Palatine Hill, home of former emperors and could act as an important marker on the route to the future expo from the Via dei Trionfi (now Via san Gregorio) (Figure 5.4).

Like the Egyptian obelisks of the Augustan age, the Aksum Stele was a symbol of empire, but unlike the Egyptian obelisks which still mark some of Rome's most important churches, the Aksum Stele returned to Ethiopia in 2005.[30] Though taken with similar intentions to its Roman counterparts, an obvious choice by Mussolini to mimic Emperor Augustus and his seizure of obelisks, the Aksum Stele was a dominant symbol of Italy's colonialist past and a focal point of political tension between the Italian and Ethiopian governments that remained in Rome for almost seventy years.[31] This conflict led to suspended diplomatic relations and drew out the painful memory of Italian occupation for the Ethiopian people. Under the 1947 Paris Peace Treaty, Italy was to give up all of its

FIGURE 5.4 Postcard of the Aksum Stele before and after the completion of the World Headquarters of the United Nations' Food and Agriculture Organisation (former Ministry of Italian Africa) Author's collection.

colonies so by putting its notions of imperial dignity aside and swallowing its colonial pride it could enter the community of democratic nations free of the stigma of Fascist crimes.[32]

With a country in the throes of rebuilding itself, its democracy and its identity, what thoughts were given to reckoning with the colonial side of the Fascist past? Despite being aware of the Aksum Stele's psychological or symbolic value for the Ethiopian people, the government did not give the impression they wanted to repair the wrong. The ambassador of the time maintained that the Ethiopians attached no sentimental, cultural or economic value to its return while others claimed that it was a gift to the Italian people that now symbolized the unity of Italian and Ethiopian peoples.[33] However, the continued presence of both Lion and Stele in Rome affected diplomatic and trade relations between the two countries. While the Lion's return was more straightforward, the Stele remained a moral issue up against the technical issues of flying 160 tonnes of solid stone back to Ethiopia.³⁴ Over the decades numerous campaigns and debates over the Stele's return continued until the late 1990s and just as preparations were being made to send it back it was struck by lightning. Its restored pieces then lay in storage at Fiumicino airport until April 2005 and by September 2008 it was finally reconstructed and officially welcomed home.

Its traces are no longer physical but they remain in the imaginations and memories of Italians and Ethiopians alike. Today the Stele remains inconspicuous by its absence and it has taken any reckoning of Italy's colonial past away with it. Soon after its return, there was some debate about how (or even whether) it should be replaced. Should it be another, modern obelisk? Should there be a competition? Should the new monument keep its function as an urban marker and deny any colonial connection? Should there be a plaque stating 'Here stood the Stele of Aksum'? Wasn't that a bit too funereal? Big names weighed into the debate and, as Igiaba Scego has pointed out, there was no mention of the Stele as an item of war booty and no consideration of what it meant in relation to Italy's colonial past. 'Starchitect' Massimiliano Fuksas suggested we stop 'inflicting suffering on ourselves' and dismissed the idea because no-one ever noticed it anyway so why would they notice its absence. Even Italo Insolera, possibly the most Marxist of urban historians, suggested there be nothing because Rome had enough obelisks already.³⁵

The piazza did get a new monument, one to the victims of the terrorist attack on New York's Twin Towers on 11 September 2001, an important commemoration of an event that changed the course of history. Its twin columns, taken from the city's museum deposits, are supposed to represent the Twin Towers, and it is dedicated to all victims of terrorism. The monument was promised by Mayor Alemanno on a visit to New York indicating that he believed a continued relationship with the United States to be more important than how some Ethiopians might feel.³⁶ The plaque at the base of the columns displays a telling quote from the US writer George Santayana: '*Coloro che non sanno ricordare il passato sono condannati a ripeterlo*' (Those who do not know how to remember the past are condemned to repeating it). As Igiaba Scego asks, 'How can something that seems so right also feel so wrong?'.³⁷ Is it because it is assumed that the wrongs of Italy's colonial past are not at risk of being repeated or is it the sign of a continued unwillingness to confront it? Either way, the question remains: Why is there no plaque commemorating the victims of Italian colonialism? The Stele now stands alongside her sisters and its absence is yet another sign of the 'silence, absence, oblivion, forgetfulness in served in an Italian sauce' that is the country's pervading attitude towards colonialism.³⁸

Modernity/Fascist achievement

Obelisco Marconi *(the Marconi Obelisk)*

Although each monument in its own right can be understood as a Fascist achievement in itself the Marconi obelisk brings together Modernity and Fascist Achievement to celebrate one of Fascism's most important heroes: Guglielmo Marconi. The Nobel Prize-winning scientist, entrepreneur and inventor of radios who died in July 1937 was prime fodder for propaganda so less than two years after his death the Ministry of Popular Culture had hired Piacentini's friend, Arturo Dazzi, to design a funerary monument in his honour.[39] It took pride of place in the main piazza of the E42/EUR, in the very spot previously reserved for the Aksum Stele, to align Marconi with the primacy of the Expo's Science Exhibitions as a key element in the process of universal civilization.[40]

From the outside the 45-metre-high Marconi Obelisk looks like a monolith but it is actually 96 bas relief panels in Carrara marble mounted on a reinforced concrete structure (Figure 5.5). Dazzi re-interpreted the ancient obelisk form as modern antenna, as metaphor for the wonder of radio and

FIGURE 5.5 Arturo Dazzi, Marconi Obelisk. Photograph by author.

its capacity to bring the people of the world together under the aegis of a resurrected Christ.[41] No mention of the crucial role played by radio in the formation of consent, no mention of how tens of thousands of government-sponsored Bakelite boxes projected the barking voice of the *Duce* into every home. Dazzi began work on the panels for what he affectionately called 'Marconi's Antenna' in 1939 ready to be attached to the concrete armature which stood waiting in what was to be the Piazza Imperiale, E42/EUR's most grandiose space (see Chapter 2, p. 47 & Chapter 4, pp. 85 & 92).

When the Second World War interrupted work Dazzi had only started on the first two rows and the new Ministry of Public Works, who did not consider the expenditure justified, decided they would demolish the armature. When Rome was preparing to host the 1953 *Esposizione dell'Agricoltura* (Agriculture Exposition – EA53) in E42/EUR, it was not the thriving directional centre we see today (see Chapter 4, pp. 83–5), it was still a void punctuated by the metaphysical volumes of the recently completed Fascist-era buildings. To be worthy of global attention it needed more spatial landmarks and the semi-complete obelisk easily fit the bill.[42] Dazzi was brought back to finish the job and because time was of the essence he was asked to complete his work in plaster but the artist refused and the ministry considered pulling the whole Obelisk down once more but there was no time for that either. Thanks to the 1960 Olympics, a new opportunity for funding came about in the late 1950s so Dazzi was able to finish all the panels in marble and it was finally inaugurated in December 1959 in plenty of time for the opening ceremony to signify the modernity and achievement of the First Republic.[43]

Despite his known Fascist sympathies, Marconi was, and remains, a national hero.[44] He was honorary president of the London Fascist Association (active in Britain since August 1921), was nominated *Accademico d'Italia* and awarded the 1931 Mussolini prize for Science and was known to discriminate against Jewish scientists (Figure 5.6). Like many other industrialists, he had to make some kind of deal with the regime in order to pursue his career but all this was eclipsed by his standing as a universal figure of Italian history and innovation.[45]

Moral behaviour/social control

Moral behaviour and social control were key elements of the culture of consent and were instrumentalized through the various *Opere* dedicated to different groups. They took on architectural form in the various *Case del Fascio* or *Case Balilla* (see Chapter 3, pp. 73–7), were translated into quotes and aphorisms on building façades (see Chapter 6, pp. 164–7) and were celebrated in monuments. The two case studies in this chapter both merge Militarism with Moral behaviour/social control with one aimed primarily at women and the other two designed to bind aspects of Fascist to practice by creating monuments as ritual destinations.

FIGURE 5.6 Guglielmo Marconi in his *Accademico d'Italia* uniform with Marchioness Maria Cristina Marconi in a rather fetching turban at the Piazza del Campidoglio after being awarded the Mussolini Prize. Luce Historical Archive.

Monumento ad Anita Garibaldi
(Monument to Anita Garibaldi)

If one decides, after admiring the view and the giant statue of Garibaldi on the apex of the Janiculum Hill, to wander down a little bit towards the Villa Lante they will notice an unusual equestrian statue, of a woman pointing pistol in the air with one arm and holding a baby at her breast with the other (Figure 5.7). The idea to build a statue for Anita Garibaldi preceded fascism and its completion by Mussolini could be chalked up to the long list of his achievements. Mussolini 'adopted' the Anita monument as a special project so he could appropriate both its realization and its triple symbolism. It was a Fascist Achievement that could demonstrate the inefficacy of the Liberal State (the idea dated back to 1905 – he was going to make it happen!), bolster

FIGURE 5.7 Monument to Anita Garibaldi. Photograph by Ian Woodcock.

Militarism by absorbing the spirit of the Garibaldi movement and celebrate this warrior-mother to prop up traditional gender roles to reinforce moral behaviour/social control.[46] In parallel to the interment of Mameli in the Janiculum Ossuary, the body of Anita was brought to Rome and placed under the new monument. During his inauguration speech, Mussolini said: 'If the bronze knight nearby [Garibaldi] could come alive once more and open his eyes I like to hope that he would recognise the descendants of his red shirts in the soldiers of Vittorio Veneto, and in the Blackshirts that for ten years now continue his voluntarism.'[47]

There was no need to modify either the myth or the monument of Anita after the fall of the regime. Her acts of heroism transcend it because they belong to Italy's universal history and at best it is a monument to the multi-tasking abilities of today's working mothers.

Ara Caduti Fascisti *(Altar of the Fascist Martyrs)*

Moral behaviour and social control were strongly tied to Militarism and these were reinforced with the newly invented Cult of the Fascist martyrs or *Caduti per la Rivoluzione* (the Fallen for the [Fascist] Revolution) and, although the actual numbers of people who died for this new faith were relatively small, their importance was highly inflated.[48] The idea to extend the Cult of First World War Martyrs to those who fell in the name of the Fascist Revolution came as early as 1923.[49] Local individual martyrs like Giovanni Berta were commemorated in Florence while *Sacrari* (shrines) were built throughout the country to honour the idea of Fascist martyrdom by fulfilling a similar function to that of the Tomb of the Unknown Soldier. Some were set up in existing buildings and purpose-built ones were designed into all newly built *Case del Fascio* (Fascist Party Headquarters) from Aosta to Agrigento. Their post-war fate and eventual re-use were usually linked to how the actual *casa* itself was adapted and they usually ended up as store-rooms, their artworks stripped away or hastily boarded up (see Chapter 3, pp. 73–4).[50]

Rome also had two public versions of this ritual space: a 'pagan'-style altar on the Campidoglio and a Christian-style mausoleum at the Verano cemetery. The *Ara Caduti Fascisti* was created as a multi-purpose altar for worship on the important ritual dates of the Fascist calendar and in 1926 a small section of land on Rome's most sacred hill was set aside for this new purpose.[51] Its proximity to Piazza Venezia and the *Vittoriano* with the Tomb of the Unknown Soldier, was crucial to its political importance and its connections to Militarism. Along with the usual trappings to make it look and feel like a war monument, it had to remain distinct. By using an altar type, common in front of ancient Roman temples, there was also the opportunity to link the monument to the rhetoric of *Romanità*. A relatively smooth and undecorated granite block, preferably one connected to the ancient emperors, was considered ideal. Fortunately, and this could only happen in Rome, the Governorate just happened to have one lying forgotten in the basement of a tramways building among cornices, papal stemma and pipes.[52] In the 1890s the Boncompagni-Ludovisi family had offered up a massive block of granite recently excavated from their Villa for the Dogali monument but the architect thought it was too imposing so now the 4.56 x 5m block was given a new lease of life. It was also Egyptian so could easily be tied to Augustus.[53] At its first inauguration, on 29 October 1926 it was still a simple block of granite on a travertine base and by the same date in 1927 it had been decorated with fragments of other ancient monuments accompanied by imperial eagles and fasces (to connect to ancient Rome) and lions – the common iconography of war monuments that conveniently coincided with Leo, Mussolini's star sign.[54] Its importance at the time can also be measured by its inclusion in a Latin poem that takes the reader on a tour of Rome's historic centre in 1933. Francesco Giammaria's *Capitolium Novum* includes the *Ara dei caduti fascisti* on an itinerary that includes big-ticket items like the Circus Maximus, the Colosseum and the Arch of Constantine.[55] His description underpins its intention to regulate moral behaviour and exert social control:

> Here a new altar, which rises up between the laurel-trees, celebrated with sacred devotion and an eternal cult, has deservedly been dedicated, as the

Dux wished, to the strength of the unsubdued youth, which, slain by an unspeakable crime, shed its blood and offered its life to the Fatherland. Here then it is now honoured with dignity, so that it may become both an example and a warning for future generations.[56]

Its last documented use as a shrine was soon after 8 January 1944. The Ministry of the Interior had just nominated a new Governor of Rome: the Podestà of Naples, Giovanni Orgera. *Capitolium* reports that soon after being sworn in he went to pay tribute to the Tomb of the Unknown Soldier and the *Ara Caduti Fascisti* indicating that two opposing ideals still reigned in the city.[57] After the fall of the regime it was stripped of its decorative elements that were sent back to the storage vaults and turned onto its side so we do not know if its inscription was erased or not. Anyone wandering about in the interstices of space between the back of the *Vittoriano* and the Forum of Julius Caesar would find it lying forgotten once more, up against a section of the Republican walls, accosted by a broken column and behind a railing (Figure 5.8).

FIGURE 5.8 Altar of the Fascist Martyrs all forlorn in the back blocks of the *Campidoglio*. Photograph by Francesca de Caprariis.

Mausoleo dei Martiri Fascisti
(Mausoleum of the Fascist Martyrs)

As Rome's monumental cemetery Verano is home both to the graves of established families and to the famous Italians from the novelists Natalia Ginzburg and Sibilla Aleramo to Rome's first Jewish Mayor Ernesto Nathan; from Mussolini's lover Clara Petacci to the Resistance hero Bruno Buozzi. You will also find a host of national monuments to the war dead: from those who gave their lives to the Roman Republic in 1848 to the fifty-four sailors who died in 1925 in the Sebastiano Veniero submarine as a result of a tragic accident. Located just off the avenue that leads from the main entrance the Mausoleum of the Fascist Martyrs, which doubles as a chapel, has a shallow dome with cornices and columns in travertine enclosing shallow niche in tufa (Figure 5.9). Sculpted heads wearing the

FIGURE 5.9 Mausoleum of the Fascist Martyrs, Verano Cemetery. Photograph by author.

fez with the tell-tale tassel worn by both the *Balilla* (Fascist Youth) and the *Squadristi* (Fascist crack squads) look out from the frame and the columns feature a triangular stone towards the top to symbolise the axe element of the fasces. A bas relief of Victory holding the laurel crown flies above the entrance and a pristine Latin inscription honours those who died for the Fascist faith entrusting them to the protection of Christ. The interior is modelled on a Christian altar to elevate martyrdom for the Fascist cause to the same level as the saints. The plain white wall bears the inscription 'To the Fascist Martyrs' and a window in the shape of a cross sheds light on the dim interior while a small Christ statue looks with benevolence over the space.

The Mausoleum was built in conjunction with the *Mostra della Rivoluzione Fascista* (Exhibition of the Fascist Revolution) and was inaugurated on 25 March 1933 to hold the remains of Roman martyrs to the Fascist cause. Designed by the architect Mascanzoni and with sculptures by Giovanni Prini, it was designed to hold twelve bodies although in reality only four men were killed in Rome during the times of the Fascist Revolution. Others, killed during other conflicts both in Italy and overseas, were added later – including the body of 'La Capitana' Ines Donati a young woman from the Marche who was the only official female *squadrista* and one of the nine women who participated in the March on Rome. She wanted desperately to join the ranks of the *Milizia Volontaria per la Sicurezza Nazionale* (Voluntary Militia for National Security – MVSN) but Mussolini would not allow it and she died of typhus in 1924 supposedly caused by the fervent efforts and enthusiasms of those heady days.[58] *Partito Nazionale Fascista* (National Fascist Party – PNF) secretary Achille Starace had her body exhumed on the auspicious date of 23 March 1933 and her remains were placed in the Mausoleum with great ceremony.[59] After the war, they were taken back to her hometown in the Marche.

Evidence of its continued importance to neo-Fascists is indicated on the marble plaque in its interior that bears the names of other Fascist martyrs who died for the 'Honour of Italy' including – at the top and in the largest letters – Benito Mussolini. Three names have been added to the bottom: Stefano and Virgilio Mattei who died in the 1973 *Rogo di Primavalle* (the Primavalle Pyre) and Michele (Mikis) Mantakas, the Greek student who was shot dead in the violent clashes that occurred during the trial of its alleged perpetrators.[60] They are, like the martyrs to the Fascist Revolution – *Presente!* Not even the Mattei family themselves know for certain who added the names but they were pleased nonetheless. As Amy King has also argued, this clearly indicates a continuity of the Cult of the Martyrs and belief in the Fascist cause. It is most likely the *Fratelli d'Italia* (Brothers of Italy) party who hold annual ceremonies at the Mausoleum.[61] They follow in the footsteps of dedicated Fascists who continued to march there nine months after the fall of the regime to commemorate the foundation of the *fasci* on 23 March 1944 by placing laurel crowns in front of both mausoleum and altar.[62]

The presence of fresh laurel crowns as well as candles and photographs on the altar further demonstrates its continued importance. They could have been left there by another group calling themselves *Comunità di avanguardia* who visit the shrine on 28 October. When interviewed by the press on the hunt for a bit of drama, they proclaimed to be peaceful – there were no salutes, no Party flags or symbols just what they called a tribute to 'their' dead.[63]

National Unity

Vittoriano *(Monument to Victor Emanuel)*

As we saw above Rome has many a monument dedicated to the *Risorgimento* and its heroes, in particular the main trio who made it happen: Garibaldi the soldier, Mazzini the philosopher and Cavour the politician but the Monument to Victor Emanuel II, the first of Italy's three kings, is both the best known and the least loved. Begun in 1885 and made of gleaming white peperino stone, it pulls out all the Neoclassical stops but because it was not completed until 1935, it is most often thought of as a Fascist monument and, in many ways, it was. As a monument about patriotism and the Nation it was primarily about National Unity, as home to the Tomb of the Unknown Soldier it contributed to the climate of Militarism and, thanks to its location next to the Palazzo Venezia, it became protagonist in the spectacle of the Cult of the *Duce* when the piazza was appropriated as a space of mass rallies.

The *Vittoriano* has had many shifting meanings in the course of its existence. Originally meant as a tribute to Italy's new King, even during this first phase its very form shifted from an architectural and sculptural interpretation of the Capitoline to receptacle for complex allegorical programme of sculptures, mosaics and bas reliefs to instil in each visitor a sense of being, not Siennese, Sicilian or even Slav, but Italian. The second shift came about when the symbolic body of the Unknown Soldier transformed the *Vittoriano* from political to civic monument and it was renamed *Altare della Patria* (Altar of the Fatherland) to act as intersection between the patriotism of the Italian nation, national participation in the First World War and Fascist Nationalism.[64]

The Fascists strengthened their claim on the *Altare della Patria* during the African Campaign by choosing the 24 May 1935, the twentieth anniversary of Italy's entry into the First World War, to move the Unknown Soldier into a specially built crypt designed by Armando Brasini. This space became part of a new ceremonial ritual where soldiers, on leaving for campaigns, were to collect their flag from a special gallery within the monument, have it blessed symbolically by the Unknown Soldier by walking past his tomb and return it to its place after their (presumably always victorious) return.[65] The crypt was decorated with contemporary Venetian mosaics of a crucified Christ, the Madonna of Loreto and four 'military' saints: Barbara, George, Martin and Sebastian.[66] The phrase *Victores victuri* (Those who win shall be the winner) inscribed above the doorway that is often used on War monuments rang awfully hollow at the end of the Second World War. The winners were not the Italian army that Mussolini sent to war on 6 June 1940 but the partisans and the Allies.

The *Vittoriano* and the former Via dell'Impero were soon claimed back on 7 December 1947 when a parade of tens of thousands of *Volontari della Libertà* (Volunteers for Freedom) delivered a strong militaristic and anti-Fascist message by assembling in front of the tomb of the Unknown Soldier and then proceeding to pay homage at Italy's newest post-war Monument to Rome's biggest Nazi massacre at the Fosse Ardeatine. In this way, they performed what Dogliani has called a 'symbolic reconquest of those patriotic places which Fascism had once adapted to its own cause'.[67] In 1968, the *Vittoriano* inaugurated more than a decade of violence, fear and death that became known as the *anni di piombo* (Lead/Bullet Years). Two bombs on either side of the colonnades exploded within ten minutes of each other, causing damage to the entrances. Unlike the other bombs planted in banks and offices that exploded at roughly the same time, the intent of the *Vittoriano* bombs was not to kill or injure anyone but to attack the symbolism of the monument. Initially thought to be planned by a group of anarchists, it was later found to be the work of neo-Fascist cells.[68]

In 1969 it was closed to the public and became a kind of arcane mastodon of Brescian marble whose steps were only walked on by a handful of dignitaries to mark the armistices of the First and Second World Wars. Its imposing yet distant presence inspired Peter Greenaway to use it as a set for his film *Belly of an Architect* where the main character Storley Kracklite reflects on his obsession with Étienne Louis Boullée whose projects were of a similar size but never realized.

In 2000 the *Vittoriano* was re-opened to the public and throughout the twenty-first century it continues to be the focus of commemoration for the war against Fascism. On Holocaust Remembrance Day in 2005, a plaque dedicated to the 650,000 soldiers sent to concentration camps was installed in one of the main interior halls and at the monument's feet, where Via dei Fori Imperiali meets Piazza Venezia another plaque to the Partisans stakes its claim.

The 150th anniversary celebrations of Italian Unification in 2011 were a new opportunity for the *Vittoriano*'s return to the political stage with

FIGURE 5.10 Giuseppe Sacconi, Monument to Victor Emanuel and Altar of the Fatherland with some presidential pomp and ceremony in progress. February 2022, Presidenza della Repubblica.

a re-creation of the 'Hero's Journey' of 1921. Then President Giorgio Napolitano and groups of youngsters waved Italian flags to welcome a select group who had re-lived the original journey of the Unknown Soldier from Aquileia to Rome and unveiled a plaque on Platform 1 of Termini station to commemorate the event. The Minister of Defence's speech highlights the *Vittoriano*'s continued role in defining Italian identity (Figure 5.10):

> Today, 90 years on, national unity is just as important when we remember our fallen. Remembering how the Italian people wanted to come together around the symbol of the Unknown Soldier bodes well in a difficult moment like this one where it is essential to find unity once more.[69]

The *Vittoriano* is a multi-valent monument that merged the *Risorgimento*, exalted the monarchy who had also legitimized Fascism and became a central node of commemoration for the First World War. Its temporary appropriation by Fascism is only partially obscured by its post-war vicissitudes and it remains, in the imaginary of many, a Fascist monument.

The cult of the *Duce*

Obelisco Mussolini *(the Mussolini Obelisk)*

When news got around on 25 July 1943 that Mussolini had been deposed, people poured into the streets to celebrate and 'depose' as many monuments, inscriptions and plaques as possible connected to him. A second wave of iconoclasm followed after 8 September armistice with a series of smaller ones in 1945 whose ripples followed the geography of liberation. As we saw in Chapter 1 images of Mussolini were the first to disappear in the waves of iconoclasm that swept the nation in 1943 but one thing is to fling a portrait or plaster bust out the window, an enormous marble monument is quite another matter. It is safe to say that the obelisk dedicated to Mussolini remains one of the best-known and most controversial extant monuments of the Fascist period. Standing tall and stark against the green backdrop of Monte Mario and the triangular frames of the Olympic stadium, its chiselled profile of Carrara marble remains a key element of the *Foro Mussolini/Italico*, the new sporting complex built to the north of Rome on the western bank of the Tiber (see Chapter 2, 38–42). Begun in 1928, this City of Sport was a node of Fascist Rome that acted as the headquarters of the Fascist Youth Organization (*Opera Nazionale Balilla* and later *Gioventù Italiana del Littorio*), a place of learning and physical training to mould the new generations of Fascists. Symbolically, it conveyed associations with Moral Behaviour/Social Control, *Romanità* and Empire.[70]

Architect Enrico Del Debbio included an obelisk in his overall layout for the complex to act as both urban marker and heir to a genealogy that included the monuments brought over by Augustus and then restored and re-erected by Pope Sixtus V Peretti in the 1580s.[71] The idea to dedicate it to Mussolini came about when *Opera Nazionale Balilla* President Renato Ricci and a group of his industrialist friends were taking the *Duce* on a tour of the site of the future sporting complex.[72] Their gift would both emulate and outdo Rome's existing obelisks and feed both the Cult of the *Duce*, with Mussolini as the personification of fascism, and the rhetoric of *Romanità* by connecting him with the emperor Augustus.[73] In the context of a sporting complex for Italian youth Mussolini served as a role model (particularly for boys) with the modern interpretation of an ancient phallic object to allude to *Duce's* virility, his self-domination and physical activity in general.[74] Designed by the engineer Costantino Costantini in 1928, this 'pure, white flag of this city of youth' or 'plastic interpretation' of the fasces was erected on 29 October 1932, just one day after the tenth anniversary of the March on Rome.[75]

After the fall of the regime, the Mussolini Obelisk was reportedly saved from destruction by American soldiers who were using the former *Foro Mussolini/Italico* as a rest centre (Figure 5.11).[76] At the same time legends

FIGURE 5.11 Constantino Costantini, Mussolini Obelisk, *Foro Italico/Mussolini*, c. 1944 while in use as the United States Army Rest Centre with flags of the Allies: Great Britain, the United States of America and France in the foreground. From *The United States Army Rest Center, Foro d'Italia, Rome 1944–45* pamphlet, Casa Editrice Dalmatia di Luciano Morpurgo, Rome 1945. No page number.

abounded around the 32 kilograms (or perhaps 132 kilograms) of gold on its apex. The idea of 132 kilograms (or even 32 kilograms) of gold in 1943 seemed an almost impossible amount of wealth that the *Banca d'Italia* (Bank of Italy) could use well. But that legend went up in smoke when it was discovered that the cap was merely gold-plated bronze becoming a case where some people wished that Mussolini's megalomania was even greater than it was revealed to be.[77]

Like with the Aksum Stele its continued presence may also be a case of moral imperative at odds with practicality: how does anyone go about moving or destroying a sixty-four-tonne monolithic block of Carrara marble? They managed to at least move the marble blocks with the dates on them into different positions (see Chapter 6, p. 157) and turn the *Ara Caduti Fascisti* on the Campidoglio onto its side so why not here? One suggestion was to slice it like a salami to make memorial plaques for partisans who died fighting fascism, a suggestion that was never seriously considered.[78] And what about keeping its usefulness as an orientation device but deleting the inscription? Most of the furore around the erasure (or retention) of the Fascist past was centred around the mosaics of Piazzale dell'Impero. It seems that Fascist slogans and dates that chart the rise of the Fascist empire were far more contentious than defeated Ethiopian leaders or a single obelisk proudly displaying the words 'Mussolini Dux'.[79]

It may seem shocking that such a monument still exists in Rome today and a quick scan of online comments of the right-wing paper *Il Giornale* on whether the Obelisk should come down reveals a range of attitudes. At one extreme, the absurdist notion that if we remove the signs of Italian fascism then we also need to remove all references to Soviet Russia, if we remove Mussolini then we remove Togliatti, if we remove the Obelisk then we remove all the schools, highways and railway stations built by the Fascist regime as well. Others blithely state 'you can take away all the inscriptions you like but there are still 6,000,000 [Fascists] alive today' while others take a more measured approach that history is nothing to be scared of.[80] *Corriere della Sera* journalist Manlio Lupinacci summed it up well in 1959:

> The fifteen years that have passed since the fall of the regime are worth centuries. The world's imperatives have changed so much that the Mussolini monolith is now a contemporary of a Scala family column [of Verona] or a plaque of the Borgias. It is anachronistic to imagine that they can still represent anything today the goes beyond their brief life as a symbol.[81]

An appraisal that the 2022 right-wing Meloni government may have just turned on its head.

Monuments after the Fall

Apart from a few memos emanating from the Presidency of the Council of Ministers in 1944, there is no evidence of a national policy or legislation on de-fascistization in the State Archives.[82] As for monuments, Minister of Education De Ruggiero put forward a proposal for a set of norms to govern the removal of monuments and artworks whose subject matter aimed at exalting fascism and its ideals. In his proposal, the Superintendence of Monuments for each region was to make the presence of these artworks and monuments known to an inter-ministerial committee who would decide its fate after having taken into account: its political meaning, artistic value and the possibility of removal without causing too much aesthetic damage to the building.[83] Other than a response from the Presidency of the Council of Ministers, approving the proposal there is no evidence that neither norms nor committee were ever realized.[84] Individual monuments (and for that matter artworks and inscriptions remained subject to decisions at a local level and their removal happened sporadically over a long period while many still stand today.[85]

Conclusion

Rome's many monuments narrate the slices of its millennial history, and cutting through the twenty or so years of the Fascist era reveals a legacy that continues to be complex. Some of its monuments, like the Mussolini Obelisk, still gleam in the sun as they did the day they were inaugurated, others like the *Ara Caduti Fascisti* lie hidden in plain sight while those honouring the heroes of other times like Anita Garibaldi or the *Bersagliere* have been claimed by the Republic as part of universal history. But the story does not end there.

Italians who stayed faithful to fascism were left out of the official memorialization programmes of the First Republic but clandestine (and not so clandestine) groups of neo-Fascists keep their memory alive through private monuments or in special parts of cemeteries, like the Verano shrine.[86] The advent of the Second Republic with its more right-wing leanings gave sanction to these groups to come out in the open thus making this remains an unresolved tension in Italian society manifest.

Protests by far-right groups are held on anniversaries of 25 April on the part of far-right groups who continue to ask, 'Where are the monuments for OUR dead?'[87] Fascist or anti-Fascist, Italians who were executed, deported or massacred during the regime, the civil war or the *anni di piombo* (Lead/Bullet Years) remain individuals whose death is harnessed to serve a greater cause and have become an integral part of Italy's collective memory and remain, at the same time, individuals that their families and loved ones continue to mourn.[88]

CHAPTER SIX

Aspirations and illusions of control

Re-contextualizing Rome's Fascist epigraphy

Non voglio qui esaltare Rome perché poeti, filosofi, pensatori prima di me e in modo magnifico lo hanno fatto; ma noi fascisti non possiamo dimenticare che Roma, questo piccolo territorio, è stato una volta il centro, il cervello, il cuore dell'impero.
I don't want to exalt Rome here because poets, philosophers and thinkers have done so before me and magnificently so. But we Fascists cannot forget that this little territory of Rome was once the centre, the brain and the heart of the empire.

MUSSOLINI – 'FOR REAL RECONCILIATION', 1 DECEMBER 1921[1]

Introduction

If you studied Latin at school, you may delight in deciphering the many inscriptions on Rome's ancient monuments as you pick your way along the cobblestones of the Roman Forum. But if you look a little harder, perhaps on the way back to your hotel, you will also find all manner of mottos, quotes and inscriptions on Rome's twentieth-century buildings. Some may be hard to read, faded or partially scratched off. If that is the case, then chances are it is a Fascist slogan. But not all traces of such inscriptions are gone, you only need to catch the Metro to E42/EUR to see the words of Mussolini himself still clearly visible on the heights of its buildings. Epigraphy as an integral part of the urban experience of Rome dates back to the times of the Roman Republic. Definitive tomes like the *Corpus Inscriptionae Latinae* record the use of epigraphy across the former Roman empire up until the fifth century, but the practice did not die with the fall of the Roman empire and was part of more widespread revivals of Classical culture most notably during the Renaissance, nineteenth century and, of course, the Fascist era.[2] During the Fascist period they were used for the most part to reinforce Moral Behaviour/Social Control, but they also expressed *Romanità*, bolstered Militarism and exalted Empire. They were like the icing on the cake for Rome's most representative nodes where they spoke to the elites at the *Città Universitaria* and tourists or fairgoers at E42/EUR, but they really came into their own when used to indoctrinate the more impressionable audience – youth at the *Foro Mussolini/Italico* and in the *Quartieri/Borgate* nodes where they had to work on Fascism toughest audience – the working classes.

Words and symbols on buildings are a form of mass media where the past is conceived and presented, rethought and repackaged to communicate a range of messages: commercial, commemorative or conflictual. Whether scratched in the stucco, attached to buildings or sprayed onto walls they draw us out of our everyday state of distraction in urban space and transport us to another space and time, to another emotional state.[3] Plaques, inscriptions and symbols can turn an ordinary building into an *architecture parlante* amplifying its message into the highly charged public space of the city.[4]

For big business, governments and institutions, lettering on buildings is used to shape and govern behaviours and can play an important role in writing history, manipulating memory and forming identity. The construction of a unified memory, history and identity was fundamental to consent building for Italy's nineteenth-century Liberal State, Fascist regime and the post–Second World War democratic republic alike. Architecture's capacity to communicate a precise political message was crucial to the propagandists of the Fascist period who co-opted architecture and architects, art and artists, within the various processes and techniques of building consent. The voice of Mussolini that already resounded in the ears of every Italian who attended rallies, turned on the radio or watched a newsreel also barked at them from the facades of buildings. Inscriptions were recognized as a valuable measure of control carried on from the Nationalist project of the *Risorgimento* (Italian Unification). The Fascist regime used epigraphy as a form of official political discourse that added Mussolini to the mix of peremptory phrases by Cicero, Dante and Garibaldi instructing the population on how to be good (Fascist) Italians and build a national (Fascist) identity.[5]

Inscriptions were integrated into facade compositions from the early design phases and were most often in the stark sans serif font known as *bastone* (stick). Its use was part of the rhetoric of modernity; it was 'rational', 'universal' and flew in the face of convention and *bourgeois* snobbery; it was clear, almost brutal and virile. Its name also recalled the *manganello* (club) favoured by the *squadristi* (Fascist crack squads).[6] On a practical level, this modern form of lettering lent itself to monumental inscriptions because it was easy to carve, allowed for strong shadows and could be easily read from below.[7] This, together with their lofty locations, also made the inscriptions very difficult to modify or erase. In fact, a surprising amount remain and their presence (or otherwise) today is dependent on various factors like author, content, meaning, origin, context and physical location which is most often the prime hurdle to removal.

Immediately after the fall of the Regime, during the chaotic forty-five days of the Badoglio government, people were climbing up on ladders with hammers and scalpels to remove inscriptions and change street names. Together with an official, albeit somewhat haphazard, campaign to remove Fascist era plaques and inscriptions, Italy's new Republic employed epigraphy as a key strategy to re-write the narrative of Italian identity as founded in anti-Fascism. In the post–Second World War period, official writing on the walls came in the form of memorial plaques for partisans killed during the war of Resistance, deportees and victims of Nazi-Fascist violence from the period of the 'civil war' (1943–46). These were placed on the homes of individual citizens, on selected buildings connected to the Nazi occupation like on the former German War Tribunal, now a trade union headquarters in Via Lucullo, but not on the Hotel Flora (now the Marriott) which was used as the Nazi command headquarters. Plaques can also be found at sites of massacres and reprisal killings of partisans and civilians at the hands of both Nazi and Fascist soldiers during Italy's period of civil war and remain key to guide dominant readings of post-Fascist history.

It is not possible to discuss the nearly 1000 inscriptions, symbols and plaques that bedecked Rome's many public and private buildings during the Fascist era. Instead, a representative selection of examples found in the highly charged representative nodes of the *Città Universitaria*, the *Foro Mussolini/Italico* and E42/EUR will be juxtaposed with their use in the everyday spaces of life under Fascism for working and lower middle classes who lived in the Residential nodes many of which were forcibly removed there from the *centro storico* (see Chapter 2, pp. 48–9). The examples will be discussed under the four more prevalent themes of Fascist rhetoric: *Romanità*, Militarism, Empire and Moral Behaviour/Social Control.[8] Because the most common author of inscriptions was Mussolini himself, the very act of inscribing buildings with his words also reinforced the Cult of the *Duce*.

Fascist-era inscriptions: The range in Rome

The stark and clean surfaces of modern Fascist architecture acted as convenient canvases for propaganda. They added another channel of communication for the Fascist message with enormous murals or mosaics, stylized fasces and imperial eagles and giant block letters, often in combination. Inscriptions, plaques and symbols were most common on public buildings built during the *ventennio* (twenty years of Fascism) especially if connected to education or commemoration (see Chapter 5) as well as Fascist building types like *Case Balilla* or *Case della GIL* (Fascist Youth Centres), *Case del Fascio* (Fascist Party Headquarters) and *Dopolavoro* (After-work circles) (see Chapter 3, pp.73–7). Many existing buildings and monuments also had plaques affixed to them in places of maximum visibility, like those that decried the economic sanctions placed on Italy by the League of Nations after the invasion of Ethiopia. The Minister for the Interior had these put up on all public buildings in a bid to whip up hate and scorn for the Allies. After the war, when Italy had been liberated from Fascism by the very Allies being decried on the plaques, Prime Minister Ivanoe Bonomi instructed each Italian city to have them immediately taken down.[9]

The themes of the inscriptions follow those central to Fascist rhetoric: *Romanità*, Militarism, Empire and Moral Behaviour/Social Control. There were citations from Classical or contemporary authors (like Virgil or d'Annunzio) or mottoes of noble families that were often shortened or re-ordered to fit into the space available. Some were composed for the occasion in emulation of ancient styles showing that historical accuracy was less important than allowing monuments and architecture to bind past and present in a meaningful dialogue.[10] Selected snippets of speeches by the *Duce* and slogans mimicking catechism abounded and were primarily aimed at children. Those he supposedly crafted himself (like Believe Obey Fight) were popular while other inscriptions were taken from landmark speeches such as the one proclaiming empire. Their presence on buildings reinforced both the Cult of the *Duce* and the messages his speeches conveyed and were part of a general fetishization that transformed his words into politically charged commodities.[11]

Inscriptions were mostly in Italian but Latin was also used for its effect on particular audiences. At the *Città Universitaria* (new campus of Rome *La Sapienza* university) it was assumed the elite body could read and understand the erudite Latin of the ancient authors but when it came to the less educated working classes the preference went towards aphorisms and phrases to promote domestic bliss, ennoble labour and promote moral behaviour.[12] Apartment buildings, especially those built by the *Istituto Case Popolari* (Worker Housing Institute), used Latin inscriptions to lend an air of nobility with the aim of improving minds. On public buildings they added an air of *gravitas* and solemnity that was universally understood even if the precise meaning was not because the similarities between Italian and Latin are enough to convey a basic comprehension.

Finally, these plaques and inscriptions were often accompanied by the two symbols most closely connected with the Regime: the fasces and the imperial Eagle. These were also used as decorative elements for everything from bollards to lamp posts and applied in highly stylized forms on buildings to break up the monotony of the blank facades of *Stile Littorio* buildings, decorate a balcony and, in the case of Palazzo Venezia, actually added to the doorframe that the *Duce* himself would emerge from to deliver his rousing speeches. The eagles – temporarily co-opted as Imperial eagles for the Fascist empire – have gone back to being eagles but fasces have been almost entirely erased. A bit like the noses and penises of ancient Roman statues, they tend to stick out and are within easy reach so have only very rarely remained intact. Two examples are the highly stylized fasces that form the columns of the Mausoleum of Fascist Martyrs in the Verano cemetery and on the doorways of the Ministry of Aeronautics (Figure 6.1).

FIGURE 6.1 Gallery of (Contradictory) fasces. Montage and photographs by author. a. Extant fasces and inscription on Ministry of Aeronautics; b. extant fasces on the Mausoleum of Fascist Martyrs, Verano Cemetery; c. fasces hacked off a lamp post on the Via dei Fori Imperiali; d. fasces hacked off a sign for Lot 21, Garbatella.

Romanità

Romanità is intrinsic to the practice of inscription and embedded in the use of Latin and ancient authors in the same way as the frescoes and mosaics in the public art gallery of the city revived ancient practices of fresco and mosaic. It therefore pervades the other examples presented in this chapter although two examples of *Romanità* in inscriptions need to be mentioned: the assemblage of inscriptions around the Augustan Mausoleum and the one on the entry portico of the *Città Universitaria*.

Piazza Augusto Imperatore

When Augustus's mausoleum was denuded and brought back to its 'necessary solitude' his *Ara Pacis* (Altar of Peace) was reconstructed nearby in its own purpose-built pavilion (see Chapter 5 pp. 116–8). On the side of its platform facing the mausoleum was an extract from Augustus's *Res gestae* that listed, among other great feats, the transformations he had wrought on Rome. The other three sides of the piazza were defined by new buildings in a nondescript *Stile littorio* embellished with mosaics and inscriptions: two in Latin and a third in Italian.

The first, by Livy, is an extract adapted from the preface of his history *Ab urbe condita* and the second is written in the manner of the *Res gestae* but this time lauding the transformations of the area by Mussolini. It reads:

HUNC LOCUM UBI AUGUSTI MANES VOLITANT PER AURAS/ POSTQUAM IMPERATORIS MAUSOLEUM EX SAECULORUM TENEBRIS/EST EXTRACTUM ARAEQUE PACIS DISIECTA MEMBRA REFECTA/MUSSOLINI DUX VETERIBUS ANGUSTIIS DELETIS SPLENDIORIBUS/VIIS AEDIFICIIS AEDIBUS AD HUMANITATIS MORES APTIS/ORNANDUM CENSUIT ANNO MDCCCCXL A.E.R. XVIII

[In this place, where the manes of Augustus fly in the air, after the Emperor's mausoleum had been rescued from the obscurity of centuries and the dispersed fragments of the *Ara Pacis* had been reunited, Musso**lini Dux**, having demolished the old slums, decided that it should be decorated with more beautiful streets, buildings and houses suitable to a civilised form of life 1940].[13]

Opposite is an extract from an April 1923 speech by Mussolini:

IL POPOLO ITALIANO È IL POPOLO IMMORTALE/ CHE TROVA SEMPRE UNA PRIMAVERA/ PER LE SUE SPERANZE PER LA SUA PASSIONE/ PER LA SUA GRANDEZZA

[The Italian people are the immortal people who will always find a Spring [as in the season] for their hopes, for their passion, for their greatness]

After the fall of the Regime, the brick relief fasces on the facades of the buildings and the above inscription became a target for iconoclasts intent on 'purifying' the city from the taint of Fascist symbols and inscriptions. But whoever was up on the ladder wielding a trowel sometime in July 1943 decided to be quite selective and inject a note of humour to the proceedings. Rather than destroy the whole inscription they decided to cover the section of the date referring to the Fascist Era (A.F.R. XVIII) and the last four letters of Mussolini's name with cement. The inscription would read: 'Now the slums were demolished and the *Ara Pacis* was reconstructed by Musso', the Roman dialect for donkey or jackass. This was *damnatio memoriae* with a twist. Leaving the inscription there, but for this small detail, was a much more powerful gesture than deleting all of it because it effectively undermined all that the former *Duce* had done.[14] But why attack the Latin inscription and leave the Mussolini quote intact? (Figure 6.2)

The answer could be in its polyvalent meaning. Leaving the author entirely aside it could just as well be interpreted in the post-war context. The Italian people had, after all, resisted thanks to their hopes and passions driving out the Nazi-fascists and into the 'spring' of a democratic Republic.

If you go to the Piazza Augusto Imperatore today, perhaps to visit the interior of the newly restored mausoleum, you will notice that the new home of the *Ara Pacis* has kept the text of the *Res gestae* intact. After all, Augustus is Augustus. But you may also notice that Mussolini's full name is there once more and the date of the Fascist era (anno XVII) have been restored. This occurred sometime between the late 1990s and 2002 but who restored it and how remains a mystery.[15]

Entry Portico, Città Universitaria

Students of *La Sapienza* university are more likely to be looking at their phones than reading the inscription on the entry portico of the *Città Universitaria*. This form of latinizing text mimicked the inscriptions on triumphal arches, but its length and altitude meant that it was not so easy for the iconoclasts to attack. As we will see below, inaccessibility was used as an excuse for not removing Mussolini's speech from the Square Colosseum, but this argument did not hold at the *Città Universitaria* where it was deemed imperative to cancel his name and that of the King from the top of the Entrance Gate (Figure 6.3). The original inscription dated 1935 read:

VITTORIO EMANUELE III REGNANTE BENITO MUSSOLINI REM ITALICAM MODERNATE VETUS URBIS STUDIUM IN HANC SEDEM ROMANA MAGNIFICENTIA DIGNAM TRANSLATUM EST

ASPIRATIONS AND ILLUSIONS OF CONTROL 147

FIGURE 6.2 Assemblage of inscriptions at Piazza Augusto Imperatore. Montage and photographs by author. a. Extant quote in Italian by Mussolini; b. restored quote in Latin by Mussolini; c. extract of Augustus's *Res gestae* re-installed on the side of Richard Meier's *Ara Pacis* Museum (with admirer).

FIGURE 6.3 Arnaldo Foschini, Entrance Portico of *Città universitaria* with Fascist-era inscription framed either side with stylised fasces. From *Architettura. Numero speciale – La Città Universitaria di Roma*, 1935, p. 25.

[During the reign of Victor Emanuel III and when Benito Mussolini was governing the Italian state/the old university was moved to this site worthy of Roman magnificence]

With neither King nor *Duce* reigning the country, Piacentini was brought back to supervise the general 'de-fascistisation' of the university. This included chipping away the stylised fasces and relief letters in the severe *bastone* font and sculpting a new inscription was into the travertine in a rounder, friendlier and more Roman-style:

VETUS STUDIUM URBIS QUOD PER TOT HOMINUM SAECULA MAGNA GLORIA FLORUIT ANNO MDCCCCXXXV IN HANC SEDEM ROMANA MAGNIFICIENTIA DIGNAM TRANSLATUM EST

[The old university, which flourished with great glory through so many centuries of mankind, was moved in 1935 to this place worthy of Roman magnificence]

At the same time the stylized fasces adorning the parapet either side of the inscription were replaced by the new logo of La Sapienza University: the *Angelo della Sapienza* (Angel of Knowledge/Wisdom) inspired by the angels with wings of fire that decorate the cupola of Borromini's S. Ivo alla Sapienza.[16] It is clear that in this instance, cost, labour and difficulty of

ASPIRATIONS AND ILLUSIONS OF CONTROL

FIGURE 6.4 Arnaldo Foschini, Entrance Portico of *Città universitaria* with new post-war inscription. Zoonar/Valerio Rosati, Alamy Foto Stock, PHCG7C, Zoonar GmbH.

access were no object to ensuring that the university as the training ground for a new generation of anti-Fascists be divested of all associations with Fascism and the monarchy (Figure 6.4).

Militarism

As to be expected, militaristic phrases abounded on war monuments (see Chapter 5, pp. 118–20) and on the various buildings associated with the military: the *Milizia Volontaria per la Sicurezza Nazionale* (Voluntary Militia for National Security – MVSN) headquarters, barracks for soldiers and other paramilitary corps such as the fire brigades and the *carabinieri* (military police) who would later play such a decisive role in the Resistance. They were an important feature of the many *Case del Fascio* (Fascist Party Headquarters) *Case dei Mutilati* (National Association of War Wounded) and Rome's *Casa Madre dei Mutilati* (Mother House of the War Wounded) was no exception. Buildings and other spaces such as sports grounds connected to the education of Fascist Youth like the *Case Balilla/GIL* (Fascist Youth Organisation Headquarters) and the *Foro Mussolini/Italico* were also common sites for militaristic phrases and this continued in more subtle forms on the walls of Rome's new university, the *Città Universitaria* where militarism imbued the education of the new Fascist elite through the use of Latin phrases from Cicero, Horace and Quintilian.[17]

Inscriptions were not just for new buildings. Mussolini's most famous slogan *Credere Obbedire Combattere* (Believe Obey Fight) was added to the headquarters of existing barracks for tank and fire brigades as if to replace the voice of the military commander with that of the nation's leader.[18] This was often accompanied in these contexts with a second part *e se occorre morire* (and if necessary die).[19] General Diaz's Victory Bulletin from the First World War was also given much prominence and small versions are still around today. Still bearing the stemma of the Savoia kings, these ornate bronze plaques can be found, for example, at the entrances of the *carabinieri* training barracks in Prati where they have continued relevance for today's defence forces.[20]

Ossario del Gianicolo (*Janiculum Ossuary*)

Monuments built to honour the First World War tended to follow the usual conventions of the roll call for the dead or used the repetition of the word

FIGURES 6.5 Gabriele d'Annunzio inscription around altar at the Janiculum Ossuary. Photograph by Ian Woodcock.

Presente! (Here!) common on shrines for Fascist Martyrs, the most famous being the giant ossuary at Redipuglia.[21] These were subsequently adapted to also pay homage to the Italians who died both during the Spanish Civil War and the invasion of Ethiopia.[22] One example still proudly displaying inscriptions of the Fascist era is the ossuary on the Janiculum. It was built in 1941 to honour the soldiers of the *Risorgimento* in a bid to appropriate their myth for Fascist propaganda aims at a time when there was very little public appetite for entry into the Second World War (see Chapter 5 pp. 118–20). The design included a complex set of inscriptions 'curated' by the vice president of the Garibaldi society and a descendant of one of the original *Garibaldini*: Antonio Reggiani. He did not, however, agree with the inclusion of the Garibaldean battle cry ROMA O MORTE (Rome or death) that Mussolini often referred to in his speeches (Figure 5.2).[23] Still visible on the body of the monument itself are a quote from Ezio Garibaldi (the hero's own grandson who went from being a dedicated Fascist to opposing the Pact of Steel with Nazi Germany) and on the inner walls around its altar there are extracts from *Delle Laudi* by Gabriele d'Annunzio the so-called Warrior Poet who led his legionaries to claim the Fiume peninsula back for Italy in 1920 (Figure 6.5). On the central pillar of the crypt there is a quote taken from Livy's history of Rome, *Ab urbe condita*: ET FACERE ET PATI

FIGURES 6.6 Italian quote attributed to Mussolini and Latin quote by Livy in the crypt of the Janiculum Ossuary. Photograph by author.

FORTITA/ ROMANUM EST (To act and to suffer bravely is Roman). It is part of a longer declaration attributed to Mucius Scaevola that was strongly tied to the Nationalist movement and became even more popular during the First World War (Figure 6.6).[24]

On the walls Giuseppe Mazzini (the philosopher of the *Risorgimento*) speaks of the angel of victory and opposite is an intact quote attributed to Mussolini but also common to many other war monuments:

RESTINO PERENNEMENTE SCOLPITI NEI CUORI I NOMI DI COLORO CHE MORIRONO COMBATTENDO PER FARE PIÙ BELLA E PIÙ GRANDE LA PATRIA

[May the names of those who dies to make our Fatherland grander and more beautiful be forever engraved upon our hearts]

We know that the symbols of the fasces were swiftly removed after the fall of the Regime to firmly disconnect the continued honour that Resistance forces and post-war Italian culture pay to Garibaldi and the *Risorgimento* but the iconoclasm did not extend to the inscriptions. Ezio had redeemed himself, d'Annunzio had a track record that went beyond his Fascist convictions and the Mussolini quote was only an attribution. The crypt is also barely accessible to the public and has a holy character that would have stopped the hammer of even the most fervent anti-Fascist.

Casa Madre

Though built in the Fascist era and designed by the architect most firmly identified with it, the *Casa Madre dei Mutilati* by Marcello Piacentini stands almost exactly as it was built (see Chapter 3, pp. 62–3). This building was literally the Mother House of nearly 100 *Case dei Mutilati* built along the length of the peninsula for the *Associazione Nazionale*

FIGURE 6.7 Marcello Piacentini, National Association of War Wounded, side façade showing a triad of mottoes above the windows. Photograph by Ian Woodcock.

Mutilati e Invalidi in Guerra (National Association of War Wounded – ANMIG) that was founded by independent groups of First World War veterans in 1917 and soon co-opted into the mechanisms of the Fascism propaganda machine.[25]

Its decorative programme was partially censored and modified after the war but the inscriptions on the outside are untouched. The triangular building has three long facades composed according to Classical rhythms and pierced on the *piano nobile* by six long arch-shaped windows. Carved into the top of each window frame are six Latin inscriptions in elegant Roman Square Capitals and of a quasi-religious tone to convey the idea of sacrifice for the Fatherland as secular martyrdom (Figure 6.7). Some can be traced to long-standing noble families and bear similarity to the pithy mottoes of military brigades like the ME NE FREGO (I don't give a damn) of the famously fearless *Arditi* corps of the First World War. They also recall slogans penned by d'Annunzio and later appropriated by Fascism such as the untranslatable EIA! EIA! EIA! ALALA which was a kind of Hip Hip Hurrah! The mottoes were chosen by the President of the association, Carlo Delcroix, a practised orator who was able to elevate himself to hero status after being blinded during the First World War by a faulty hand grenade (and not in battle as it was commonly thought).[26]

The sequence is repeated on each facade and begins with: CITRA CRUOREM (This side/just short of bloodshed) implying a non-fatal wound. Derived from a medieval hymn, CITRA CRUOREM weaves into the rhetoric of both Fascism and Catholicism.[27] Seen in its context – 'Eternity must be feared by good men; beyond the bloodshed, it is thought that the lofty summit of the martyrs was obtained by virtuous behaviour' – it is clear why Delcroix chose it. It is clearly linked to martyrdom and, for the regime, it had the bonus of directing behaviour.[28] The reference to blood is, of course, highly charged and used to political advantage for its threefold significance: it referred to donating blood in Red Cross drives, the concept of bloodlines in racial theory and Catholic iconography of bloodied Christ and the saints.[29] Martyrdom and sacrifice crossed over three identity-building cultural constructs of the period: war heroism, Catholicism and the Fascist Revolution (see Chapter 5, pp. 128–33). The quote illustrates the regenerative powers of spilt blood to justify the spilling of more blood and, literally, create new blood to be spilt through the embedding of the belief system in new generations.[30]

Next in the sequence is: MICAT IN VERTICE (It shines at the summit), the famous motto of the Chigi family. The phrase refers directly to the star at the top of their coat of arms but could also allude to stars on a medal, to glory and/or as guides in moments of despair. This can be seen throughout Delcroix's writings, like for example: 'glory is the … Hearth of the suffering, could you not see how the golden medal shone on your mourning clothes like a star in the dead of night?'[31] This is followed by: PERCUSSA VIVIT (Having been struck she (patria?) lives) from the stemma of the Archbishop of Toledo. This is the wounded soldier who continues to live despite being struck down but could also refer to the Fatherland that relives thanks to Fascism. It is closely connected to the next inscription: GEMENDO GERMINAT (In lamenting it blossoms). This is the motto of the Carassi family of Turin and alludes to the blossoming of a new life after the war thanks to the efforts of ANMIG and the Fascist regime. ARDEO NAM CREDO (I am inflamed for I believe) is also a family motto used by noble families hailing from both Florence and Sicily and would have had the strongest resonance with the idea of Fascism as a lay faith.[32] The belief in the glory of the Fatherland is what ideally inflames the spirit and helps send the body into battle. This spirit was kept alive by the dominant militaristic propaganda of the Fascist era. The final motto, CONCUSSUS SURGO (Having been knocked down I get up) continues this dual theme. Together, the mottoes summarise the myth of the war experience. Their collective meaning recalled ideals that allowed soldiers, their families and the Nation to transcend the horrors of their experience to retain meaning for their individual lives in the knowledge that their suffering was for a greater cause.[33]

The mottoes on the *Casa Madre* are all related to concepts of war heroism loosely linked by themes of sacrifice and resurrection that were shared by Fascist and Catholic culture based on the concept that a death on the battlefield or during the days of the Revolution, became a life given to the Fatherland much in the same way that Christ's death upon the cross was a life given as redemption for sin.[34] In a post-war democracy dominated by Christian Democrats, the Catholic part of the meaning persists but this time its parallels are limited to war heroism which enjoyed a resurgence after the Second World War and the Resistance as the many plaques around the city dedicated to partisans attest. On one level, these inscriptions act as a memorial for the public of both the sacrifice made by the soldiers and the plight of invalids, widows and orphans. Their continued presence on the building negates their temporary appropriation during the Fascist period because the universality of the meaning behind them allowed them to remain untouched. They spoke (and continue to speak) to the community of invalids and their families who experienced the building as a collective home where they could receive concrete financial assistance, participate in events and worship at the altar of their fallen comrades as part of a 'fraternity of the trenches'.[35]

Case Balilla/GIL *(Fascist Youth Organisation Headquarters)*

Slogans were an integral part of indoctrinating the future fraternity of the trenches, Italy's youth, to discipline, obedience and combat. This started in the school room and continued at summer camp and in the sports fields all the way to university. Each *Casa Balilla/GIL*, or headquarters of the Fascist

Youth Organisation, would the feature the Fascist oath on their facade as well as the same *Credere Obbedire Combattere* we saw on the military barracks. As we saw in Chapter 3, these buildings continued to provide the post-war populace with much-needed sports facilities but without the Fascist rhetoric. Highly charged and overt inscriptions such as the Fascist oath were quickly removed either by bottom up initiative or top-down directive but, as with other examples it is difficult to pinpoint a pattern. At the *Casa Balilla/GIL* in Forlì, the outline of the relief lettering still remains and the same goes for the *Casa Balilla/GIL* in Trastevere where the slogan *Necessario vincere. Più necessario combattere* (It is necessary to win. It is more necessary to fight) is still faintly visible above the small *arengario* of the building's *Torre littoria* (Figure 3.8). Moretti had the same quote on the main facade on the *Casa delle Armi* at the *Foro Mussolini/Italico* but that one has been decisively removed.[36] While at Trastevere the inscription was reinterpreted in 2022 by artist Andrea Lo Giudice whose site-specific project *A+G* used phosphorescent pigment to highlight the letters A, M, A, R and E from the inscription so that it reads 'to love', a creative and ironic way to deal with difficult heritage.[37]

Piazzale dell'Impero/Foro Italico, Foro Mussolini/Italico

An entirely different approach was taken with the inscriptions on a configuration of twenty-four marble blocks that, together with the Mussolini obelisk and the sphere fountain demarcate the mosaicked Piazzale dell'Impero (now Piazzale Foro Italico). Eleven blocks either side face towards the Tiber while two larger blocks rotated at ninety degrees are oriented towards the centre. The dates form a summary history lesson for the uniformed youth in militarized formations marching towards an imagined destiny of eternal Fascism. The dates were to be memorized like a litany together with the coordinated marching, salutes and physical exercises that were intended to mould the new generation through a coded set of gestural systems that stipulated their affiliation to Fascist society. For children it was especially important to take ideology out of the abstract realm and bind it to a set of images and actions and, in the case of the Piazzale dell'Impero it was a sequence of dates that coincided with the new ritual dates that marked the calendar of Fascist society (Figure 6.8).[38]

The primarily militaristic narrative begins on the right-hand side and is interspersed with instances of Fascist Achievement related to acts of foundation of specifically Fascist organizations – the MVSN and the ONB; the *Popolo d'Italia* newspaper and the Pontine Marsh towns. It begins with Italy's entry into the First World War (24 May 1915) followed by the Battle of Vittorio Veneto (24 October 1918), the Battle for Grain policy (30 July 1925) and the inaugural *leva fascista* or Fascist draft (21 April 1926) which,

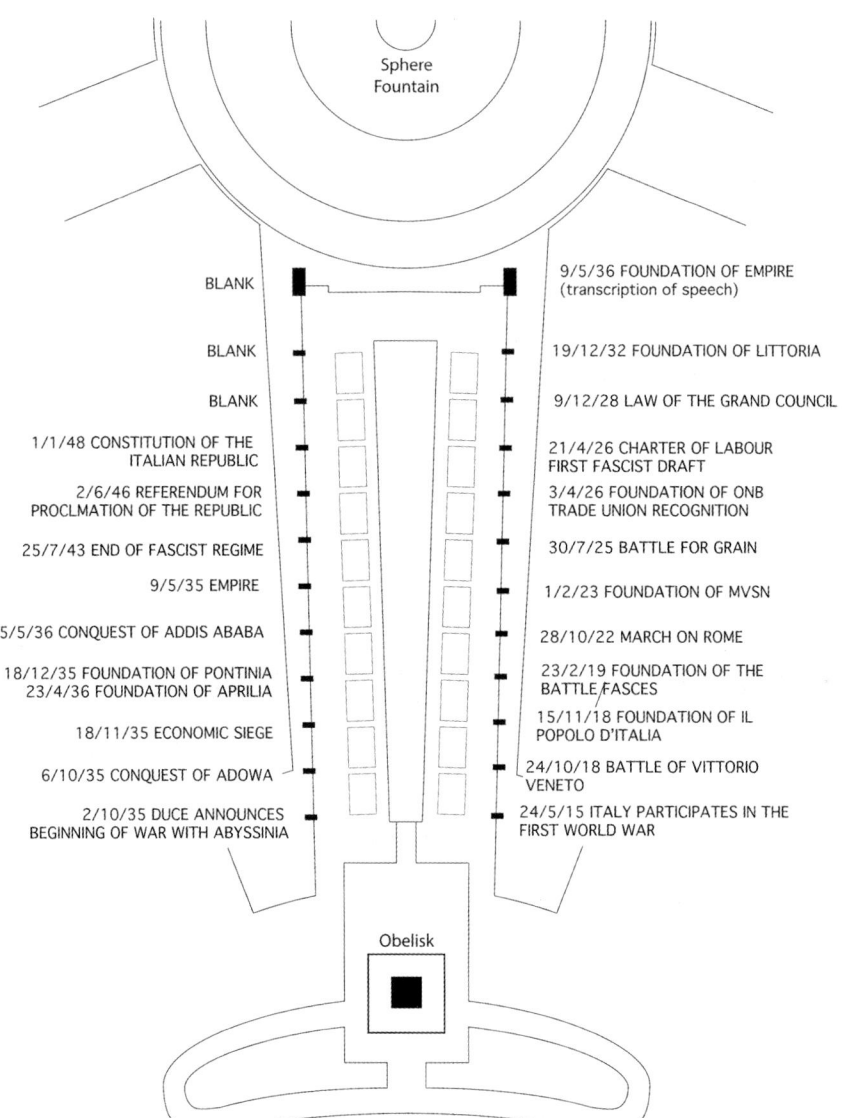

FIGURE 6.8 Diagrammatic plan indicating dates shown on the marble blocks at Piazzale dell'Impero/Foro Italico. Drawing by author.

like the Catholic confirmation ritual, confirmed an adolescent's Fascist faith and subsequent entry into the Party. The chronology then continues on the left-hand side with specific episodes in the lead up to the declaration of empire in May 1936, which will be discussed in the following section on Empire.

Empire

Piazzale dell'Impero/Foro Italico, Foro Mussolini/Italico

The sequence of marble blocks on the left-hand side of the former Piazzale Impero begins with another entry into war, this time with a proclamation from Mussolini of a war against Abyssinia (as Ethiopia was also known) on 2 October 1935 (Figure 6.8). The martial narrative continues with the Battle of Adowa, the League of Nations sanctions – framed as an *assedio economico* (economic siege) – and the conquest of Addis Ababa with the foundation of Pontinia and Aprilia thrown in for good measure. The sixth block in the sequence proclaims empire and this is reiterated in the large block facing the centre of the avenue off the left-hand side which bears a large section of the Empire speech that Mussolini delivered from the balcony of Palazzo Venezia on 9 May 1936 (Figure 6.9). Five blocks remained to be filled, five blocks that Mussolini perhaps dreamed would bear dates of

FIGURE 6.9 Luigi Moretti, Piazzale dell'Impero/Foro Italico. Marble block displaying extract from Mussolini's Proclamation of Empire speech. Photograph by author.

rousing victories against Greece and Albania and alongside Nazi Germany in the Second World War, dates of more new towns, bigger and better social and economic reform. But it was not to be.

The Olympics provided the impetus to finally take action on an issue that had been problematic for some time: removing this set of remaining inscriptions that celebrated a universally condemned past lest they be thought of as a form of glorification.[39] Reasons ranged from possibly offending members of the former League of Nations with a reminder of the sanctions placed on Italy after it invaded Ethiopia to being generally laughed at for still having the word *Duce* repeated over and over in mosaic.[40] Did the continued presence of these artefacts signify that Fascism had never gone away and that democracy was a passing phase or did their very presence in what was a solid, democratic Republic only strengthen it?[41]

While left-wing papers like *Paese sera* and *l'Unità* clamoured to have them removed and right-wing papers like *Il messaggero* asserted that Fascism was a part of Italian history that could not be cancelled, the more open-minded *Corriere della Sera* had a more measured approach. Leaving them there was an act of faith in Italian democracy itself because they acted as testimonies of a past marked by inconsistent rhetoric, a rhetoric that the blocks themselves help to reveal.[42] When it came to the removal or otherwise of the inscriptions it was more a question of common sense and civil education than of politics. Their continued presence did not necessarily signify the permanence of Fascist ideology nor was a refusal to delete the inscriptions a signal of being in cahoots with the far right. Lupinacci argues that of all cities it should be Rome to best accommodate layers of history because if you look around that is all you see so why should the layer of history proper to the *ventennio* be any different?[43] After all the lay state of a unified Italy, whose most stringent agitators wanted to throw the coffin of the Pope into the Tiber, did not go around hacking every papal stemma or inscription off the walls. He did not believe that the murder of Matteotti or the sufferings of the soldiers sent to fight in the Second World War without adequate weapons or clothing could be redeemed by ripping fasces off architraves. He has no problem with the frenzy of iconoclasm – either by the people or by the government – if that frenzy is fed by the excitement of overturning a tyrant and a hate towards both him and the Allies turned enemies who caused so much suffering during the days of occupation. But to do it fifteen years later to ostensibly pander to the sensibilities of 'democratic' foreign tourists was another matter. It was not a problem when the *Foro Mussolini/Italico* hosted the 1951 NATO meeting or when popular Japanese travel writer Kaoru Kanetaka walked across the tiles in her kimono so what made the Olympics different?

In the end only the block referring to the League of Nations sanctions was covered up for the Olympics and it was decided instead to contextualize the sequence of dates within a broader arc of history. The seventh block was inscribed with the Fall of the Regime on 25 July 1943. This was followed by the Referendum for the Republic on 2 June 1946 which consigned

FIGURE 6.10 Luigi Moretti, Piazzale dell'Impero/Foro Italico. Marble block displaying freshly minted inscription to commemorate the referendum for the republic. Luce Historical Archive, Rome.

the Savoia Royal family – who had been seen to twice betray the Italian people – to history. The final date in the sequence is a new foundation, that of the Italian Republic on 1 January 1948. *Istituto Luce* photographs dated August 1960 show the blocks with the new dates contemporary to the 1959 debates surrounding the removal of the 'offensive' mosaics from the Piazzale (Figure 6.10).

But this approach did not necessarily quell debate. It continued in a more informal way through waves of graffiti when the marble blocks became a favourite 'battle' site between left- and right-wing groups. Tim Benton documented the state of the blocks in 1976 showing that the ongoing presence of these dates from the Fascist era in the contemporary city retain significance.[44] Other photographic evidence from the 1970s shows that some blocks are more polemic than others. The one with the date of the League of Nations sanctions (that was uncovered once more after the Olympics) and the one with the proclamation of empire showed signs of repeated graffiti, erasure and re-writing. The same went for the new blocks: the fall of Fascism was denied by crossing out the statement while the declaration of the Republic was overwritten with *Evviva il Duce* (Hooray for the

FIGURE 6.11 Luigi Moretti, Piazzale dell'Impero/Foro Italico. Marble block displaying graffiti denying the fall of the Fascist regime and exalting the Duce. Photograph by Edward Schröter. Foto: Bibliotheca Hertziana – Max-Planck-Institut für Kunstgeschichte, Rom.

Duce) (Figure 6.11).[45] The blocks have been since restored and now display occasional signs of the ongoing feud between Rome's rival football teams: Roma and Lazio. Two more blocks at the end of the sequence remain blank waiting for a history that is yet to be written.

Corso Rinascimento

While the common extract from Mussolini's 9 May Empire speech '*Il popolo italiano ha fondato con il suo sangue, l'impero*' (the Italian people have founded the empire with their blood') was systematically removed from the many schools and *Case Balilla/GIL* around the country, other less obvious references to Empire remain. One example can be found just behind Piazza Navona on the Corso Rinascimento on a building formerly belonging to the National Insurance Institute and up until 2020 at least, home to a university study abroad programme (Figure 6.12). The familiar *bastone* font above the main entrance of the building's stripped-back Classical composition reads: ITALIAE FINES PROMOVIT BELLICA VIRTUS/ ET NOVUS IN NOSTRA FUNDITUR URBE DECOR (The confines of Italy have been extended with war-like valour/and a new beauty

ASPIRATIONS AND ILLUSIONS OF CONTROL

FIGURE 6.12 Arnaldo Foschini, INA Building, Corso Rinascimento displaying an inscription about Empire. Photograph by author.

is bestowed upon our city). Drafted for the purpose by the obscure poet Raffaello Santarelli, it is dated in the year of the Lord 1937 and in the usual language of ancient Roman inscriptions, also *imperii primo* – the first year of empire.[46] There are two things happening here: the Latin text and the comforting presence of the she-wolf suckling Romulus and Remus on the top floor balcony allow this inscription to fade into the general context of *Romanità* and could easily be perceived as belonging to another time. Secondly, like the Duca d'Aosta Bridge and other monuments discussed in Chapter 5, it fits into a general atmosphere of convenient oblivion and self-sympathizing attitude towards Italy's colonialist past.[47]

The Palazzo della Civiltà Italiana *(Italian Civilisation Building)*

Nowhere is the continued presence of empire more outspoken than at E42/EUR with two of the most famous extant inscriptions on the parapet of the *Palazzo della Civiltà Italiana* (Italian Civilisation Building) and above the colonnade of the *Palazzo Uffici* (Office Building) in the south-western suburb of E42/EUR. Planned as the site of Rome 1942 World Exposition, it has fulfilled its prophecy of a modern government, commercial and residential area of the city (see Chapter 2, pp. 43–8 and 4).

The 'Square Colosseum', as it is affectionately known, is one of the first signs of arrival into the city when either travelling in by train or speeding by on the freeway (i.e. when it is not clogged with traffic). Originally built for the Exhibition of Italian Civilisation, it was to become a permanent museum at the close of the Expo and after years of abandonment and many plans for its re-use it is currently the headquarters of the Fendi fashion label (see Chapter 4, pp. 89–91). Looking up at its stark, square form it is easy to notice that its parapet has a phrase proudly expounding the noble pursuits of the Italian people in bringing civilization to the world as poets, artists, heroes, saints, thinkers, scientist, navigators and migrants – less evident is the fact that this is a quote by Mussolini. The inscription was not part of the original competition entry by the trio of Guerrini, La Padula and Romano whose initial perspectives show a block masonry solution with an even border framing its array of sixty-three arches.[48] At one point the parapet was going to boast a frieze of Victory holding a Roman military standard but apart from an archival photograph showing a trial image, not much else is known.[49] Like many other buildings at E42/EUR, its perceived flaws were fixed by Piacentini who played around with its proportions to make it a perfect square and increased the height by adding a blind storey thus creating a bespoke surface for the building to, literally, speak.

The original plan was to have it display extracts from Augustus's *Res gestae* but it was decided that the words of the ideal Emperor would be better placed on the plinth of the new pavilion being built to house the reconstructed *Ara Pacis* right alongside his newly excavated and denuded mausoleum (see Chapter 5, pp. 116–8).[50]

It was replaced by an extract from the *Res gestae* of the 'ideal' *Duce* himself, his 1935 'Ascension Speech' where he addressed the (estimated) 20 million people in the piazzas of Italy and railed against the League of Nations and the 'blackest injustice' of economic sanctions against Italy for the invasion of Ethiopia that would take that 'place in the sun' away from the Italian people 'to whom humanity owes some of its greatest conquests' (Figure 4.5).[51] It reads:

UN POPOLO DI POETI DI ARTISTI DI EROI/ DI SANTI DI PENSATORI DI SCIENZATI/ DI NAVIGATORI DI TRASMIGRATORI

[A people of poets, of artists, of heroes, of saints, of thinkers, of scientists, of navigators, of migrants]

That same people of poets, etc., were Italian troops who brought tear gas, looting, rape and death along with their 'civilisation'. Once placed on the parapet of the planned Expo's most visible building Mussolini's explicit call to arms (that any Italian visiting the fair would have well remembered) became an innocuous statement to help describe exhibits that traced a history of Italian civilization from the birth of Rome to the triumphs of Fascism. Yet it remained, as Benton has argued, 'a defiant claim for universal supremacy, a statement of Imperialism'.[52] But without an Imperialist climate pervading society in general is it not possible to consider that post-war Italy was still that same nation of poets and scientists? Is it not conceivable that now they could speak to the achievements of a democratic republic?

Palazzo Uffici *(Office Building) at E42/EUR*

The second building at E42/EUR still bearing a Mussolini quote is not far away. It is the *Palazzo Uffici* which still fulfils its original function as the administrative centre of E42/EUR, now a private company (see Chapter 4, pp. 91–2). Built in less than two years the executive, administrative staff and the architects drawing up the plans for the Expo layout moved in while the paint was literally still drying. This was both a practical and a symbolic gesture because the building acted as a foundation stone for the future Expo, the Third Rome of Fascism and Italy's further expansion across the seas.[53] Inside the main hall a Latin inscription commemorating the building's completion by Mussolini and honouring the King was removed and covered with a wall panel by Gino Severini (possibly one for the 1953 Agricultural Exhibition).[54] Another, far more visible instance on the building's exterior exemplifies the many mysteries behind the treatment of Fascist-era inscriptions. The Mussolini quote emblazoned along the colonnade comes from his 1925 *La nuova Roma* speech and also makes a reference to empire but perhaps a more oblique one. It is still early days and this speech was being given in the halls of the Campidoglio on the occasion of the swearing-in of Rome's first Fascist governor when the idea of a Fascist empire was still a twinkle in Mussolini's eye (Figure 4.6).[55] It talks of Rome both as city and concept and reads:

> LA TERZA ROMA SI DILATERÀ SOPRA ALTRI COLLI LUNGO LE RIVE DEL FIUME SACRO SINO ALLE SPIAGGE DEL TIRRENO

> [The third Rome will expand over other hills along the banks of the holy river [Tiber] to the beaches of the Tyrrhenian [Sea]]

This speech was therefore appropriated in order to present E42/EUR itself as a synecdoche for empire, the magnificent Third Rome which will expand beyond its hills, along the shores of the sacred river (the Tiber) to the shores of the Tyrrhenian Sea. Its location was important as the colonnade would serve as the ticket office during the time of the Expo giving visitors plenty of time in queues to absorb the meaning of the words, though without the help of a translation app.

Together with *Palazzo Uffici*, the *Palazzo della Civiltà* was the only building completed before work was abandoned on the site in 1943 and this may explain, firstly, why they have inscriptions and, secondly, why they are still there. During the first wave of iconoclasm that swept Italian cities in the heady days of 1943 and 1944 E42/EUR was basically a half-built ghost town where the homeless took cover from the elements, the Nazis stole toilet bowls from the basilica and the odd flock of sheep grazed among piles of unused building material. Quite apart from the fact that they are impossibly high, it would not have occurred to people to target these inscriptions at that time and later, when E42/EUR was being used as a base for Allied troops inchoate inscriptions from a dead leader would have been the last thing on anyone's mind. The interim Commissioner of E42/EUR in fact wrote to the prime minister in December 1944 explaining that a large number of symbols and insignia on buildings had been removed (including seven large fasces at the entrance of the Office Building) or at least covered over but that they could not proceed with removing inscriptions and mosaics because the buildings were being used by Allied troops. He then promised to see to it as soon as practicable.[56] But it never became practicable and now enough time has passed to render its politics less urgent.

If you did not know these quotes were by Mussolini, you could be excused for thinking they were simply a proud description of the Italian people. They were, and continue to be, poets, artists, heroes, saints, thinkers, scientists, navigators and transmigrators. As for the inscription about the Third Rome, when read out of context, it simply states a fact. Rome has expanded, thanks to the threads of the Fascist matrix, towards the sea. But if we recall the case of the *Città Universitaria*, this demonstrates that hard to get at locations of substantial size that take considerable time, effort and expense to remove are not enough of an explanation for why a Fascist-era inscription should remain. While the portico inscription made specific mention of a fallen *Duce* and a deposed King using the Fascist calendar, the writing on the *Palazzo Uffici* and the *Palazzo della Civiltà* – especially if one does not know the source of the quote – are more open to interpretation. Also, the university was used virtually without interruption and is located in the *centro storico* node while E42/EUR lay in disuse for decades and remains peripheral despite the efforts of Virgilio Testa and his successors to make it an integral part of the city (see Chapter 2, pp. 43–8 and 4, 83–7).

Moral behaviour/social control

Inscriptions prescribing moral behaviour and social control are mainly found on apartment buildings, particularly on social housing built by the *Istituto di Case Popolari* (Worker Housing Institute – ICP). Many of them were hand-picked to express the virtues of Fascist society but some of them pre-date the Fascist era and are more closely connected to the politics of the ICP whose aim was to build good houses for happy workers and ennoble their souls with Latin inscriptions that they only partially understood.[57] But they were also used on high schools and the *Città Universitaria* for an audience who knew Latin.

Apartment buildings

Latin inscriptions common on apartment buildings were intended to infuse specific notions of moral behaviour and in that way exert forms of social control (Figure 6.13). How successful they were can never be truly known but what we can do is analyse their intended meaning and how it could be re-interpreted in the post-war political context. Overall they exalted the values of work, deserved rest and the peace of being at home with such lines as NIHIL SENZA LABORE, adapted from Horace's Satires (1,9,59–60); NIHIL SINE MAGNO LABORE VITA DEDIT MORTALIBUS – life has given humans nothing without great labour). This notion of domestic bliss was also inscribed on apartments built for workers in 1929 out in the new Prenestina district next to the SNIA Viscosa factory. Adapted from Cicero *Pro domo sua*, XLI it reads NIL SANCTIUS QUAM DOMUS UNIUSCUIUSQUE CIVIUM – there is nothing more holy than each citizen's own home. Owners of private villas also liked to show off their status, education and, while they were at it, their morals like the Professor Mario

FIGURE 6.13 Latin inscriptions for all classes. a. 'LABOR OMVIA VINCIT' on an apartment building in Via dei Ciceli, Quadraro. b. 'DOMINUS CUSTODIAT DOMUM' on a Villa in Via dei Monti Parioli. Photographs by author.

Francesco Oddasso who adapted this quote from Horace's Epistles (I, 11) for his villa in the San Saba quarter: QUOD PETIS, HIC EST, ANIMUS SIT TE NON DEFICIT AEQUUS. (Here is that tranquillity you seek; if you are good cheer, tranquillity will not forsake you).

The provision of housing by the State was a linchpin of the consent-building process and this was reinforced with such quotes as could be seen in INCIS housing for state employees like the apartments at Piazza Mazzini 8 built in 1924, DOMUM AEDIFICAT SAPIENS INSIPIENS DEXTRUET (The wise man builds a home the foolish man destroys it). Given the context of the thousands of homes destroyed by the *sventramenti*, this would come off as unintentionally ironic.

Other common phrases exalting domesticity were: PULCHRA DOMUS FAMILIAM LAETAT (A beautiful home brings the family cheer), DOMUS TUETUR ET VITAM LAETIFICAT (The home protects us and cheers up our lives) and DULCE POST LABOREM DOMI MANERE ... (How sweet to remain at home after work). The concept of good cheer also appears with quotes from the poet Gabriele d'Annunzio: SUFFICIT ANIMUS (Good cheer is sufficient), whose work was used to effect on the Janiculum Ossuary (see Chapter 5, pp. 118–20 and above). In some cases, these remain clearly visible but in others when, for example, the year of construction 1933 XI E. F. (eleventh year of the Fascist Era) is alongside it, the quote inscribed into the stucco has been repainted in a common terracotta shade to make it less noticeable.

Some quotes were related specifically to women's behaviour. For example, ANTIQUAM EXQUIRITE MATREM (Seek out the ancient mother) from Virgil's *Aeneid* (III, 96) on a house on Via Aventina. Based on the literary context, the injunction to the Trojans to seek out their mother country, Ferraironi surmises that the mother in question could both be the Italian race and the *patria* (Fatherland). In the context of the sexual politics of the time, it referred to the mother of the household whose prime job was to raise the next generation of Fascists. In any case, the true master of the home was the man as exemplified with quotes such as DOMUS REGATUR SENIORE (May the house be governed by its elder).

The true master of the nation, however, remained Mussolini and his quotes also made it onto worker housing such as the tenement on Viale Scalo San Lorenzo: DIAMO DEL SOLE, DELLA LUCE, DELL'ARIA AL POPOLO (Let us give the People sun, light and air). This quote from an overall speech outlining the renewed grandeur of Rome on the tenth anniversary of the regime greeted inhabitants returning home. Save for a barely discernible LUCE DELL'ARIA the letters have been scalpelled off and painted over. The Latin version SOLIS ET AERIS (of sun/light and air) taken appropriately from Vitruvius's *De architectura* (Book 8 chapter 10) escaped the wrath of the scalpel and can be clearly seen on a marble plaque above the door of housing on the Prenestina.[58]

Rectory, Città Universitaria

Phrases governing moral behaviour started in schools and on *Case Balilla/GIL* and for the elite it continued into university where there was an opportunity to use highly erudite quotes. As I have articulated elsewhere, the *Città Universitaria* used inscriptions as part of an overall assemblage of art, architecture and inscription to give the new university campus an overwhelmingly militarist air. The select use of Latin authors on the principal building also overlaps with the rhetoric of *Romanità*. Pride of place is given to Cicero with a phrase adapted from *De officiis* (1.13) and *De oratore* (3.57) broken in the middle by the Latinized name for Rome's university. Unfurling across a good 120 metres of parapet it reads: IN PRIMIS HOMINIS EST PROPRIA VERI INQUISITIO ATQUE INVESTIGATIO [STUDIUM URBIS] DOCTRINA EADEM VIDETUR ET RECTE FACIENDI ET BENE DICENDI MAGISTRA (To search for the truth and seek it out is the first duty of mankind [The University of Rome] Education, by the same route, is seen to be the instructress of both behaving correctly and speaking well). On the rear facade, students were given more suggestions on the right type of moral behaviour from Horace with an

FIGURE 6.14 Marcello Piacentini, Rectory Building, *Città Universitaria*. Rear façade with extract from Horace's *Odes* on the virtues of education. Photograph by author.

extract from *Odes* (4.4). The line was chosen because it celebrated national pride and lauded youthful vigour in the service of the state. It also made direct reference to the Augustan education programme which would be read as the precursor to the contemporary Fascist one that was based on the 'right/correct'; culture to strengthen the spirit. It reads: DOCTRINA VIM PROMOVET INSITAM RECTITUDE CULTU PECTORA ROBORANT (Education promotes an innate vigour and morals give physical strength to the spirit) (Figure 6.14).

These lines were chosen by Latin professor Vincenzo Ussani in an effort to link education to Roman morality, which Horace contrasts in his poem with barbarian degeneracy. This aligned with the supposed 'civilising mission' at the heart of the Ethiopian invasion where the aim was to promote virile, resolute and combative moral attitudes among both the Italian and the Ethiopian population over territorial conquest.[59]

Graffiti

In opposition to the official inscriptions that pervaded public space, there are documented instances of another type of writing on the walls: subversive graffiti. During the *ventennio* anyone expressing anti-Fascist sentiment – whether an opinion over an aperitivo or a scrawled hammer and sickle in the change rooms of a factory – faced arrest, a trial by a special tribunal followed by jail, execution or exile. And dissent did exist. One young girl was stopped by the police for writing anti-Mussolini sentences in chalk and was ordered to stop and redeem herself by shouting '*Viva il Fascio! Viva Mussolini*' (Hooray for the fasces! Hooray for Mussolini!). Instead, she shouted back '*Morte al fascio*' (Death to Fascism) and ran away so fast the policeman could not stop her.[60] Documents in the State Central Archives show a number of instances of clandestine publication and subversive graffiti in bathrooms and factories of the Ostiense quarter and on the walls of the Garbatella area where large numbers of these workers lived. A decline in consent in the late years of the regime is evident in these areas and police reports from October 1942 documented the existence of graffiti in pencil in Viale Guglielmo Massaia and Via Ansaldo: '*A morte Mussolini*', '*Morte a Benito*', '*Viva Lenin*' and '*Fuori i tedeschi*' ('Death to Mussolini', 'Death to Benito', 'Hooray for Lenin' and 'Germans out') (Figure 6.15). Around the corner, the hammer and sickle had been scratched onto the window of a railway worker's apartment.[61] Located near significant infrastructure related to gas works, electricity generation, markets, the abattoir and tram depots, Garbatella would later become a crucial player in the armed Resistance.

Once the Regime had fallen and the city was occupied by Nazis there was a new licence to take to the streets to express dissenting opinions. The armed struggle of the civil war of bombs, rifles and ammunition was also

FIGURE 6.15 Restored graffiti at the back of an apartment building Garbatella. It reads 'Down with the Nazi fasces' and 'Down with Adolf Hitler'. Photograph by author.

played out with other less violent forms of attack and resistance in the form of graffiti, posters and leaflets that have long since washed away but the sentiments they expressed are still alive and well today.[62]

Conclusion: Epigraphy today

The meanings of quotes and inscriptions on buildings are dependent on the socio-political context. Semiotics teaches us that the relationship between signifier (in this case the texts) and signified (what we take them to mean) is susceptible to various combinations of distortion, instability and substitution. The literal meaning of these inscriptions, or what they denote remains relatively static while their rhetorical and symbolic meaning, or what they connote is both mobile and malleable.[63] If living under a repressive regime where the lives of workers and women are under direct control their meanings will have that nuance. In a modern democracy their meaning can become more universal or, in the case of the domestic mottoes, on the apartment buildings revert to platitudes or quaint documents of the past. Other quotes regulating behaviour from the ancient authors also revert to their literal meaning and remain monuments to the writers themselves.

This overview of Fascist-era epigraphy still present in Rome's urban landscape shows similar patterns of the post-war legacy that we have seen in the art and architecture. Epigraphy was also erased, modified or kept visible according to a multitude of factors like author, meaning content or location. But, again, there is not necessarily a correlation: the voices of Cicero and Horace still speak clearly from the main buildings of Rome's *Città Universitaria* campus but you only need to go take nine stops on the Metro B to E42/EUR to see the words of Mussolini on the parapet of the Square Colosseum. The genesis, meaning, re-inscription and erasure of Rome's Fascist-era epigraphy tell a story of politics and counter-politics, heroes and villains, memory and forgetting. As journalist Manlio Lupinacci observed, in the midst of the polemics around removing inscriptions in the lead up to the Olympics:

> There is little evidence of the art of the stonecutter sent by the *Campidoglio* [Rome City Council] to hammer away signs in stone to render them as ephemeral as the pride of those who put them there. And if your eyes rest upon a lictoral fasces you can never know what era it is from and you need to ask yourself was it decreed by a consul, an emperor, a senator, the [left-leaning and only Jewish mayor of Rome] Nathan or the [only non-aristocratic] Governor Bottai.[64]

Inscriptions were removed through frenzies of iconoclasm in the immediate wake of the fall of the Regime and later by haphazard or systematic removal which was both popularly led and directed by government. Parallel to this was a re-inscription of new values onto the urban landscape that commemorated and celebrated a new set of heroes and events from the Resistance a process that continues into the 2020s.

CHAPTER SEVEN

A conclusion for a centenary

Ho voluto che accanto alla Roma antica, che deve risorgere in tutto il suo splendore poiché è cosa unica al mondo, ci fosse anche la Roma moderna, viva, operosa, vibrante, degna capitale del grande Stato fascista.

Next to ancient Rome, that must rise again in all its splendour because it is unique in all the world, I wanted a modern Rome, a living, hard-working, vibrant and worthy capital of the Fascist State.

MUSSOLINI – AL POPOLO DI ROMA PER IL 28 OTTOBRE, 28 OCTOBER 1926[1]

I finished writing this book in July 2022, just a few months short of the centenary of the day Mussolini and his rag-tag groups of followers in Blackshirts marched on Rome to 'seize' power in the name of Fascism. The Draghi government who shepherded the country through the worst of the COVID pandemic had recently fallen and three months later Giorgia Meloni, the leader of Italy's neo-Fascist party *Fratelli d'Italia* (Brothers of Italy), became Italy's prime minister.[2]

One hundred years ago very few people had even heard of Fascism and Rome had barely changed in size or population since becoming capital of a United Italy in 1870. In the twenty-one years of its regime, Fascism anchored its image onto Rome through multiple interventions that re-engineered spatial and temporal relations across the urban fabric. This was done through a dual process of demolition and construction that borrowed heavily from the city's existing palimpsests and myths. These were taken apart and re-assembled in new narrative frames to tell the story of a new society through the lens of Fascist rhetoric (Figure 1.2).[3] Fascism remapped the space of the city centre, drew up new plans, drafted the legislation to enact them and expanded the city three-fold with new representative nodes and residential quarters.

Together with creating new architectural and urban space, each of the Seven nodes of Fascist Rome aimed to communicate one or more key elements of Fascist rhetoric: modifications around Piazza Venezia in Node 1: the *centro storico* helped prop up the Cult of the *Duce* and Node 2: the Vatican was the urban and legislative representation of Catholic Power. Militarism and National Unity were a central theme in Node 3: the *Foro Mussolini/Italico* and Node 4: the *Città Universitaria*, Node 6: E42/EUR encapsulated *Romanità* & Empire while Node 5: *Cinecittà* and Node 7: the *Quartieri/Borgate* both exerted and represented Moral Behaviour/Social Control (Figure 1.3). Each node was concurrently a testament to Modernity and Fascist Achievement. These themes were also intrinsic to individual buildings, monuments and inscriptions and affect the relationship between political content and continuity. Together, their aesthetic, political and utilitarian functions became a measure of control, thus transforming Rome into both gallery and channel through which to broadcast the Fascist message into the everyday life of citizens.

Regimes and their leaders may fall but built heritage remains as an assemblage that continues to transmit Fascist rhetoric into the urban realm of the twenty-first century. Its voice is still heard by an audience whose political consciousness has changed (or not) with the times. The Fascist matrix of legal, economic, political and social threads has continued to shape the city beyond the existence of the regime. Converging into nodes, they have significantly impacted the city's ongoing development and architectural identity. Cleansed of its propaganda elements and either completed or modified, architecture has enjoyed continued use serving the needs of an ever-growing suburban population and acting as testament to the nation's capacity to rebuild. Thanks to historical distance and a surging interest in modern architecture these everyday buildings are now celebrated as jewels of Italian Rationalism. E42/EUR wrestles with the ghost of the unrealized Expo while standing its ground as architectural expression of post-war modernity and Democratic Achievement. Monuments continue to negotiate their original meanings with their Fascist and post-Fascist appropriations while inscriptions linger on its facades as testimonials to the aspirations, mandates and illusions of the Fascist regime.

As for the content of Fascism's rhetorical broadcast, its meanings also have different degrees of continuity. *Romanità* is evident in the overall plan of E42/EUR, architecturally it is in the overall form and composition of the Ministry of Foreign Affairs down to the stylized fasces whose shadows remain on everything from building facades to bollards. The Militarism of the *Città Universitaria* means little without a martial climate to feed it and buildings like the *Casa Madre dei Mutilati*, with its Latin phrases and battle frescoes, take on a documentary and celebratory function for Italy's national war narrative. A narrative whose switch was flipped to honour the battle against, not for, Fascism. The same cannot be said for traces of Empire. Rome is no longer an urban showcase for Fascism's colonial 'triumph' and although its most glaring examples have been taken down or brought home many traces remain. The street names of the *Quartiere Africano* still read as a list of 'conquests', the Amedeo Duca d'Aosta bridge is still named after the former Viceroy of Ethiopia while inscriptions in the *centro storico* remind us that Italy still has a way to go in reconciling with its colonial past. As EUR's new Museo delle Civiltà shows, the myth of *Italiani brava gente* cannot hold forever.

As capital of a revolutionized Fascist nation, Rome's duty was to encapsulate the full gamut of the Regime's achievement. From its transformation into a 'hygienic' city free of traffic to new residential areas filled with light, air and all (Fascist) mod cons. From high-speed trains that (mostly) run on time to ready-made Olympic infrastructure at the *Foro Italico/Mussolini* tourists and Romans alike continue to enjoy the fruits of Fascist labour. City growth, architecture, monuments and inscriptions worked together to uphold moral behaviour and maintain social control. Democracy obviated the need for social control and the remit for moral behaviour went back to the Catholic church. All that remains is the geography of privilege and the political leanings that come with it.

Fascist rhetoric did not disappear with the regime and many of its elements continued across (Figure 1.2). The post-war concept of National Unity relied heavily on reclaiming existing Nationalist discourses of the *Risorgimento* and the First World War on one hand and firmly repudiating Fascist discourses on the other by bringing the nation together under a shared rubric of Resistance, Democracy, Peace and Catholicism. Together with *Romanità*, Catholic Power remains the strongest element of the Fascist legacy manifest through the physical and juridical entity of the Vatican State. It is expressed along the length of Via della Conciliazione and in the imposing presence of the Basilica of Sts. Peter and Paul at E42/EUR. Less obvious but nonetheless highly impactful were the changes wrought on the city for the various instances of Holy Year and the knock-on effect of the Via Olimpica that kickstarted the highly profitable land speculation by the Vatican's real estate arm that radiates into the expanding northwestern suburbs. Outlawed and pushed underground, only the Cult of the *Duce* continues to pose difficulty. Consistently covered, defaced or destroyed his image has come out of hiding but not without continued controversy.

As the future becomes the present and the present becomes the past, the meanings of the urban assemblage of Fascist Rome have changed along with the values, ideals and aspirations of the people. Architecture and monuments do more than signify and commemorate, they remain expressions of the ideals, aims and actions of their creators. The Fascist regime has left behind a complex layer to neutralize, explain, re-claim, demolish or simply ignore and leave to join the ruins. In each case, the concrete realizations of the Third Rome continue to tell their story in the urban space of collective experience. The city plays an important role in keeping the social function of history and memory active and its Fascist heritage continues to hold evidential, historical, aesthetic, communal and social value within the changing affective *milieu* in which it is perceived and experienced.[4]

Semiotics teaches us that the relationship between signifier (in this case the urban assemblage of Rome's Fascist layer) and signified (what we take it to mean) is susceptible to various combinations of distortion, instability and substitution. Its literal meaning, or what it denotes, has remained relatively static while its rhetorical and symbolic meaning, or what it connotes, is both mobile and malleable and dependent on individual readings in different socio-political contexts.

Rome as a unique repository for iconic overproduction has shown that the heritage of Fascism has been organically dealt with, by either the people or the government, on a case-by-case basis. This is, ironically, in accordance with a 1944 proposal for an inter-ministerial commission for the removal of monuments and artworks whose 'subjects exalted the aims and ideas of Fascism' (Figure 7.1). A commission that would take into account

> the political meaning of each work, its artistic value, the possibility of removing it without causing too much artistic damage to the building and suggesting any necessary precautions.[5]

The legacy of Fascism in contemporary Rome is an instance of what we term a difficult heritage. Starting on the cusp of the twenty-first century there has been a surge of interest in this topic with monographs, edited collections, special issues of journals and individual articles dedicated to how former totalitarian regimes, and Italy in particular, have dealt (or are continuing to deal with) with their difficult past.[6] How it is approached depends on a complex interweaving of factors related to chronology, location and rhetorical content. Chronology is related to the socio-political context or the 'when' are we dealing with the difficult heritage of Fascism. For example, 1950s Italy in the throes of post-war reconstruction considered this heritage in a very different way to the 2020s Italy hosting the COVID era G20 meeting. Its physical context, whether public or private, central or remote, essential to survival or simply decorative is a key determinant especially when it comes to audience. For example, the removal or otherwise of a Fascist monument in an out-of-the-way part of the city suddenly becomes an issue when international visitors arrive. Content is related to how it was harnessed in the service of propaganda and its polyvalency for a contemporary audience. Images of Mussolini that were covered, almost with a sense of shame in the 1950s, have been restored in the 1990s for their artistic merit.

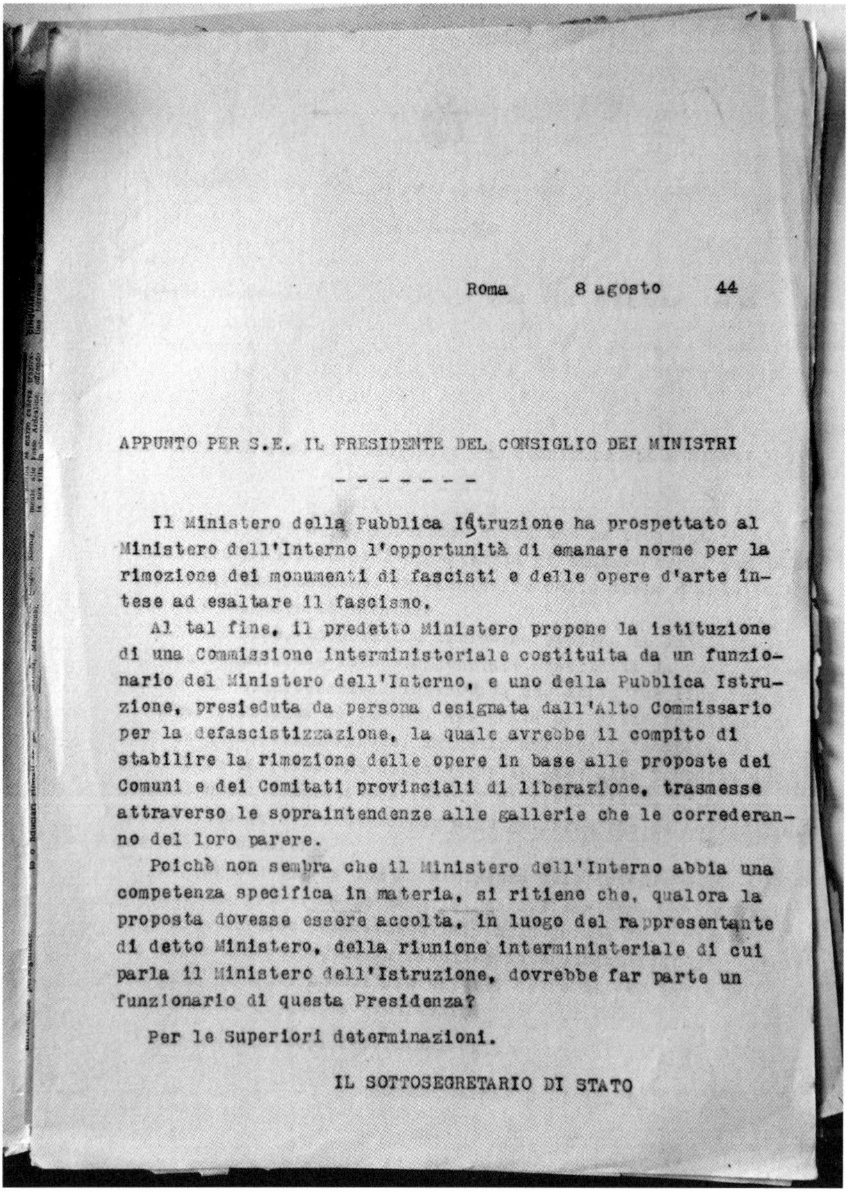

> Roma 8 agosto 44
>
> APPUNTO PER S.E. IL PRESIDENTE DEL CONSIGLIO DEI MINISTRI
> --------
>
> Il Ministero della Pubblica Istruzione ha prospettato al Ministero dell'Interno l'opportunità di emanare norme per la rimozione dei monumenti di fascisti e delle opere d'arte intese ad esaltare il fascismo.
> Al tal fine, il predetto Ministero propone la istituzione di una Commissione interministeriale costituita da un funzionario del Ministero dell'Interno, e uno della Pubblica Istruzione, presieduta da persona designata dall'Alto Commissario per la defascistizzazione, la quale avrebbe il compito di stabilire la rimozione delle opere in base alle proposte dei Comuni e dei Comitati provinciali di liberazione, trasmesse attraverso le soprintendenze alle gallerie che le correderanno del loro parere.
> Poiché non sembra che il Ministero dell'Interno abbia una competenza specifica in materia, si ritiene che, qualora la proposta dovesse essere accolta, in luogo del rappresentante di detto Ministero, della riunione interministeriale di cui parla il Ministero dell'Istruzione, dovrebbe far parte un funzionario di questa Presidenza?
>
> Per le Superiori determinazioni.
>
> IL SOTTOSEGRETARIO DI STATO

FIGURE 7.1 1944 Proposal to the President to draft a set of norms and set up an inter-ministerial commission to remove monuments and artworks exalting Fascism. PCM44-47 1/7 f.11240/2. Archivio Centrale di Stato, Rome.

Of the many layers that form the palimpsest of Rome's urban identity, the one belonging to the Fascist period is at the same time the most obvious and the most well-hidden. It remains, 100 years on from the March on Rome, the most impactful and the most fascinating. I hope those reading this book in 2043 whilst celebrating the centenary of the fall of Fascism will see this layer not as discordant or difficult but as an integrated testament to Rome's complex millennial urban history.

NOTES

Introduction

1 Benito Mussolini, 'Il primo anniversario della marcia su Roma' in E. Susmel and D. Susmel eds., vol. 20 *Opera omnia di Benito Mussolini* (Florence: La Fenice, 1972), 65.
2 James E. Young, ed., *The Art of Memory. Holocaust Memorials in History* (Munich: Prestel Verlag, 1994), 2.
3 Maurice Halbwachs, *On Collective Memory*, ed. Lewis A. Coser (Chicago: University of Chicago Press, 1992), 172–3.
4 The subject of monumental art and its difficult heritage is beyond the scope of this book and will form the subject of a forthcoming volume.
5 Filippo Marinetti, 'The Futurist Manifesto', trans. James Joll, http://cscs.umich.edu/crshalizi/T4PM/futurist-manifesto.honl (accessed 12 September 2012), Emilio Gentile, *Il culto del littorio: la sacralizzazione della politica nell'Italia fascista* (Rome: Laterza, 1993), 27; Jan Nelis, 'Constructing Fascist Identity: Benito Mussolini and the Myth of *Romanità*', *The Classical World* 100, no. 4 (2007): 399–400.
6 Martina Ercolano, 'I giocattoli dei figli della borghesia fascista. Uno spaccato sulla Napoli di inizio novecento', *Rivista italiana di educazione familiare*, no. 1 (2017): 210–11 and Gian Franco Venè, *Mille lire al mese: vita quotidiana della famiglia nell'Italia fascista* (Milan: CDE, 1991), 75–89.
7 Ercolano, 'I giocattoli dei figli della borghesia fascista', 210–11; Flavia Marcello and Paul Gwynne, 'Speaking from the walls: Militarism, Education and *Romanità* in Rome's Città Universitaria (1932–35)', *Journal of the Society of Architectural Historians* 75, no. 3 (2015): 338.
8 On Italian colonialism, see Angelo Del Boca, *L'Africa nella coscienza degli Italiani: miti, memorie, errori, sconfitte* (Rome: Laterza, 1992), 111–12; Greg Blake, 'Ethiopia's Decisive Victory at Adowa', *Military History* 14, no. 4 (1997): 62. For more on the Italian colonialism in Libya, see Muhammad T. Jerary, 'Damages Caused by the Italian Fascist Colonization of Libya' in Ruth Ben-Ghiat and Mia Fuller eds. *Italian Colonialism* (New York: Palgrave Macmillan, 2005), 203–8; Eileen Ryan, 'Violence and the Politics of Prestige: The Fascist Turn in Colonial Libya', *Modern Italy* 20, no. 2 (2015): 123–35; Amedeo Osti Guerrazzi, 'Italians at War: War and Experience in Fascist Italy', *Journal of Modern Italian Studies* 22, no. 5 (2017): 587–603; Christopher Seton-Watson, 'Italy's Imperial Hangover', *Journal of Contemporary History*

15, no. 1 (1980): 170; Robert Gale Woolbert, 'Italian Colonial Expansion in Africa', *Journal of Modern History* 4, no. 3 (1932): 430 & Giampaolo Calchi Novati, 'Italy in the Triangle of the Horn: Too Many Corners for a Half Power', *Journal of Modern African Studies* 32, no. 3 (1994). Most recently the special issue of *Modern Italy* 27 (2022) edited by Carmen Belmonte and Laura Moure Cecchini, 'Critical issues in the study of visual and material culture of Italian Colonialism'.

9   Roger Griffin, *Modernism and Fascism: The Sense of a Beginning under Mussolini and Hitler* (London: Palgrave Macmillan, 2007), 232.

10 Griffin, *Modernism and Fascism*, 233.

11 For a short and sharp definition see P. V. Cannistraro, *Historical Dictionary of Fascist Italy* (Westport, CT: Greenwood Press, 1982), 139–40.

12 Vittorio Vidotto, 'I luoghi del fascismo a Roma', *Urbs: Concepts and Realities of Public Space / Concetti e realtà dello spazio pubblico, l'Istituto Olandese di Roma*, 2–4 aprile 2003.

13 Gentile, *Culto del Littorio*, 242. For a range of perspectives on the Cult of the *Duce*, see Christopher Duggan and Giuliana Pieri and Stephen Gundle, eds., *The Cult of the Duce: Mussolini and the Italians* (Manchester: Manchester University Press, 2013) & Ann Thomas Wilkins, 'Augustus, Mussolini and the Parallel Imagery of Empire' in Claudia Lazzaro and Roger Crum eds. *Donatello among the Blackshirts: History and Modernity in the Visual Culture of Fascist Italy* (Ithaca: Cornell University Press, 2004), 53–65.

14 Gentile, *Culto del Littorio*, 242.

15 On the iconography of the *Duce*, see Giuliana Pieri, 'Portraits of the Duce' in C. Duggan, G. Pieri and S. Gundle eds. *The Cult of the Duce: Mussolini and the Italians* (Manchester: Manchester University Press, 2013), 161–77.

16 G. Procacci, *Storia degli italiani* (Bari: Laterza, 1978), 512.

17 Vincenzo Ceppellini and Paolo Boroli, eds., *Storia d'Italia. Cronologia 1815–1990* (Novara: Istituto Geografico De Agostini, 1991), 427; Phillip V. Cannistaro, *Historical Dictionary of Fascist Italy* (Westport, CT: Greenwood Press, 1982), 298–300. See also Denis Mack Smith, *Italy. A Modern History* (Ann Arbor: University of Michigan Press, 1969), 96–7 and 440–1.

18 For the full text, see *Inter sanctam sedem et italiae regnum conventiones initae die 11 februarii 1929*, https://www.vatican.va/roman_curia/secretariat_state/archivio/documents/rc_seg-st_19290211_patti-lateranensi_it.html#CONVENZIONE_FINANZIARIA (accessed 14 June 2021) & Cannistraro, *Historical Dictionary of Fascist Italy*, 50–2.

19 Vittorio Vidotto *Roma Contemporanea* (Bari: Laterza, 2001), 213–15.

20 See Gerard Noel, *Pius XII: The Hound of Hitler* (London: Bloomsbury Publishing, 2009).

21 Mario Isnenghi, *Breve storia dell'Italia unita a uso dei perplessi (e non)* (Bari: Laterza, 2012), 131.

22 Roma Today, 'A Roma 8,2 miliardi per il Giubileo, ma nel 2025 ci saranno cantieri ancora aperti', *Roma Today*. 30 March 2022, https://www.romatoday.it/politica/cantieri-aperti-giubileo-2025.html (accessed 13 July 2022).

Chapter 2

1. Benito Mussolini, 'Le città tentacolari' in E. Susmel and D. Susmel eds., vol. 2, *Opera omnia di Benito Mussolini* (Florence: La Fenice, 1972), 209.
2. Paola Gigli Padellaro and Mario Panizza, *Roma formale e informale* (Napoli: Editoriale Scientifica, 1976), 36, 42 & 54.
3. For the phenomenon of 'oil stain' expansion see Italo Insolera, *Roma moderna. Da Napoleone I al XXI secolo* (Turin: Piccola Biblioteca Einaudi, 2011), 144–58.
4. Suet. Aug 29.
5. Cited in Richard Bosworth, *Whispering City: Modern Rome and Its Histories* (New Haven: Yale University Press, 2011), 173.
6. Bosworth, *Whispering City*, 188.
7. It mirrored the totalitarian structure of the nation and made Rome part and parcel of the structure of the Fascist government. The Governor, Deputy Governor and Secretary were nominated by Royal Decree and answered directly to the Minister for the Interior (who just happened to be Mussolini).
8. Benito Mussolini, 'La nuova Roma' in E. Susmel and D. Susmel eds., vol. 22, *Opera omnia di Benito Mussolini* (Florence: La Fenice, 1972), 47–9.
9. For example, in the 1993 mayoral elections 54.3 per cent inhabitants of Aurelio-Boccea, Parioli-Trieste and Cassia-Flaminia voted for the exteme right wing candidate while 59.6 per cent of inhabitants in Tiburtina voted to the left. Vittorio Vidotto, *Roma contemporanea* (Bari: Laterza, 2001), 353.
10. LEGGE 17 agosto 1942, n. 1150 Legge urbanistica. (042U1150). First amended in 1952, latest update: *20/05/2022*. For full text see: *Gazzetta Ufficiale* n. 244, 16th October 1942.
11. Insolera, *Roma moderna*, 28.
12. See also Flavia Marcello, 'Forma Urbis Reconsidered: The Making of Fascist Rome' in Helen Roche and Demetriou Kyriakos eds. *Companion to Classical Reception in Fascist Italy and Nazi Germany* (Leiden: Brill Academic Publishers, 2017), 325–69 & Aristotle Kallis, *The Third Rome, 1922–43 the Making of the Fascist Capital* (London: Palgrave Macmillan UK, 2014), 30–2.
13. For the phenomenon of 'oil stain' expansion see Insolera, *Roma Moderna*, 144–58 & Gigli Padellaro and Panizza, *Roma formale e informale*, 43–7.
14. Benito Mussolini, 'Per la cittadinanza di Roma', in E. Susmel and D. Susmel eds., vol. 24, *Opera omnia di Benito Mussolini* (Florence, La Fenice, 1972), 235.
15. Antonio Cederna, *Mussolini urbanista. Lo sventramento di Roma negli anni del consenso* (Bari: Laterza, 1979), xi.
16. Cederna, *Mussolini urbanista*, 192.
17. Insolera, *Roma moderna*, 177.
18. Insolera & Mancini, 'Roma. La "variante generale" del 1942', *Urbanistica. Rivista trimestrale dell'Istituto Nazionale di Urbanistica* 62, no. April (1974): 64–5.

19. Leonardo Benevolo, 'Le discussioni e gli studi preparatori al Nuovo Piano Regolatore', *Urbanistica. Rivista trimestrale dell'Istituto Nazionale di Urbanistica* 29, no. October (1959): 93.
20. Cited in Benevolo, 'Le discussioni e gli studi', 93.
21. Piero Ostilio Rossi and Ilaria Gatti, *Roma: Guida all'architettura moderna 1909–2000* (Bari: Laterza, 2005), 72.
22. Insolera, *Roma moderna*, 193.
23. Insolera, *Roma moderna*, 231.
24. Benevolo, 'Le discussioni e gli studi', 70.
25. Vidotto, *Roma contemporanea*, 334–44.
26. Laura Francescangeli, 'I trasporti pubblici a Roma. Dall'omnibus alla metropolitana' (2003), http://www.archiviocapitolino.it/cdrom/i_trasporti_pubblici_a_roma/index.htm#indice (accessed 10 May 2019).
27. 'Voi toglierete dalle strade monumentali di Roma la stolta contaminazione tranviaria, ma darete modernissimi mezzi di comunicazione alle nuove città che sorgeranno, in anello, attorno alle antichità …'. Mussolini, 'La nuova Roma'.
28. Francescangeli, 'I trasporti pubblici a Roma'.
29. Arnaldo Geraldini, 'Da oggi si viaggia a cento all'ora sotto i palazzi dei cesari e dei papi' *Corriere d'Informazione*, 9–10 February 1955, 7.
30. Insolera, *Roma moderna*, 186–9.
31. Insolera, *Roma moderna*, 194–5.
32. Testa also exerted substantial influence as chief editor of the journal *Capitolium*, co-founder of the Istituto Nazionale di Urbanistica (National Urban Institute – INU), Professor of Urban Studies at the University of Rome *La Sapienza* and principal (though not officially recognized) author of the 1942 National Planning Law and the *Manuale di legislazione urbanistica*. Italo Insolera and Luigi Di Majo, *L'Eur e Roma dagli anni trenta al duemila* (Bari: Laterza, 1986), 83; Insolera, *Roma Moderna*, 134.
33. Francesco Erbani, ed., *Antonio Cederna. I vandali in casa. Cinquant'anni dopo* (Bari: Laterza, 2006), xxiv–xv.
34. Insolera, *Roma moderna*, 238–40.
35. Giovani Russo, 'Gronchi visita gli impianti sportivi in costruzione a Roma per le Olimpiadi', *Corriere della Sera*, 5 March 1959: 7.
36. Indro Montanelli, 'Una sfida ai secoli con aquile e "bustarelle"', *Corriere della Sera*, 30 August 1959, 3.
37. The principal wave of migration was to the industrial triangle in the north-west but Rome was still the single city with the fastest growing population. Vera Zamagni, 'Evolution of the Economy' in Patrick McCarthy ed. *Italy since 1945* (Oxford: Oxford University Press, 2000), 42–68.
38. Vittorio Vidotto, 'I Luoghi Del Fascismo a Roma'. *Urbs: Concepts and realities of public space / Concetti e realtà dello spazio pubblico*, l'Istituto Olandese di Roma, 2–4 aprile 2003.

39 Mario Isenghi, *Italia in piazza: i luoghi della vita pubblica dal 1848 ai giorni nostri* (Milan: Mondadori, 1994), 311.

40 Paolo Monelli, *Roma 1943*, 153 cited in Isenghi, *Italia in piazza*, 329.

41 Nuova Luce, 'Piazza Santi Apostoli: manifestazione del CLN dell'Italia dell'Alta Italia; partecipano militanti del partito comunista e democristiano', Notiziario Nuova LUCE, NL00101, 26/7/1945.

42 Adriano Ballone, 'La Resistenza' in M. Isenghi ed. *I luoghi della memoria: Strutture ed eventi dell'Italia unita* (Bari: Laterza, 2010), 413–14.

43 Vidotto, *Roma contemporanea*, 379.

44 Marino Bisso, 'A Roma la medaglia d'Oro al Valore Militare, 11 giorni di iniziative dell'Anpi nel nome della libertà e dei diritti', *La Repubblica*, 4 June 2019, https://roma.repubblica.it/cronaca/2019/06/04/news/a_roma_la_medaglia_d_oro_al_valore_militare_11_giorni_di_iniziative_dell_anpi_nel_nome_della_liberta_e_dei_diritti-227908423/?ref=search (accessed 5 February 2021).

45 John F. Pollard, *The Vatican and Italian Fascism, 1929–32* (Cambridge University Press, 1985), 43.

46 Amato Pietro Frutaz, *Le piante di Roma* (Rome: Istituto di studi romani, 1962), vol. 2 plates 597 & 598 and vol. 3 290–1.

47 Cited in Insolera, *Roma moderna*, 184.

48 Antonio Cederna, *Mussolini urbanista: lo sventramento di Roma negli anni del consenso* (Bari: Laterza, 1981), 233.

49 Insolera, *Roma moderna*, 186.

50 Cederna, *Mussolini urbanista*, 242.

51 Insolera, *Roma moderna*, 186, 322.

52 Cederna, *Mussolini urbanista*, 242–5.

53 'la più alta espressione plastica del cattolicesimo come il "Magnificat" di Monteverde è la più gloriosa esaltazione musicale della stessa religione.' Calzini, Raffaele, '"Non sventrare più" dice il chirurgo di Roma', *Corriere della Sera*, 29 July 1951, 3.

54 'Foro Italico e non "Foro Mussolini"', *Il pomeriggio. Corriere della Sera*, 26–27 August 1943: 1.

55 Rossi and Gatti, *Roma: Guida all'architettura moderna*, 203; Lilli Garrone, 'Roma 1960, l'eredità per la città: l'Olimpica, l'arteria della Capitale', *Corriere della Sera*, 15 February 2016.

56 See Insolera, *Roma moderna*, 186–9; Insolera and Di Majo, *L'Eur e Roma*, 111–12.

57 Lilli Garrone, 'Hilton, cinquanta candeline e festa grande per l'hotel delle star', *Corriere della Sera*, 20 June 2013.

58 Insolera, *Roma moderna*, 240–4.

59 Insolera, *Roma moderna*, 240.

60 Rossi and Gatti, *Roma: Guida all'architettura moderna*, 209–11. G. f, 'Villaggio Olimpico Vittorio Cafiero, Adalberto Libera, Amedeo Luccichenti,

Vincenzo Monaco, Luigi Moretti, Via Portogallo, 00196 Roma, Italia, 1957–1960', ArchiDIAP, https://archidiap.com/opera/villaggio-olimpico/ (accessed 25 June 2021).

61 Redazione, 'Stazione Vigna Clara, Comitati a Calabrese: "Dal Campidoglio il nulla"', *VignaClaraBlog.it*, 19 April 2021, https://www.vignaclarablog.it/2021041998487/stazione-vigna-clara-comitati-a-calabrese-dal-campidoglio-il-nulla/ (accessed 29 June 2021). Stephanie Kirchgässner, 'Mayor of Rome Announces Opposition to City's 2024 Olympic Bid', *The Guardian*, 22 September 2016, https://www.theguardian.com/sport/2016/sep/21/virginia-raggi-mayor-of-rome-announces-opposition-city-olympic-bid (accessed 28 June 2021).

62 Kirchgässner, 'Mayor of Rome Announces Opposition to City's 2024 Olympic bid'.

63 Insolera, *Roma moderna*, 323.

64 Rossi and Gatti, *Roma: Guida all'architettura moderna*, 281–4.

65 Virgilio Testa, 'Centri direzionali e parcheggi sotterranei. Dichiarazioni del Prof. Virgilio Testa, Commissario dell'Ente Autonomo Esposizione Universale di Roma al Dr. Mario Del Viscovo', *Automobilismo e automobilismo industriale. Rivista bimestrale dell'Ufficio Studi dell'ACI*, no. 1 (January–February 1963): 22.

66 Flavia Marcello, 'All Roads Lead to Rome: the universality of the Roman ideal in Achille Funi's incomplete fresco cycle for the Palazzo dei Congressi in EUR, 1940–43', *Civiltà romana. Rivista pluridisciplinare di studi su Roma Antica e le sue Interpretazioni* 3 (2016): 156–9. For the latest work on the plan of EUR see also Alessandra Tarquini, 'Il progetto dell'E42 per una nuova Roma fascista' in Vittorio Vidotto ed. *Esposizione Universale Roma: una città nuova: dal fascismo agli anni '60*. Roma De Luca editori d'arte, 2015, 33–41, Quilici, *EUR: una moderna città di fondazione*, 31–8; for a synthetic history of the site and its main buildings see Rossi and Gatti, *Roma. Guida all'architettura moderna*, 133–49.

67 Testa, 'Dichiarazioni', 3–4.

68 Testa, 'Dichiarazioni', 6–8.

69 Testa, 'Dichiarazioni', 9.

70 Testa, 'Dichiarazioni', 8–9.

71 "Quattro anni di operosa attività nella zona dell'E.U.R.", 2. ACS, "Leggi, utilizzazione EUR Relazioni Commissario", Testa Archive Box 31.

72 Virgilio Testa, *Relazione sull'attività svolta nel decennio 1951–1961* (Rome: Ente autonomo Esposizione Universale di Roma. E.U.R., c. 1962).

73 Virgilio Testa, *La vita di un urbanista e un capolavoro* (Spoleto: Arti grafiche Pavetto & Petrelli, 1976), 92.

74 Gigli Padellaro and Panizza, *Roma formale e informale*, 54 & 60.

75 A. Bianchi, 'Il lido di Ostia nel quadro dello sviluppo cittadino', *Capitolium* 25, 7/8, July–August 1950: 207–8.

76 'a portare un po' di vita in quella monumentale appendice di Roma, fatta di spazi esagerati, di marmi freddi, di vuoti paurosi in cui anche la numerosa

popolazione di statue sembra assalita dall'angoscia dell'agorafobia'. Gino Visentini, 'Centomila romani abiteranno la città satellite delle Tre Fontane', *Corriere della Sera*, 10 June 1953, 6.

77 Antonella Greco, 'Eur 1953. La mostra dell'agricoltura' in S. Aldini, C. Benocci, S. Ricci and E. Sessa eds. *Il segno delle esposizioni nazionali e internazionali nella memoria storica delle città. Padiglioni alimentari e segni urbani permanenti* (Rome: Kappa, 2014), 158.

78 Greco, 'Eur 1953. La Mostra dell'Agricoltura', 162–2.

79 Insolera, *Roma moderna*, 237.

80 Fernando Salsano, 'La seconda vita dell'Eur: da expo a centro direzionale' in Vidotto ed. *Esposizione Universale Roma: una città nuova: dal fascismo agli anni '60*, 99.

81 Visentini, 'Centomila romani', 6.

82 Bosworth, *Whispering City*, 254.

83 Nick Carter, "'What Shall We Do with It Now?': The Palazzo Della Civiltà Italiana and the Difficult Heritage of Fascism', *Australian Journal of Politics & History* 66, no. 3 (2020): 381–2.

84 Kallis, *The Third Rome*, 175.

85 P. V. Cannistraro, *Historical Dictionary of Fascist Italy* (Westport, CT: Greenwood Press, 1982), 162–4.

86 Insolera, *Roma moderna*, 150–1.

87 Kallis, *The Third Rome*, 176–7.

88 Percy Allum, 'Italian Society Transformed' in Patrick McCarthy ed. *Italy since 1945*, (Oxford: Oxford University Press, 2000), 12–20.

89 Leonardo Benevolo, 'La distruzione del piano' in Alberto Clementi and Francesco Perego eds. *La metropoli 'spontanea': il caso di Roma, 1925–1981. Sviluppo residenziale di una città dentro e fuori dal piano*, (Bari: Dedalo, 1983), 69.

90 Benevolo 'La distruzione del piano', 69–70.

91 Alberto Clementi and Francesco Perego, 'Questioni dell'abusivismo' in Clementi and Perego eds. *La metropoli 'spontanea'*, 29–30.

92 Mauro Olivieri, '1925–1981: La città abusiva' in Clementi and Perego eds. *La metropoli 'spontanea'*, 290–331, 291.

93 Emilio Gentile, *Fascismo di pietra* (Rome: Laterza, 2007), 258.

94 Kallis, *The Third Rome*, 16.

95 Henri Lefebvre, *The Production of Space*, trans. D. Nicholson Smith (Oxford: Blackwell, 1991), 221.

96 Robert C. Fried, *Planning the Eternal City; Roman Politics and Planning since World War II* (New Haven: Yale University Press, 1973), 201–2.

97 Joshua Arthurs, '"Voleva essere Cesare, morì Vespasiano": The Afterlives of Mussolini's Rome', *Civiltà romana. Rivista pluridisciplinare di studi su Roma antica e le sue interpretazioni* 1 (2015): 300.

Chapter 3

1. Benito Mussolini, 'Al popolo di Roma' in E. Susmel and D. Susmel eds., vol. 20, *Opera omnia di Benito Mussolini* (Florence: La Fenice, 1972), 229.
2. Vittorio Vidotto, 'I luoghi del fascismo a Roma'. Paper presented at the *Urbs: Concepts and realities of public space / Concetti e realtà dello spazio pubblico* (Rome: l'Istituto Olandese di Roma, 2003); F. Hermanin, 'La Sala del Mappamondo nel Palazzo di Venezia', *Dedalo* 11 (1930–1): 466–7.
3. Associazione Roma Sotterranea, 'Il bunker di Palazzo Venezia', https://www.bunkertorlonia.it/il-bunker-di-palazzo-venezia.html (accessed 27 July 2020).
4. Paolo Monelli, *Roma 1943* (Rome: Migliaresi, 1945), 91–2.
5. Emilio Gentile, *Fascismo di pietra* (Rome: Laterza, 2007), 256.
6. Mattia Feltri, 'Veltroni: "I luoghi del fascismo"', *La Stampa*, 23 March 2013.
7. Richard Bosworth, *Whispering City: Modern Rome and Its Histories* (New Haven: Yale University Press, 2011), 189.
8. Annapaola Agati, 'La residenza di Mussolini a Villa Torlonia' in A. Campitelli ed. *Villa Torlonia. Guida* (Rome: Electa, 2007), 183–7; Bosworth, *Whispering City*, 190.
9. Bosworth, *Whispering City*, 189–90.
10. Agati, 'La residenza di Mussolini', 185–6; Musei di Villa Torlonia (2014), 'Il Bunker e i rifugi antiarei di Villa Torlonia', http://www.museivillatorlonia.it/it/servizi/news/il_bunker_e_i_rifugi_antiarei_di_villa_torlonia (accessed 27 July 2020).
11. 'E villa Torlonia non è più il luogo del mito. I bambini vanno in bicicletta lungo i sentieri che Mussolini percorreva a cavallo. Si va a mangiare la pizza nella Limonaia. Se però uno ha la passione, va e se la guarda con gli occhi dello storico. La villa era fatiscente. Abbiamo fatto rimettere i pochi mobili rimasti, compreso il letto di Mussolini. O i disegni dei soldati americani che la occuparono. E adesso che la villa è com'era, uno può veramente cogliere il disgusto all'idea che il Duce facesse colazione in giardino mentre i nostri soldati morivano di freddo in Russia'. Feltri, 'Veltroni: "I luoghi del Fascismo"'.
12. The final design was the result of a collaboration between Vittorio Cafiero, Giulio Rinaldi, Ettore Rossi, Wolfang Frankl, Alberto Legnani and Armando Sabatini. Flavia Marcello and Aidan Carter, 'The Axum Obelisk: Shifting Concepts of Colonialism and Empire in Fascist and 21st-Century Rome' in D. Coslett ed. *The Colonial Past in the Neocolonial Present: Inherited Built Environments in Africa, Asia, the Middle East and Europe* (London: Routledge, 2019), 42–64, 50.
13. ACS PCM 1951–54 B4467 7.2 50058 2/16 – Ministero Poste e Telecomunicazioni.
14. Ralph Phillips, *FAO: Its Origins, Formation and Evolution* (Rome: Food and Agriculture Organisation of the United Nations, 1981), 48.

15 The Italian government offered permanent occupancy of building and grounds also recognized as an inviolable extra-territorial zone, free utilities, tax exemptions, special privileges and immunities for FAO officers, discounted rail tickets, a special contract with the Italian Lines to transport staff and families, asking only a nominal rent of US$1 per annum in exchange. Law n.713, 10 August 1950, GU 210, 13 September 1950, 2644.
16 Phillips, *FAO: Its Origins, Formation and Evolution*, 49.
17 Arturo Escobar, *Encountering Development: The Making and Unmaking of the Third World* (Princeton: Princeton University Press, 2011), 125.
18 Gianfranco Angeleri and Umberto Mariotti Bianchi, *Termini. Dalle botteghe di Farfa al dinosauro* (Rome: Edizioni Abete, 1983), 268.
19 Angeleri and Mariotti Bianchi, *Termini*, 253–61.
20 Manfredo Tafuri, *History of Italian Architecture, 1944–1985*, trans. Jessica Levine (Cambridge, MA: MIT Press, 1989), 11.
21 Lilli Garrone, 'Roma, rinasce la stazione Termini', Cronache, *Corriere della Sera*, 30 January 2000, 19.
22 Mario Lupano, *Marcello Piacentini* (Bari: Laterza, 1991), 29–30.
23 Nick Carter and Simon Martin, 'The Management and Memory of Fascist Monumental Art in Postwar and Contemporary Italy: The Case of Luigi Montanarini's Apotheosis of Fascism", *Journal of Modern Italian Studies* 22, no. 3 (2017): 346–8.
24 Patrizia Marchetti, 'Il vincolo del Foro Italico nel cinquantesimo anno dal termine dei lavori', *Monumenti di Roma* 2, nos. 1–2 (2004): 136.
25 For the story of the *Palazzo Littorio* competition, see Flavia Marcello, 'The Politics of Place: Siting and Re-Citing Mussolini's New Party Headquarters, the Palazzo Littorio', *Architectural Theory Review* 12, no. 2 (2007): 146–72; Manfredo Tafuri, '"Giuseppe Terragni: Subject and Mask,"' *Oppositions* 11, (Winter 1977): 1–24; Dennis Doordan, *Building Modern Italy* (Princeton: Princeton University Press, 1988), 134–7; Richard Etlin, *Modernism in Italian Architecture* (Cambridge, MA: MIT Press, 1991), 426–34; Terry Kirk, *The Architecture of Modern Italy, Vol. II: Visions of Utopia, 1900s to Present* (New York: Princeton University Press, 2005), 109–13; Giorgio Ciucci, *Gli architetti e il fascismo, Architettura e città 1922–1944* (Turin: Einaudi, 1989), 139–46; Paolo Ostilio Rossi and Ilaria Gatti, *Roma. Guida all'architettura moderna, 1909–1991* (Bari: Laterza, 1991), 104–7, 122–4; Carolo Cresti, *Architettura e fascismo* (Florence: Vallecchi, 1986), 185–8; Gianni Accasto, Vanna Fraticelli and Renato Nicolini, eds., *Architettura di Roma capitale* (Rome: Edizioni Golem, 1976).
26 Architettura, 'Il concorso di secondo grado per la Casa Littoria in Roma', *Architettura. Numero speciale – Architettura e urbanistica nella capitale e nell'impero* 16, no. 12 (December 1937): 702.
27 Nadia Salvatori, *Il palazzo della Farnesina e le sue collezioni* (Rome: Palombi, 2011), 40–6.
28 Arnaldo Geraldini, 'Più Grande Del Colosseo', *Corriere d'informazione*, 24–25 August 1959, 3.

29 Salvatori, *Il palazzo della Farnesina*, 42.
30 Geraldini, 'Più grande del Colosseo', 3.
31 Salvatori, *Il palazzo della Farnesina*, 61–75.
32 Salvatori, 'Il palazzo della Farnesina e la Collezione di arte contemporanea', https://www.esteri.it/mae/it/ministero/farnesina (accessed 3 September 2021); Rossi and Gatti, *Roma. Guida all'architettura moderna*, 123. Salvatori, *Il palazzo della Farnesina*, 59.
33 Corriere della Sera, 'Il palazzone della Farnesina', *Corriere della Sera*, 30 April 1954, 5; Cesco Tomaselli, 'Sensazionali architetture per le olimpiadi di Roma'. *Corriere della Sera*, 15 March 1958, 5; Silvio Negro, 'Non sarà più "Palazzo Chigi" la sigla della nostra politica estera'. *Corriere della Sera*, 13 August 1959, 2.
34 Arrigo Levi, 'Non si potrà più dire: "Palazzo Chigi" comunica …'. *Corriere d'informazione*, 11–12 September 1959, 3.
35 For more on the Brigades and the Moro assassination see Paul Ginsborg, *A History of Contemporary Italy: Society and Politics, 1943–1988* (New York: Palgrave Macmillan, 2003), 384–5, 386, 400–1 and Bosworth, *Whispering City*, 267–71.
36 Corriere della Sera, '"L'aula Bunker deve tornare allo Sport" Chiesto l'intervento del Ministro Veltroni per liberare l'ex palestra di scherma'. *Corriere della Sera. Cronaca di Roma*, 3 February 1998, 45 and Cesare De Simone, 'Alla sbarra gli "squadroni neri". Saranno 164 gli imputati nel più grosso processo ai gruppi terroristici neofascisti', *Corriere della Sera*, 16 April 1985, 4.
37 David Homewood, 'Exhuming the Archive: Interview with Rossella Biscotti', *Un Magazine* vol. 5, no. 2, http://unprojects.org.au/magazine/issues/issue-5-2/exhuming-the-archive-interview-with-rossella-biscotti/ (accessed 1 March 2021).
38 Lauretta Colonnelli, 'I trent'anni che sconvolsero la Casa della Scherma', *Corriere della Sera. Cronaca di Roma,* 25 June 2005, 51.
39 Renato Nappi, 'Foro Italico, la Casa delle Armi non sarà più aula bunker', *Corriere Roma. Cronaca/Sport/Spettacoli*, 17 June 2000, 47.
40 Stefano Petrucci, 'Casa della scherma, stesso iter della Galleria Borghese', *Corriere della Sera. Cronaca di Roma,* 16 April 2005, 51.
41 Associazione Culturale Ordine Architetti Roma, 'Roma: un Museo dello Sport nell'Accademia della Scherma di Luigi Moretti', 2020, https://www.aloarchitettiroma.it/roma-un-museo-dello-sport-nellaccademia-della-scherma-di-luigi-moretti/ (accessed 31 July 2020).
42 'La Casa della Scherma non restituisce, infatti, solo uno dei caratteri fondanti di una stagione della nostra architettura, l'ordine classico che governa serenamente, in forme inedite, l'universo moderno dei volumi puri. Rappresenta anche un nodo vitale nel percorso artistico di Luigi Moretti. Moretti, in realtà, si dedicava a celebrare l'altra Italia, quella della destra cinica e imprenditoriale, della speculazione fondiaria'. Giuseppe Strappa, 'Quell'omaggio all'incoerenza', *Corriere della Sera. Cronaca di Roma,* 25 June 2005, 50–1.

43 See Flavia Marcello and Paul Gwynne, 'Speaking from the Walls: Militarism, Education and *Romanità* in Rome's *Città Universitaria* (1932–35)', *Journal of the Society of Architectural Historians* 75, no. 3 (2015): 325 & 336–8.

44 Archidiap, Istituto Nazionale Luce, http://www.archidiap.com/opera/istituto-nazionale-luce/ (accessed 18 June 2020). Gianpiero Brunetta, *Storia del cinema italiano. 2. Il cinema del regime 1929–1945* (Rome: Editori Riuniti, 2001).

45 Noa Steimatsky, 'The *Cinecittà* Refugee Camp (1944–1950)', *October* 128 (2009): 31 & ACS, MI DG PS RSI Chierici (1943–1945), b. 70, fasc. 'Questura di Roma mattinali 1944 gennaio-febbraio'.

46 ACS, MI DGPS ct A5G II gm, b. 121, fasc.82 'Truppe tedesche' s.fasc. 'Alloggi'.

47 'Incolonnato insieme con gli altri fui portato a Cinecittà: i miei compagni di sventura, molti dei quali erano stati presi di sorpresa in mezzo alla strada, in fretta e furia scrivevano dei bigliettini per dare notizie di sé ai propri familiari che non sapevano.', Marisa Musu and Ennio Polito, *Roma ribelle, La resistenza nella Capitale 1943–1944, Il racconto di tre deportati del Quadraro in una ricerca della scuola 'Moneta'* (Milan, Teti editore, 1991), 295–7.

48 Adriano Baracco, 'L'amante grassa', *Star*, no. 1 (August 1944): 3. Cited in Steimatsky, 'The *Cinecittà* Refugee Camp', 32.

49 Ginsborg, *A History of Contemporary Italy*, 78–9.

50 Letter from the Ministry of Post-War Assistance to the Ministry of Finance, 13 December, ACS PCM 1944–47, 7/2 55915 – 433.

51 Steimatsky, 'The *Cinecittà* Refugee Camp', 35.

52 Steimatsky, 'The *Cinecittà* Refugee Camp', 40 and 46–7.

53 Letter from Minister of Post and Communications to Minister of Public Works, 8 August 1946, ACS PCM 1951–54, 7.2 50058 2/16.

54 Steimatsky, 'The *Cinecittà* Refugee Camp', 47–8.

55 'chiama a un più alto grado di vita civile' ... 'un mezzo semplice e naturale di educazione ed elevazione delle masse operaie, ricreando lo spirito, rendendo più comoda l'esistenza e più salda la coesione familiare'. A. Calza Bini, *Il fascismo e le case per il popolo*, Rome, Tipografia Sociale, 1927, 32–3 cited in Francesca Romana Stabile, *Regionalismo a Roma. Tipi e linguaggi: il Caso Garbatella* (Rome: Editrice Librerie Dedalo, 2001), 132. 'Nuovi ariosi imponenti quartieri sorgono nella zona di P Bologna. (Giornale Luce B0576, November 1934) – ex Quartiere Italia'.

56 On the borgate see Italo Insolera, 'Le borgate', *Urbanistica* 28–9, June (1959): 45–60 and Rossi and Gatti, Roma. *Guida all'architettura moderna*, 76–8.

57 Sergio Poretti, 'Dal piano al patrimonio Ina Casa', in Rinaldo Capomolla and Rosalia Vittorini eds. *L'architettura Ina Casa (1949–1963). Aspetti e problemi di conservazione e recupero*, 9–17 (Rome: Gangemi, 2003), 9.

58 Poretti, 'Dal piano al patrimonio', 9.

59 See Capomolla and Vittorini, *L'architettura Ina Casa (1949–1963)*.

60 Angela Raffaella Bruni, 'Cinema Nuovo-Sacher' in Gaia Remiddi, Antonella Greco, Antonella Bonavita and Paola Ferri eds. *Il moderno attraverso Roma: Guida a 200 architetture e alle loro opere d'arte* (Roma: Fratelli Palombi, 2000), H106.

61 Marina Docci, '"Case Del Fascio": Forgotten "Fragments" in Contemporary Rome' in Cristiana Bartolomei, Alfonso Ippolito and Simone Helena Tanoue Vizioli eds. *Digital Modernism Heritage Lexicon* (Cham: Springer International Publishing, 2022), 164–6.

62 Flavio Mangione, *Le Case del Fascio in Italia e le terre dell'oltremare* (Rome: Ministero per i beni e le attività culturali, Direzione generale per gli archivi, 2003), 3–8 & 20–3; Docci, '"Case Del Fascio"', 165–8. These include the new 'Franco Baldini' headquarters of the Tiburtino Group, the 'Pierino del Piano' Appio headquarters, the 'Manlio Cavagnaro' Latino Metronio Group and the 'Fulcieri Paolucci di Calboli' headquarters in Monte Mario.

63 Docci, '"Case del Fascio"', 169–70 & 173–4. For the re-use of *Case del Fascio* around Italy see Lucy Maulsby, 'Drinking from the River Lethe. *Case Del Fascio* and the Legacy of Fascism in Postwar Italy', *Future Anterior. Journal of Historic Preservation History Theory & Criticism* 9, no. 2 (2014): 18–39.

64 LC, Redazione, 'Rino Daus, i miti del fascismo e la fine della memoria', *il lavoro culturale*, 21 April 2017, https://www.lavoroculturale.org/rino-daus/redazione-lc/2017/ (accessed 8 July 2022).

65 Cited in Tim Benton, 'Rome Reclaims Its Empire' in Dawn Ades, Neal Ascherson and Eric J. Hobsbawm eds. *Art and Power: Europe under the Dictators 1930–45* (London: Thames and Hudson, 1995), 120–7, 126.

66 Giuseppe Strappa and Gianni Mercurio, *Architettura moderna a Roma e nel Lazio: 1920–1945: Atlante* (Rome: Edilstampa, 1996), 203.

67 Sara Mechelli, 'Restyling completo per la Palestra Agnini: sarà polo dello sport del Montesacro', *Romatoday*, 29 August 2014, https://www.romatoday.it/zone/montesacro/ex-gil-ristrutturata (accessed 8 July 2022) & Sara Mechelli, 'A Montesacro arriva Salagnini: il nuovo spazio della cultura e del "Tempo Insieme"', *Romatoday*, 19 October 2018, https://www.romatoday.it/zone/montesacro/montesacro-sala-agnini-polo-culturale-viale-adriatico.html (accessed 8 July 2022).

68 Architettura, 'Casa della Gioventù Italiana Del Littorio a Roma in Trastevere', *Architettura. Rivista del Sindacato Nazionale Architetti Fascisti* 20, no. 9–10, September–October (1941): 373–5.

69 Edoardo Sassi, 'Ma è in abbandono l'altro capolavoro di Moretti: l'ex Gil a Trastevere', *Corriere della Sera. Cronaca di Roma*, 25 June 2005, 51.

70 Lilli Garrone, 'Trastevere, quanti bei progetti', *Corriere della Sera. Cronaca di Roma*, 18 May 2000, 49; Giuseppe Pullara, 'La "Casa Della Regione" Nel Cuore Di Trastevere', *Corriere della Sera. Cronaca di Roma*, 17 May 2007, 9 & Paolo Brogi, 'L'affresco nascosto di Mafai su una parete della ex Gil', *Corriere della Sera. Cronaca di Roma*, 7 December 2004, 53.

71 'Wegil – Storia', Updated 2021, https://wegil.it/la-storia/ (accessed 11 July 2022).

72 Corriere d'Informazione, 'L'istruttoria per la deportazione di tremila carabinieri in Germania', *Corriere d'Informazione*, 19–20 February 1946, 1.

73 Gastone Mazzanti, *Roma violata: dagli archivi segreti angloamericani i bombardamenti della seconda guerra mondiale* (Rome: Teos, 2006), 407–8.

74 Augusto Guerriero, 'Il Presidente Gronchi oggi a Parigi per rinsaldare l'amicizia fra Italia e Francia', *Corriere della Sera*, 25 April 1956, 1; 'Gronchi riceverà Coty alla stazione', *Corriere della Sera*, 9 May 1957, 1; 'Il re e la regina di Grecia accolti da Gronchi a Roma', *Corriere d'Informazione*, 19–20 May 1959, 1–2; 'L'itinerario della visita in Italia di Elisabetta II e del principe Filippo', *Corriere della Sera*, 12 April 1961, 2. Ostiense station stood in for Naples railway station in the 1960 film *La baia di Napoli* (*It started in Naples*). P. B., 'Per la Loren e Clark Gable "ciak" alla stazione Ostiense', *Corriere d'Informazione*, 18–19 August 1959.

75 Alfonso Madea, 'Due momenti difficili in una giornata di tensione', *Corriere della Sera*, 29 Novembre 1969, 1–2.

76 Alessandra Arachi, 'Un errore la chiusura della stazione Ostiense', *Corriere della Sera. Corriere Roma*, 22 April 1987, 24; M. Pan., 'Treni in partenza sull'"anello"', *Corriere della Sera. Corriere Roma*, 6 June 1990, 30.

77 Roberto della Rovere, 'Roma: il trenino dei Mondiali è già da buttare', *Corriere della Sera, Cronache Italiane*, 16 January 1993, 17; Monica Guerzoni, 'Fiumicino s'alllontana', *Corriere della Sera, Cronaca di Roma*, 27 September 1993, 48; Corriere della Sera, 'L'Air Terminal diventerà sede di Eataly', *Corriere della Sera, Cronaca di Roma*, 9 April 2010, 5; Luca Zanini, 'Roba alla guerra dei sapori Eataly contro Città del Gusto', *Corriere della Sera, Cronaca di Roma*, 3.

Chapter 4

1 Benito Mussolini, 'La Roma di Mussolini' in E. Susmel and D. Susmel eds., vol. 25, *Opera omnia di Benito Mussolini* (Florence: La Fenice, 1972), 87.

2 The E42 board (or Ente E42) was set up under Law 2174, 26 December 1936. *Raccolta ufficiale delle leggi e decreti del Regno d'Italia*, 1936, 4254.

3 Italo Insolera and Luigi Di Majo, *L'Eur e Roma dagli anni trenta al duemila*. (Bari: Laterza, 1986), 71; Cesare De Simone, *Roma, città prigioniera i 271 giorni dell'occupazione nazista: 8 Settembre '43–4 Giugno '44*. (Milan: Mursia, 1994), 15.

4 Nick Carter, '"What shall we do with it now?": *The Palazzo della Civiltà Italiana* and the difficult heritage of Fascism', *Australian Journal of Politics & History* 66, no. 3 (2020): 383–4.

5 Insolera and Di Majo, *L'Eur e Roma*, 72.

6 ACS E42 B306 f.4922 sf. 5 & B309 f. 4933 sf. 4.

7 ACS E42 B306. F. 4922/5-6 & B307 f. 4927 sf. 3.

8 Insolera and Di Majo, *L'Eur e Roma*, 75–6.

9 'Alla vista dei terreni coperti da erbacce, in mezzo alle quali giacevano tronchi di statue abbandonate e resti di opere d'arte vandalicamente frantumate, osservando le molte baracche abitate da povera gente priva di mezzi di sostentamento, e ponendo attenzione agli edifici per intero smantellati o mostranti tronconi che avrebbero dovuto essere anch'essi eliminati, il Testa

ebbe un attimo di autentico scoraggiamento e mormorando all'autista "Chi me l'ha fatto fare!"'. Virgilio Testa, *La vita di un urbanista e un capolavoro*. (Spoleto: Arti grafiche Pavetto & Petrelli, 1976), 78.

10 'Grandi cose, nuove cose si potranno fare utilizzando il già "fatto" in quella che doveva essere la "E-42" spingendo, come si è già osato, la città verso il mare'. Raffaele Calzini, '"Non sventrare più" dice il chirurgo di Roma', *Corriere della Sera*, 29 July 1951, 3.

11 Monica Pignatti Morano, 'Palazzo dell'Istituto Italo-Latino Americano' in A. Alberini, N. Di Santo, M. Pignatti Morano and A. Zanuttini eds. *EUR. Guida degli istituti culturali* (Milan: Leonardo Arte, 1995), 63.

12 Gian Paolo Consoli, 'Istituto Forestale A. Mussolini' in M. Calvesi, E. Guidoni and S. Lux eds. *E 42, Utopia e scenario del regime* (Venice: Marsilio, 1987), 505. For the story of the Palace of Water and Light see Angelo Maggi 'Architecture of Light and Water at the Universal Exhibition of Rome of 1942' in Rika Devos, Alexander Ortenburg and Vladimir Paperny eds. *Architecture of Great Expositions 1937–1959: Messages of Peace, Images of War* (London: Routledge, 2016): 99–114.

13 Paul Ginsborg, *A History of Contemporary Italy* (New York: Palgrave Macmillan, 2003), 212–17.

14 'Lenta, cupa agonia del regime fascista', Pino Scaglione, *Eur a Roma controguida d'architettura* (Vicenza: Testo & Immagine, 2000), 20.

15 Alessandra Muntoni, 'Piazza con le Esedre e Porta Imperiale. Il progetto' in M. Calvesi, E. Guidoni and S. Lux eds. *E 42, Utopia e scenario del regime* (Venice: Marsilio, 1987), 472–5.

16 Adachiara Zevi, ed., *Una guida all'architettura moderna dell'EUR* (Rome: Fondazione Bruno Zevi, 2008), 102.

17 Flavia Marcello, 'All Roads Lead to Rome: the universality of the Roman ideal in Achille Funi's incomplete fresco cycle for the Palazzo dei Congressi in EUR, 1940–43' *Civiltà romana. Rivista pluridisciplinare di studi su Roma Antica e le sue Interpretazioni*, 3, 2016, 151–2 and 160.

18 Antonella Greco, 'Eur 1953. La mostra dell'agricoltura' in S. Aldini, C. Benocci, S. Ricci and E. Sessa eds. *Il segno delle esposizioni nazionali e internazionali nella memoria storica delle città. Padiglioni alimentari e segni urbani permanenti* (Rome: Kappa, 2014), 162.

19 Testa (attr.), *Quattro anni di operosa attività nella zona dell'E.U.R.*, ACS Testa Archive Box 31.

20 Italo Insolera, *Roma moderna: Un secolo di storia urbanistica* (Turin: Einaudi, 1971), 241–4.

21 Gino Visentini, 'Centomila romani abiteranno la città satellite delle Tre Fontane', *Corriere della Sera*, 10 June 1953, 6.

22 ACS, EUR, SG, '23.7 Concorso Palazzo civiltà italiana' cited in Muntoni, *Palazzo della Civiltà italiana*, 354; Gio Ponti, 'Stile dell'architetto Adalberto Libera', *Stile* 20, no. 17 (May 1942): 17.

23 Carter, 'What shall we do with it now?', 384, 386 and 389.

24 Greco, 'Eur 1953. La mostra dell'agricoltura', 163.

25. Gino Visentini, 'Centomila romani abiteranno la città satellite delle Tre Fontane', *Corriere della Sera*, 10 June 1953, 6.
26. 'La più alta virtù civile, quella che sorregge la patria.' Corriere d'informazione, 'Saragat consegna le "stelle del lavoro" Moro auspica un "ordinato progresso"', *Corriere d'informazione*, 2–3 May 1966, 2.
27. Paola Somma, 'The *Palazzo della Civiltà Italiana*. From Fascism to Fashion' in K. B. Jones and S. Pilat eds. *The Routledge Companion to Italian Fascist Architecture: Reception and Legacy* (London: Routledge, 2020), 80, 82, 85–6.
28. Alberto Zambenedetti, 'Filming in Stone: *Palazzo della Civiltà Italiana* and Fascist Signification in Cinema' *Annali d'Italianistica*, Special issue 'Capital City: Rome 1870–2010', 28 (2010): 201, 206–7, 213 and Somma, 'The *Palazzo della Civiltà Italiana*', 81–2.
29. Zambenedetti, 'Filming in Stone', 213.
30. Paola Mocci, 'Palazzo Degli Uffici. L'arredamento' in M. Calvesi, E. Guidoni and S. Lux eds. *E 42, Utopia e scenario del regime* (Venice: Marsilio, 1987), 305.
31. Giuseppe Pullara, 'Eur, il mistero della Quadriga', *Corriere della Sera, Cronaca di Roma*, 8 July 2003, 50.
32. Insolera and Di Majo, *L'Eur e Roma*, 71–2 & 75.
33. Virgilio Testa, *Relazione sull'attività svolta nel decennio 1951–1961* (Rome: Ente autonomo Esposizione Universale di Roma. E.U.R., c. 1962), 7.
34. Eur Spa., 'Company Profile', https://www.eurspa.it/en/about-us/profile (accessed 1 May 2023).
35. Eur Spa., 'Il salone delle fontane', https://www.salonedellefontane.com/ (accessed 1 May 2023).
36. Insolera and Di Majo, *L'Eur e Roma*, 101.
37. Corriere della Sera, 'Giornalisti e dirigenti inglesi visitano "l'Esposizione permanente"', *Corriere della Sera*, 23 September 1959, 3.
38. Giovanni Russo, 'Gronchi inaugura a Roma la mostra dello sport nell'arte', *Corriere della sera*, 15 July 1960, 7.
39. A. Alberini, N. Di Santo, M. Pignatti Morano and A. Zanuttini, eds., *EUR. Guida degli istituti culturali* (Leonardo Arte, 1995), 106.
40. Testa, *Relazione Attività 1951–61*, 9.
41. Testa, *Relazione Attività 1951–61*, 7.
42. Ernesto Menicucci, 'Quattro palazzi storici in cambio della Nuvola' and 'Sbagliato vendere gioielli del razionalismo per coprire spese folli', *Corriere della sera. Cronaca di Roma*, 17 February 2015, 3; 'L'Inail acquista quattro musei e salva il bilancio di Eur Spa', 23 December 2015, 5.
43. Igiaba Scego and Rino Bianchi, *Roma negata. Percorsi postcoloniali nella città* (Rome: Ediesse, 2014), 131–2.
44. Flavia Amabile, 'Riapre il Museo Coloniale, il gioiello di Mussolini', *La Stampa*, 1 June 2019, https://www.lastampa.it/cronaca/2019/06/01/news/riapre-il-museo-coloniale-il-gioiello-di-mussolini-1.33704991 (accessed 30 September 2020).

45 Serena Fiorletta, 'Il Museo negato. Narrazione nazionale e museografia', *Roots – Routes. Research on Visual Cultures*, 9/30 (May–August 2019), https://www.roots-routes.org/museo-negato-narrazione-nazionale-museografia-serena-fiorletta/ (accessed 30 September 2020).

46 Archeologiavocidalpassato, 'Roma-Eur. Il museo delle Civiltà cambia pelle e volto: in quattro anni da museo composto da molti musei diventerà un meta-museo che si propone di riflettere criticamente sulle stratificazioni delle collezioni e delle culture rappresentate. Prime aperture in autunno 2022', Archeologiavocidalpassato. News, curiosità, ricerche, luoghi, persone e personaggi, 30 August 2022, https://archeologiavocidalpassato.com/2022/08/30/roma-eur-il-museo-delle-civilta-cambia-pelle-e-volto-in-quattro-anni-da-museo-composto-da-molti-musei-diventera-un-meta-museo-che-si-propone-di-riflettere-criticamente-sulle-stratificazioni-delle-co/ (accessed 9 February 2023).

47 For the Augustan Exhibition see Ferdinand Scriba, 'Archaeology as History – The *Mostra Augustea della Romanità* 1937/38 as an example of the relation between archaeology and fascism' in K. Gilliver, W. Ernst and F. Scriba eds. *Archaeology, Ideology, Method: Inter-Academy Seminar on Current Archaeological Research* (Rome: Canadian Academic Centre in Italy, 1996), 55–75; Flavia Marcello, 'Mussolini and the Idealisation of Empire: The Augustan Exhibition of *Romanità*', *Modern Italy. The Journal of the Association for the Study of Modern Italy* 16, no. 3 (2011): 223–47; Joshua Arthurs, *Excavating Modernity: The Roman Past in Fascist Italy* (Ithaca, NY: Cornell University Press, 2012), 91–124.

48 Marco Noccioli, 'Edificio per la mostra della Romanità' in M. Calvesi, E. Guidoni and S. Lux eds. *E 42, utopia e scenario del regime* (Venice: Marsilio 1987), 484.

49 Archidiap, 'Museo della Civiltà Romana', http://www.archidiap.com/opera/museo-della-civilta-romana/ (accessed 20 May 2021).

50 EUR, *E. U. R.: la città parco della Roma moderna* (Rome: Rotografica romana, 1953), 35.

51 b. m., 'Manifestazioni del XXI Aprile. Viaggio inaugurale di un convoglio S.T.E.F.E.R. sul tratto della metropolitana tra le stazioni della Magliana e l'E.U.R.', *Trasporti pubblici. Rivista mensile a cura dell'ispettorato generale della motorizzazione civile e dei trasporti in concessione* 9, no. 1 (January 1952): 461.

52 Virgilio Testa, *Relazione sull'attività svolta nel decennio 1951–1961* (Rome: Ente autonomo Esposizione Universale di Roma. E.U.R., c. 1962), 13 & Noccioli, 'Edificio per la mostra della Romanità', 484.

53 Francesco Innamorati and Carlo Bertilaccio, *Eur Spa e il patrimonio di E42: manuale d'uso per edifici e opera* (Rome: Palombi, 2004), 40.

54 Sovrintendenza Capitolina ai Beni Culturali, Direzione Interventi su Edilizia Monumentale, D.D._n._408_del_13-07-2020. DIRE. '2022, Il Museo Della Civiltà Romana Riapre Con Il Planetario.' *QA. Turismo, cultura e arte.* (accessed 30 September 2021), https://www.qaeditoria.it/details.aspx?idarticle=170414&AspxAutoDetectCookieSupport=1 (accessed 5 July 2022);

RomaToday, 'Museo della civiltà romana: servono otto mesi per riaprire il plastico dell'Antica Roma', *RomaToday,* 27 April 2022, https://www.romatoday.it/politica/museo-civilta-romana-data-riapertura-plastico.html (accessed 7 February 2023).

55 Antonella La Torre and Marco Noccioli, 'Piazza ed edifici delle forze armate. Mostra dell'autarchia, del corporativismo e della previdenza sociale' in M. Calvesi, E. Guidoni and S. Lux eds. *E 42, Utopia e scenario del regime* (Venice: Marsilio, 1987), 423–7.

56 EUR, *E. U. R.: la città parco*, 35–6.

57 Elisabetta Cristallini, 'Chiesa dei SS. Pietro e Paolo' in M. Calvesi, E. Guidoni and S. Lux eds. *E 42, Utopia e scenario del regime* (Venice: Marsilio, 1987), 441–4.

58 Antonella La Torre, 'La mostra dell'abitazione' in M. Calvesi, E. Guidoni and S. Lux eds. *E 42, Utopia e scenario del regime* (Venice: Marsilio, 1987), 524.

59 La Torre, 'La mostra dell'abitazione', 524 & 528.

60 EUR, *E. U. R.: la città parco*, 13.

61 F.D.S., 'Il Papa accompagna all'EUR una "processione della pace"', *Corriere della sera*, 18 June 1965, 7.

62 Virgilio Testa, *Considerazioni economiche e criteri generali per la valutazione del patrimonio immobiliare dell'E.U.R.* (Rome: Ente autonomo Esposizione Universale di Roma. E.U.R., n.d.), 18–19; Insolera and di Majo, *L'Eur e Roma*, 96–7 & 263–70.

63 Massimo Locci, 'Palazzo delle poste all'EUR', *AR. Bimestrale dell'ordine degli architetti di Roma e provincia* 42 (July–August 2007): 10.

64 Paola Cagiano de Azevedo and Luca Veresani, 'Edificio delle RR. poste, telegrafi e TETI' in M. Calvesi, E. Guidoni and S. Lux eds. *E 42, Utopia e scenario del regime* (Venice: Marsilio, 1987), 487.

65 EUR, *E. U. R.: la città parco*, 13.

66 Locci, 'Palazzo delle poste all'EUR' 10.

67 Francesco Innamorati and Carlo Bertilaccio, *Eur Spa e il Patrimonio di E42*, 84; Domenico Pertica, 'Il nuovo lago Dell'E.U.R. e il vecchio laghetto di Villa Borghese', *Capitolium* 37, no. 1 (January 1962): 22.

68 ACS E42, B565 f. 6842/2; Maurizio de Vico Fallani, *Raffaele De Vico e i giardini di Roma* (Florence: Sansoni Editore, 1985), 169–70.

69 Testa, *Vita di un urbanista*, 97.

70 Pertica, 'Il nuovo lago dell'E.U.R. e il vecchio laghetto di Villa Borghese', 24; 'Musiche e giochi d'acqua all'EUR', *Il giornale d'Italia*, 1 July 1961; 'A completamento del più moderno quartiere di Roma. La cascata del lago artificiale all'EUR è da ieri una realizzazione compiuta', unknown newspaper, 30 June 1961. ACS Testa Archive, Box 8, f. 28 'Articoli vari sull'EUR'; de Vico Fallani, *Raffaele De Vico e i giardini di Roma*, 180.

71 Antonio Cipriani, 'Quando all'Ente EUR decideva la P2'; Teresa Trillò, 'Hotel au Lac, un processo insabbiato', *L'Unità*, 14 January 1993, 24. Insolera & Di Majo, *L'Eur e Roma*, 100–5.

72 'Ente EUR: il commissario Di Mano sentito dal magistrato', *Corriere della Sera. Cronaca di Roma*, 25 September 1982, 20; 'Anche l'ex assessore e tre funzionari incriminati per l'hotel non costruito', *Corriere della Sera*, 2 April 1982, 20.

73 Corriere della Sera, '"Hotel du Lac": assoluzione per i tre maggiori imputati', *Corriere della Sera. Cronaca di Roma*, 1 July 1983, 19.

74 Corriere della Sera, 'Sotto accusa due assessori per illeciti urbanistici', *Corriere della Sera*, 6 July 1984, 27.

75 Manuela Canestrari, 'Edificio per la mostra dell'agricoltura e bonifiche' in M. Calvesi, E. Guidoni and S. Lux eds. *E 42, Utopia e scenario del regime*, (Venice: Marsilio, 1987), 500–2.

76 Innamorati and Bertilaccio, *Eur Spa e il patrimonio di E42*, 44 and Canestrari, 'Edificio per la mostra dell'agricoltura e bonifiche', 500–2.

77 Trillò, 'Hotel au Lac, un processo insabbiato', 24.

78 Ubaldo Bertoli, 'Cresce un palazzo all'E.U.R.' *Gatto Selvatico. Mensile aziendale* 7, no. 10 (October 1961): 15–16.

79 Scaglione, *Eur a Roma controguida d'architettura*, 22–3. Rossi and Gatti, *Roma: Guida all'architettura moderna*, 232.

80 Bertoli, 'Cresce un palazzo all'E.U.R.', 11.

81 Atelier Jean Nouvel, 'Eni Head Office. Rome, Italy', http://www.jeannouvel.com/en/projects/siege-social-eni/ (accessed 5 July 2022).

82 On the role of E42/EUR and the Olympics within the history of Rome's urban planning see Italo Insolera, *Roma moderna: Un secolo di storia urbanistica* (Turin: Einaudi, 1971), 241–4.

83 Insolera and Di Majo, *L'Eur e Roma*, 276.

84 Testa, *Vita di un urbanista*, 47–8.

85 Corriere della Sera, 'I "Beatles" canteranno anche a Roma', *Corriere della sera*, 28 May 1965.

86 Rossi and Gatti, *Roma: Guida all'architettura moderna*, 217; ArchiDIAP, 'Palazzo dello Sport', http://archidiap.com/opera/palazzo-dello-sport/ (accessed 28 October 2021); Sandra Cerasale, 'Acustica nuova, l'ex Palaeur cambia musica', *Corriere della sera. Cronaca di Roma*, 19 September 2003, 54.

87 Rossi and Gatti, *Roma: Guida all'architettura moderna*, 216; de Vico Fallani, *Raffaele De Vico e i giardini di Roma*, 176.

88 Andrea Arzilli, 'Ecco il nuovo piano per l'area del velodromo' and 'Ore 17.50 del 24 luglio di nove anni fa, 120 chili di tritolo lo radono al suolo', *Corriere della Sera*, 2 June 2017, 3; 'Si alla riqualificazione dell'ex velodromo dell'Eur', *Corriere della Sera. Cronaca di Roma*, 26 June 2007, 5; Alessandro Fulloni, 'Il tritolo spazza via l'antico Velodromo', *Corriere della Sera. Cronaca di Roma*, 25 July 2008, 5.

89 Fabio Grilli, '"Comune ed Eur spa spieghino cosa intendono fare dell'ex velodromo". E spunta l'ipotesi stadio della Roma', *Roma Today*, 3 March 2021, https://www.romatoday.it/zone/eur/altre/stadio-della-roma-dove-ex-velodromo-eur.html (accessed 7 October 2021).

90 Testa, *Relazione attività 1951–61*, 9–10.
91 Zevi, *Una guida*, 68.
92 Zevi, *Una guida*, 28.
93 Monica Guerzoni, 'Eur, le "Torri" delle Finanze diventeranno un maxialbergo?', *Corriere della sera. Cronaca di Roma*, 27 August 2001, 45; Lilli Garrone, 'Le Torri dell' Eur alla cordata da 160 milioni', *Corriere della sera. Cronaca di Roma*, 18 March 2005 & 'Accelerare l'abbattimento delle Torri', *Corriere della sera. Cronaca di Roma*, 3 January 2008, 3.
94 Ernesto Menicucci, 'Prestiti bloccati, cantiere fermo la Nuvola rischia lo stop definitivo', *Corriere della sera. Cronaca di Roma*, 24 November 2014, 3.
95 Rossi and Gatti, *Roma: Guida all'architettura moderna*, 268.
96 Rossi and Gatti, *Roma: Guida all'architettura moderna* 194; Archidiap, 'Palazzo Sturzo – Ex sede della Democrazia Cristiana', http://archidiap.com/opera/palazzo-sturzo-ex-sede-della-democrazia-cristiana/ (accessed 29 October 2021).
97 G. Gh., 'Bomba a Roma contro la DC', *Corriere della sera*, 16–17 November 1964, 1–2.
98 Re. Do., 'Palazzo Sturzo all' Eur La storica sede DC si trasforma per Italease', *Corriere della sera. Cronaca di Roma*, 14 December 2009, 2.
99 Lilli Garrone, 'La Nuvola di Fuksas cala sull' Eur', *Corriere della sera. Cronaca di Roma*, 14 March 2006, 2.
100 'Rutelli: "Roma più verde pensando al Giubileo Troppe critiche ingiuste"', *Corriere della sera. Cronaca di Roma*, 8 October 1998, 17; 'Centro congressi, sette in corsa', *Corriere della sera. Cronaca di Roma*, 1 December 1998, 49; Giuseppe Pullara, 'Centro congressi Eur appuntamento al 2003', *Corriere della sera. Cronaca di Roma*, 5 November 1999, 50; Giuseppe Pullara, 'La "Nuvola" aspetta ancora la prima firma', *Corriere della sera. Cronaca di Roma*, 8 May 2003, 51; Ernesto Menicucci 'Eur, la Nuvola c'è e facciamo utili', *Corriere della Sera. Cronaca di Roma*, 15 October 2011, 1.
101 Ernesto Menicucci, 'Prestiti bloccati, cantiere fermo la Nuvola rischia lo stop definitivo', 3; 'Quattro palazzi storici in cambio della Nuvola' and 'Sbagliato vendere gioielli del razionalismo per coprire spese folli', *Corriere della sera. Cronaca di Roma*, 17 February 2015, 3.
102 Giuseppe Pullara, 'Raggi fischiata alla festa della Nuvola di Fuksas', *Corriere della sera. Cronaca di Roma*, 30 October 2016, 21.
103 'G20. I leader lanciano la monetina nella Fontana di Trevi', *Rai News*, http://www.rainews.it/dl/rainews/media/G20-I-leader-lanciano-la-monetina-nella-Fontana-di-Trevi-66ac6716-3a86-4cc0-a860-b786177749cc.html (accessed 5 November 2021).

Chapter 5

1 Benito Mussolini, 'La Roma di Mussolini' in E. Susmel and D. Susmel eds., vol. 25, *Opera omnia di Benito Mussolini* (Florence: La Fenice, 1972), 85.

2   Josep Lluís Sert, Ferdinand Léger and Siegfried Giedion, 'Nine Points on Monumentality' in Siegfried Giedion ed. *Architecture You and Me. Diary of a Development* (Cambridge, MA: Harvard University Press, 1943), 48.

3   Andreas Huyssen, 'Monument and Memory in a Postmodern Age' in James E. Young ed. *The Art of Memory. Holocaust Memorials in History* (Munich: Prestel Verlag, 1994), 9–17; Sert, Léger and Giedion, 'Nine Points on Monumentality', 48.

4   See Patrizia Dogliani, 'Constructing Memory and Anti-Memory: The Monumental Representation of Fascism and Its Denial in Republican Italy' in R. J. B. Bosworth and Patrizia Dogliani eds. *Italian Fascism: History, Memory and Representation* (London: Palgrave Macmillan UK, 1999) and John Foot, *Italy's Divided Memory* (Basingstoke: Palgrave Macmillan, 2011), 147–82.

5   Richard Bosworth, *Whispering City: Modern Rome and Its Histories* (New Haven: Yale University Press, 2011), 174–5.

6   Mario Isnenghi, *Le guerre degli italiani: parole, immagini, ricordi 1848–1945* (Milan: Mondadori, 1989) 322.

7   Foot, *Italy's Divided Memory*, 57.

8   For more on the bimillennial and the Exhibition of *Romanità* see Ferdinand Scriba, 'Archaeology as History – The *Mostra Augustea della Romanità* 1937/38 as an Example of the Relation between Archaeology and Fascism' in K. Gilliver, W. Ernst and F. Scriba eds., *Archaeology, ideology, method: Inter-academy seminar on current archaeological research* (Rome: Canadian Academic Centre in Italy, 1996), 55–75; Flavia Marcello, 'Mussolini and the Idealisation of Empire: The Augustan Exhibition of *Romanità*', *Modern Italy. The Journal of the Association for the Study of Modern Italy* 16, no. 3 (2011): 223–47; Joshua Arthurs, *Excavating Modernity: The Roman Past in Fascist Italy* (Ithaca, NY: Cornell University Press, 2012), 91–124.

9   Benito Mussolini, 'Per l'isolamento dell'Augusteo' in E. Susmel and D. Susmel ed., vol. 26, *Opera omnia di Benito Mussolini* (Florence: La Fenice, 1972), 367.

10 *Inizio delle demolizioni per l'isolamento del Mausoleo di Augusto* (1934), [Newsreel, Giornale Luce B056205] Dir. Arnaldo Ricotti, Italy: Istituto Luce.

11 See also the classic Spiro Kostof, 'The Emperor and the *Duce*: The Planning of the Piazzale Augusto Imperatore in Rome' in Henry A. Millon and Linda Nochlin eds. *Art & Architecture in the Service of Politics* (Cambridge, MA: MIT Press, 1978), 270–325; Italo Insolera, *Roma fascista nelle fotografie dell'Istituto Luce* (Rome: Editori Riuniti, 2001); John Agnew, '"Ghosts of Rome": The Haunting of Fascist Efforts at Remaking Rome as Italy's Capital City', *Annali d'Italianistica* 28 (2010): 189–92; Joshua Arthurs, '"Voleva Essere Cesare, Morì Vespasiano": The Afterlives of Mussolini's Rome', *Civiltà Romana. Rivista pluridisciplinare di studi su Roma antica e le sue interpretazioni* 1 (2015): 283–302 and Aristotle Kallis, *The Third Rome, 1922–43 the Making of the Fascist Capital* (London: Palgrave Macmillan UK, 2014), 95–105.

12 Articles on this topic abound in the various newspapers of the late 90s, I cite but one example: Francesca Giuliani, 'Quel muro è uno scempio Zurli stoppa

l'Ara Pacis', *La Repubblica*, 15 March 1998, https://ricerca.repubblica.it/repubblica/archivio/repubblica/1998/03/15/quel-muro-uno-scempio-zurli-stoppa.html?ref=search (accessed 4 February 2021).

13 Steve Rose, 'When in Rome ....', *The Guardian*,1 May 2006, https://doi.org/http://www.guardian.co.uk/travel/2006/may/01/travelnews.museums (accessed 14 November 2019).

14 Renata Mambelli, 'Roma, la guerra dell'Ara Pacis', *La Repubblica*, 20 April 2006, https://ricerca.repubblica.it/repubblica/archivio/repubblica/2006/04/20/roma-la-guerra-dell-ara-pacis.html?ref=search (accessed 4 February 2021).

15 'L'Ara Pacis riapre dopo sette anni. Ma è scontro sulla teca di Meier', *La Repubblica*, 21 April 2006, https://www.repubblica.it/2006/04/sezioni/cronaca/apertura-ara-pacis/apertura-ara-pacis/apertura-ara-pacis.html?ref=search# (accessed 4 February 2021); Bosworth, *Whispering City*, 200.

16 Enrico Regazzoni, 'La guerra degli architetti', *La Repubblica*, 17 June 1995, https://ricerca.repubblica.it/repubblica/archivio/repubblica/1995/06/17/la-guerra-degli-architetti.html?ref=search (accessed 4 February 2021).

17 See for example, 'I lettori denunciano', *La Repubblica*, 14 May 2006, https://ricerca.repubblica.it/repubblica/archivio/repubblica/2006/05/14/lettori-denunciano.041i.html?ref=search; Renata Mambelli, 'Ara Pacis, è ancora scontro', *La Repubblica*, 4 May 2006, https://ricerca.repubblica.it/repubblica/archivio/repubblica/2006/05/04/ara-pacis-ancora-scontro.html?ref=search; La Repubblica, 'Fuksas: "Errori fin dall" inizio', *La Repubblica*, 24 May 2006, https://ricerca.repubblica.it/repubblica/archivio/repubblica/2006/05/24/fuksas-errori-fin-dall-inizio.rm_003fuksas.html?ref=search and 'Calvesi: 'Luci e misure perfette', *La Repubblica*, 24 May 2006, https://ricerca.repubblica.it/repubblica/archivio/repubblica/2006/05/24/calvesi-luci-misure-perfette.html?ref=search; Gabriele Isman, 'Fra gli intellettuali è scontro è bella, anzi no, ci abitueremo', *La Repubblica*, 24 May 2006, https://ricerca.repubblica.it/repubblica/archivio/repubblica/2006/05/24/fra-gli-intellettuali-scontro-bella-anzi-no.html?ref=search (accessed 4 February 2021).

18 'La piazza e il monumento torneranno ad essere ciò che hanno sempre rappresentato: l'incontro tra passato e presente che fa di Roma una tra le città più belle al mondo', https://www.mausoleodiaugusto.it/it/il-progetto-di-restauro/ (accessed 28 July 2022).

19 Claudio Fogu, 'Fascism and Historic Representation: The 1932 Garibaldian Celebrations', *Journal of Contemporary History* 32, no. 2 (1996): 317–45.

20 Stefano Grandesso, 'Il monumento ad Anita Garibaldi a Roma' in Cristina Beltrami, Giovanni C. F. Villa and Anna Villari eds. *Garibaldi. Un eroe nel bronzo e nel marmo* (Cinisello Balsamo: Silvana Editoriale, 2012), 176–77; Mario Isnenghi, 'Garibaldi' in M. Isnenghi ed. *I luoghi della memoria: personaggi e date dell'Italia unita*, 25–45 (Bari: Laterza, 2010), 38–41.

21 Hannah Malone, 'Fascist Italy's Ossuaries of the First World War: Objects or Symbols?', *RIHA Journal*, no. 166 (2017): 2.

22 Cesare D'Onofrio, *Gli obelischi di Roma* (Roma: Bulzoni, 1967), 303–6.

23 D'Onofrio, *Gli Obelischi di Roma*, 305–6; Lars Berggren and Lennart Sjöstedt, *L'ombra dei grandi. monumenti e politica monumentale a Roma (1870–1895)*

(Rome: Artemide, 1996), 38–43. For a well-illustrated story on the various entries for the monument in what became two rounds of design competitions see Berggren and Sjöstedt, *L'ombra dei grandi monumenti*, 49–65.

24 *Scoperto il Leone di Giuda portato da Addis Abeba* (1937) [Newsreel, Giornale Luce, B1094] Dir. Arturo Gemmiti, Italy Istituto Luce.

25 Alberto Tulli, 'Il "Leone di Giuda" e l'obelisco di Dogali', in *Atti del V congresso. Nazionale di Studi Romani* Rome: Istituto dei Studi Romani (1942): 184; Igiaba Scego and Rino Bianchi, *Roma Negata. Percorsi postcoloniali nella città* (Rome: Ediesse, 2014), 62; Francesco Conte, 'A Roma c'è un monumento al colonialismo che non dovremmo ignorare', Termini TV, 26 January 2016, https://www.internazionale.it/video/2016/01/26/monumento-colonialismo-termini-roma (accessed 31 October 2018).

26 Eloi Ficquet, 'La stèle éthiopienne de Rome', *Cahiers d'études africaines* (2004): 375–76.

27 'The Lion of Judah Returns' in *Addis Reporter*, 11 April 1969, cited in Richard Pankhurst, "Ethiopia and The Loot of the Italian Invasion: 1935–1936," *Présence Africaine, Nouvelle série*, no. 72 (1969): 85–95; Scego and Bianchi, *Roma Negata*, 65.

28 Scego and Bianchi, *Roma Negata*, 49–50.

29 Marcello Piacentini, 'Piano dell'Esposizione Universale di Roma 1941', *Architettura* 16, no. 4 (1937): 184–8 and Giuseppe Pagano, 'L'esposizione universale di Roma Via', *Casabella* 114 (June 1937): 6.

30 For a full account of the Obelisk's return see Flavia Marcello and Aidan Carter, 'The Axum Obelisk: Shifting Concepts of Colonialism and Empire in Fascist and 21st-Century Rome' in Daniel Coslett ed. *The Colonial Past in the Neocolonial Present: Inherited Built Environments in Africa, Asia, the Middle East and Europe* (London: Routledge, 2019), 42–64.

31 Han Lamers and Bettina Reitz-Joosse, *The Codex Fori Mussolini: A Latin Text of Italian Fascism* (London: Bloomsbury Publishing, 2016), 52; Ann Thomas Wilkins, 'Augustus, Mussolini and the Parallel Imagery of Empire' in Claudia Lazzaro and Roger Crum eds. *Donatello Among the Blackshirts: History and Modernity in the Visual Culture of Fascist Italy* (Ithaca: Cornell University Press, 2004), 61; Peter Aicher, 'Mussolini's Forum and the Myth of Augustan Rome', *Classical Bulletin* 76, no. 2 (2000): 130–2.

32 Christopher Seton-Watson, 'Italy's Imperial Hangover', *Journal of Contemporary History* 15, no. 1 (January 1980): 171–2 and 177, Ruth Ben-Ghiat and Mia Fuller, eds., *Italian Colonialism* (New York: Palgrave Macmillan, 2005), xvii–xviii; Giampaolo Calchi Novati, 'Italy in the Triangle of the Horn: Too Many Corners for a Half Power', *Journal of Modern African Studies* 32, no. 3 (1994): 371–73.

33 See Giampaolo Calchi Novati, 'Re-Establishing Italo-Ethiopian Relations after the War: Old Prejudices and New Policies', *Northeast African Studies* 3, no. 1 (1996): 27–49 and 'La stele di Axum', *Gazzetta del Popolo*, 12 June 1954.

34 'Saluti e brindisi nel primo giorno de Negus a Roma', *Paese Sera*, 7 November 1970, 16; Dino Frescobaldi, 'Il Negus accolto da Saragat,' *Corriere della Sera*, 7 November 1970, 2; Dino Frescobaldi, 'Il Negus conferma a Roma la sua

linea di mediazione', *Corriere della Sera*, 8 November 1970, 2; *Paese Sera*, 'Per l'obelisco di Axum solo "problemi tecnici"', *Paese Sera*, 9 November 1970, 2.

35   Scego and Bianchi, *Roma Negata*, 97–8.
36   Scego and Bianchi, *Roma Negata*, 14–17.
37   Scego and Bianchi, *Roma Negata*, 17.
38   'silenzio, assenza, oblio, smemoratezze in salsa italica' Scego and Bianchi, *Roma Negata*, 18.
39   Antonella Greco, 'Gli obelischi, le piazze, gli artisti: Conversazione con Ludovico Quaroni' in Maurizio Calvesi, Enrico Guidoni and Simonetta Lux eds. *E 42, Utopia e scenario del regime* (Venice: Marsilio, 1987), 283–6.
40   Paola Cagiano de Azevedo, 'Museo delle Scienze' in *E 42, Utopia e scenario del regime*, 403. Roberto Siligato quotes the editorial from *Architettura* 16, no. 4 (April 1937): 181 which in turn quotes from Cini's 'Programma di Massima'. Roberto Siligato, 'Museo delle Scienze. La decorazione' in *E 42, Utopia e scenario del regime*, 404.
41   The themes of the bas reliefs are: Dances, The Hunt, Marconi, the Voices of the Radio, Holy Saturday and Songs of Love.
42   Vieri Quilici, *EUR: una moderna città di fondazione* (Roma De Luca editori d'arte, 2015), 103; Daniela de Dominicis and Martina De Luca, 'Arturo Dazzi, Stele a Guglielmo Marconi', in *E 42, Utopia E Scenario Del Regime*, 374.
43   de Dominicis & De Luca, 'Arturo Dazzi, Stele a Guglielmo Marconi', 374 and EUR Spa, 'Obelisco a Guglielmo Marconi', http://www.eurspa.it/it/asset-property/patrimonio/arte-e-design/opere-scultoree/obelisco-guglielmo-marconi (accessed 12 October 2018).
44   Giancarlo Masini, *Guglielmo Marconi* (Turin: Unione tipografico-editrice torinese, 1975).
45   Alfio Bernabei, *Esuli ed emigrati italiani nel Regno Unito: 1920–1940* (Milano: Mursia, 1997), 56 and 121; Antonio Armano and Stefano Biolchini, 'Quando Marconi discriminava gli scienziati ebrei', *Il Sole 24 ore*, 19 November 2013, https://www.ilsole24ore.com/art/cultura/2013-11-15/quando-marconi-discriminava-scienziati-ebrei-192555.shtml?uuid=ABqg8Td&p=2 (accessed 29 October 2018) and Rory Carroll, 'Marconi Blocked Jews from Il Duce's Academy', *The Guardian*, 19 March 2002, https://www.theguardian.com/world/2002/mar/19/physicalsciences.humanities (accessed 29 October 2018); Lauretta Colonnelli, 'Arturo Dazzi, l'uomo che plasmò l'obelisco dell'EUR', *Corriere della Sera*, 30 October 2016, 21.
46   Claudio Fogu, 'Fascism and Historic Representation: The 1932 Garibaldian Celebrations', *Journal of Contemporary History* 31, no. 2 (1996): 318–19 and 321 and Grandesso, 'Il monumento ad Anita Garibaldi', 177.
47   'Se il cavaliere di bronzo che sorge qui vicino diventasse uomo vivo e aprisse gli occhi, mi piace sperare che egli riconoscerebbe la discendenza delle sue camicie rosse nei soldati di Vittorio Veneto e le camicie nere che da un decennio continuano sotto forma più popolare e più feconda il suo volontarismo'. *A Roma l'inaugurazione del monumento ad Anita Garibaldi*

(1932), [Newsreel, Giornale Luce B009805] Dir. Arnaldo Ricotti, Italy: Istituto Luce.

48 Mabel Berezin, *Making the Fascist Self: The Political Culture of Interwar Italy* (Ithaca: Cornell University Press, 1997), 87–93.

49 Foot, *Divided Memory*, 55–8.

50 See Lucy M. Maulsby, 'Drinking from the River Lethe. *Case del Fascio* and the Legacy of Fascism in Postwar Italy', *Future Anterior. Journal of Historic Preservation History Theory & Criticism* 9, no. 2 (2014): 19–39.

51 Sylvia Diebner, 'Le trasformazioni di un blocco di granito', *Bullettino della Commissione Archeologica Comunale di Roma* L'Erma di Bretschneider 112 (2011): 153.

52 Rodolfo Bonfiglietti, 'Obelischi podisti e una base poltrona', *Capitolium*, August 1924, 347–8.

53 Diebner, 'Le Trasformazioni', 155.

54 Diebner, 'Le Trasformazioni', 163–5 and 'Il monumento ai caduti fascisti e l'apertura del Foro di Augusto', *Corriere della Sera*, 29 October 1926, 1.

55 Niccolò Bettegazzi, Hans Lamers and Bettina Reitz-Joosse, 'Viewing Rome in the Latin Literature of the Ventennio Fascista: Francesco Giammaria's *Capitolium Novum*', *Fascism. Journal of Comparative Fascist Studies* 8 (2019): 155–6.

56 Hic, nova quae lauros inter supereminet ara, / Relligione sacra et cultu celebrata perenni, / Ut voluit Dux, est merito sacrata juventae / Viribus invictae, in fando quae crimine caesa, / Obtulerat Patriae, perfuso sanguine, vitam. / Hic honor est igitur digne nunc redditus illi, / Gentibus exemplum ut fiat monitumque futuris. Translation by N. Bettegazzi, H. Lamers and B. Reitz-Joosse. Bettegazzi, Lamers and Reitz-Joosse, 'Viewing Rome', 174.

57 Capitolium. 'Giovanni Orgera nuovo Governatore di Roma', *Capitolium* 19, nos. 1–2 (January–February 1944): 4.

58 Vittorio Vidotto, 'Palazzi e sacrari: il declino del culto Littorio', *Roma moderna e contemporanea*, no. settembre-dicembre (2003): 577–8.

59 The sources on this differ. The Verano cemetery website and the *Corriere della Sera* newspaper report she was placed in the shrine while other photographic evidence shows an altar dedicated to her in the larger Chapel of the Heroes. B. A., 'La vibrante parola di Mussolini ai fedelissimi della prima adunata', *Corriere della Sera*, 25 March 1933, 1. On Donati, see also Angelo Piero Cappello, *Fasciste. Donne in marcia su Roma (1919–1922)* (Assago: Ianieri Edizioni, 2022).

60 Amy King, 'Antagonistic Martyrdom: Memory of the 1973 Rogo di Primavalle', *Modern Italy: Journal of the Association for the Study of Modern Italy* 25, no. 1 (2020): 36 & 39.

61 King, 'Antagonistic Martyrdom', 39.

62 Cesare De Simone, *Roma, città prigioniera: i 271 Giorni dell'occupazione nazista: 8 Settembre '43–4 Giugno '44* (Milano: Mursia, 1994), 108.

63 Angelo Gennaro, 'Roma, Fiori per i 'martiri fascisti' al cimitero del Verano. la comunità di Avanguardia non gradisce i giornalisti: "Come vi permettete?"', *Il Fatto Quotidiano*, no. 28, October (28 October 2017), https://doi.org/ https://www.ilfattoquotidiano.it/2017/10/28/roma-fiori-per-i-martiri-fascisti-al-cimitero-del-verano-la-comunita-di-avanguardia-non-gradisce-i-giornalisti-come-vi-permettete/3941735/ (accessed 22 October 2019).

64 Bruno Tobia, 'Il Vittoriano' in Mario Isnenghi ed. *I Luoghi della memoria: simboli e miti dell'Italia unita* (Bari: Laterza, 2010).

65 Tobia, 'Il Vittoriano', 299; Dogliani, 'Memory and Anti-memory', 15.

66 Rosella Leone, 'La cripta del Milite Ignoto e le scelte propagandistiche del regime fascista' in Pier Luigi Porzio ed. *Il Vittoriano. Materiali per una storia* (Rome: Fratelli Palombi, 1986), 50–1.

67 Dogliani, 'Memory and Anti-memory', 24.

68 Giorgio Boatti, 'Piazza Fontana' in Mario Isnenghi ed. *I Luoghi Della Memoria: Strutture Ed Eventi Dell'italia Unita* (Bari: Laterza, 2010).

69 'Oggi, a distanza di 90 anni la coesione nazionale è altrettanto importante in ricordo anche di tutti i caduti. Il ricordo di come il popolo italiano volle stringersi allora attorno al simbolo del Milite Ignoto, può essere di buon auspicio anche in un momento difficile come questo, nel quale è indispensabile ritrovare unità' Staff Pietre, '3285 – Lastra per il 90 anniversario del viaggio del Milite Ignoto – Roma', *Pietre della memoria, il segno della storia*, 26 March 2014, https://www.pietredellamemoria.it/pietre/lastra-per-il-90anniversario-del-viaggio-del-milite-ignoto/ (accessed 4 March 2021).

70 Han Lamers and Bettina Reitz, eds., *The Codex Fori Mussolini: A Latin text of Italian Fascism* (London: Bloomsbury Academic, 2017).

71 Del Debbio's archives contain 1:100 measured drawings of the four obelisks erected by Sixtus at St. Peter's, Santa Maria Maggiore, Piazza del Popolo and St. John in the Lateran. He also carried out extensive research on obelisks from all eras (including the Washington Monument), their shape, size and structure as well as different methods of construction and transportation. D'Amelio, *L'obelisco marmoreo del foro italico a Roma*, 31–9.

72 Memmo Caporilli and Franco Simeoni, *Il Foro Italico e lo stadio olimpico: Immagini Dalla Storia* (Rome: Tomo edizioni, 1990), 133.

73 Christopher Hibbert, *Benito Mussolini. The Rise and the Fall of* Il Duce (Harmondsworth: Penguin, 1986), 71.

74 Gian Franco Venè, *lire al mese: Vita quotidiana della famiglia nell'Italia fascista* (Milan: CDE, 1991), 95.

75 Cited D'Amelio, *L'obelisco marmoreo del foro italico a Roma*, 35; Antonella Greco and Salvatore Santuccio, *Il foro italico* (Rome: Multigrafica Editrice, 1991), 49–52.

76 Hannah Malone, 'Legacies of Fascism: Architecture, Heritage and Memory in Contemporary Italy', *Modern Italy* 22, no. 4 (2017) 445–70, doi:10.1017/mit.2017.51, 462; Bosworth, *Whispering City*, 243.

77 'Foro Italico e non "Foro Mussolini"', *Il pomeriggio. Corriere della Sera*, 26–27 August 1943: 1 and 'Storia inverosimile dell'oro sull'obelisco', *Il pomeriggio. Corriere della Sera*, 2–3 September 1943: 1.

78 'La cassetta d'oro sotto il monolito', *Paese Sera*, 12, 193, 13/14 August 1960.

79 Malone, 'Legacies of Fascism', 463.

80 Online commentary under: Sergio Rame, Fiano vuole cambiare l'obelisco: 'Bisogna togliere la scritta Dux', *Il giornale*, 12 September 2017, https://www.ilgiornale.it/news/politica/fiano-vuole-cambiare-lobelisco-bisogna-togliere-scritta-dux-1440734.html (accessed 9 March 2021).

81 'I quindici anni passati dalla caduta del regime fascista valgono secoli. Tutte le proposizioni del mondo sono tanto mutate, che veramente il monolito di Mussolini è diventato coevo di una colonna scaligera o di una lapide borgiana: e sono anacronistici coloro che oggi immaginano che possa rappresentare qualche cosa in cui si prolunghi ancora la breve vita di simbolo che ebbe'. Manlio Lupinacci, 'Stolto epurare le pietre a ogni svolta della storia', *Corriere della Sera*, 10 October 1959: 3.

82 Communiqué from Ivan Bonomi to all Ministries and all Prefects of the Kingdom, 1 August 1944. ACS PCM44-47 1/7 f.11240/2.

83 Letter from Minister for Education De Ruggiero to the Ministry of the Interior, 4 July 1944. ACS PCM44-47 1/7 f.11240/2.

84 Letter from Presidency of the Council of Ministers to Minister for Education, 16 August 1944. ACS PCM44-47 1/7 f.11240/2.

85 Foot, *Divided Memory*, 69.

86 Dogliani, 'Memory and Anti-memory', 21.

87 Alessandro Madron, '25 aprile, la Liberazione nera: i fascisti si ritrovano nel giorno-simbolo della Resistenza per ricordare i morti di Salò', *Il fatto quotidiano*, 22 April 2016, https://www.ilfattoquotidiano.it/2016/04/22/25-aprile-la-liberazione-nera-i-fascisti-si-ritrovano-nel-giorno-simbolo-della-resistenza-per-ricordare-i-morti-di-salo/2662216/ (accessed 25 July 2021).

88 Maurice Halbwachs, *On Collective Memory*, ed. Lewis A. Coser (Chicago: University of Chicago Press, 1992).

Chapter 6

1 Benito Mussolini, 'Per la vera pacificazione' in E. Susmel and D. Susmel eds., vol. 17, *Opera omnia di Benito Mussolini* (Florence: La Fenice, 1972), 292.

2 See for example papers presented at the Institute of Classical Studies conference *The Afterlife of Inscriptions: Reusing, Rediscovering, Reinventing & Revitalizing Ancient Inscriptions*, ed. Alison Cooley (London, 2000).

3 Walter Benjamin, 'The Work of Art in the Age of Mechanical Reproduction' in Hannah Arendt ed. *Illuminations* (New York: Fontana Press, 1992).

4 Flavia Marcello and Paul Gwynne, 'Speaking from the Walls: Militarism, Education and *Romanità* in Rome's *Città Universitaria* (1932–35)', *Journal of the Society of Architectural Historians* 75, no. 3 (2015): 323.

NOTES

5   Maria Elena Versari, 'Living among the *Duce*'s Words: The Visual Materialization of Political Rhetoric in Italian Public Space, from the *Risorgimento* to Fascism', *Word & Image* 34, no. 3 (2018): 255; Tim Benton, 'Epigraphy and Fascism', *Bulletin – Institute of Classical Studies* 44, no. S75 (2000): 163.

6   Benton, 'Epigraphy and Fascism', 167

7   Marcello and Gwynne, 'Speaking from the Walls', 323.

8   This job is being done by the Norwegian Research council funded project 'Fascist Latin Texts': https://flt.hf.uio.no/work/44

9   Letter from Ivanoe Bonomi to all Ministers and Prefects of the Reign of Italy, dated 1 August 1944, ACS PCM44-47 1/7 f.11240/1.

10 Versari, 'Living among the *Duce*'s Words', 256.

11 Versari, 'Living among the *Duce*'s Words', 258.

12 Marcello and Gwynne, 'Speaking from the Walls', 324.

13 Translation Tim Benton.

14 Benton, 'Epigraphy and Fascism', 183; Joshua Arthurs, "Voleva essere cesare, morì Vespasiano": The afterlives of Mussolini's Rome', *Civiltà romana. Rivista pluridisciplinare di studi su Roma antica e le sue interpretazioni* 1 (2015): 283.

15 Antonino Nastasi, 'Introduction. Rome (IT), Piazza Augusto Imperatore [extant] – 1940' in Han Lamers and Bettina Reitz-Joosse eds. *Fascist Latin Texts*, https://flt.hf.uio.no/work/44 (accessed 28 July 2022).

16 Andrea Nemiz, *Studium Urbis Roma novembre 1935, il Duce inaugura la Città Universitaria 'laurea 'Honoris Causa' al Re* (Rome: Litografia Covi, 1985), 15–17.

17 Marcello and Gwynne, 'Speaking from the Walls'.

18 Some examples are: the military tank department on the Via Tiburtina (formerly dedicated to Queen Elena, now Caserma Ruffo), the fire brigade on Via Nomentana (formerly dedicated to Emilio Bianchi) and the Esquiline (on what was once via Re Boris di Bulgaria).

19 P. Francesco Ferraironi, *Iscrizioni ornamentali su edifici e monumenti di Roma: con appendice sulle iscrizioni scomparse* (Rome: Industria Tipografica Romana, 1937), 298, 403 and 520.

20 For example the one inside the O. De Tommaso Barracks in Prati. Arma dei Carabinieri, '120191 - Lastra del Bollettino della Vittoria – Comando Legione Allievi CC – Roma', *Pietre della memoria. Segni della storia*, 29 December 2017, https://www.pietredellamemoria.it/pietre/lastra-del-bollettino-della-vittoria-comando-legione-allievi-cc-roma/ (accessed 4 March 2021).

21 Patrizia Dogliani, 'Constructing Memory and Anti-memory: The Monumental Representation of Fascism and Its Denial in Republican Italy' in R. J. B. Bosworth and Patrizia Dogliani eds. *Italian Fascism: History, Memory and Representation* (London: Palgrave Macmillan UK, 1999), 16; John Foot, *Italy's Divided Memory* (Basingstoke: Palgrave Macmillan, 2011), 48–9.

22 Dogliani, 'Constructing Memory and Anti-memory', 13–15.

23. Antonio Reggiani, 'Prefazione in tempo di libertà' in *Ai Caduti* (Rome, 3 July 1944), https://comitatogianicolo.it/2013/la-commissione-caduti-ripropone-il-testo-di-antonio-reggiani-del-1944-inserito-ad-integrazione-della-pubblicazione-i-caduti-per-roma/4771 (accessed 3 May 2021).

24. Antonio Nastasi, 'Introduction. Rome (IT), Garibaldian Ossuary Mausoleum [extant] – 1941' in Han Lamers and Bettina Reitz-Joosse eds. *Fascist Latin Texts*, https://flt.hf.uio.no/work/44 (accessed 28 July 2022).

25. Flavia Marcello, 'L'architettura delle case del Mutilato' in I. Simonini ed. *Storia, arte e architettura nella Casa del Mutilato di Ravenna* (Ravenna: Edizioni del Girasole, 2019), pp. 157–9.

26. Ralph-Miklas Dobler, 'Die Verarbeitung des Ersten Weltkrieges in der künstlerischen Ausstattung der Casa Madre dei Mutilati in Rom (1925–1938)', *Politische Ikonographie. E-Journal für Kunst- und Bildgeschichte* 10, no. 3 (2010): 9, http://www.anmigcomitatocentrale.com/ (accessed 4 November 2011); P. V. Cannistraro, *Historical Dictionary of Fascist Italy* (Westport Connecticut: Greenwood Press, 1982), 161.

27. H. A. Daniels, *Die Hymnen des Thesaarns Hymnologicus H. A. Daniels und anderer Hymnen-Ausgaben* (Leipzig: O. R. Reisland, 1908), http://archive.org/stream/analectahymnica51drevuoft/analectahymnica51drevuoft_djvu.txt (accessed 6 November 2011).

28. My thanks go to Professor Paul Gwynne for this and other translations from Latin in this chapter.

29. Mabel Berezin, *Making the Fascist Self: The Political Culture of Interwar Italy* (Ithaca, NY: Cornell University Press, 1997), 218; Jeremy Schnapp has also pointed out the central role of blood in the construction of the myth of the Fascist martyr and its use in the *Sacrario* of the *Mostra della Rivoluzione Fascista*.

30. Dobler, 'Die Verarbeitung', 27.

31. 'la gloria è … il focolare dei sofferenti; non vedesti come la medaglia d'oro splendeva sulle tue gramaglie sembrando una stella in mezzo alla notte?' Carlo Delcroix, *Sette santi senza candele*. With original woodcuts by A. G. Santagata (Florence: Vallecchi, 1928), 237.

32. *Percussa vivit:* On stemma of SILICEO GIOVANNI MARTINO created by Pope Paolo IV in 1555, Araldica Vaticana, http://www.araldicavaticana.com/siliceo_giovanni_martino__joann.htm; *Gemendo germinat*: Motto of Carrassi (or Carassi) family of Turin, cited in V. Spreti, *Enciclopedia Storico-Nobiliare Italiana*, 1928–1936, vol. II, 339, http://daubau.it/enciclopedia/Motti_presenti_nelle_armi_delle_famiglie_italiane. *Ardeo nam credo*: Motto of Calefati (or Calefato or Calafato) family of Florence, cited in P. Guelfi Camaiani, *Dizionario araldico* (Milan: Editore Ulrico Hoepli, 1940), 557; V. Spreti, *Enciclopedia storico-Nobiliare Italiana*, 1928–1936, vol. II, 244, http://daubau.it/enciclopedia/Motti_presenti_nelle_armi_delle_famiglie_italiane; Dott. A. Messina Mango di Casalgerardo, *Nobiliaro di Sicilia*, http://www.regione.sicilia.it/beniculturali/bibliotecacentrale/mango/calce.htm (accessed 6 November 2011).

33 George Mosse, *Masses and Man: Nationalist and Fascist Perceptions of Reality* (New York: H Fertig, 1980), 494.
34 See Berezin, *Making the Fascist Self*, Chapter 6.
35 Mosse, *Masses and Man*, 495–6.
36 Ferraironi, *Iscrizioni ornamentali*, 173.
37 My thanks to Sally Hill for alerting me to this at the Australian Centre for Italian Studies Conference in December 2022. See also Associazione AREA06, 'Andrea Lo Giudice A+G', 2023, https://www.shorttheatre.org/en/eventi/andrea-lo-giudice/ (accessed 27 February 2023).
38 Henri Lefebvre, *The Production of Space*, trans. D. Nicholson Smith (Oxford: Blackwell, 1991), 215.
39 Simon Martin, 'Rebranding the Republic: Rome and the 1960 Olympic Games', *European Review of History Revue européene d'histoire* 24, no. 1 (2017): 69. For other summaries of this debate see Arthurs, 'Voleva essere Cesare', 290–2; Richard Bosworth, *Whispering City Modern Rome and Its Histories* (New Haven: Yale University Press, 2011), 245–6; Tim Benton, 'Heritage and changes in Regime' in Tim Benton ed. *Understanding Heritage and Memory* (Manchester: Manchester University Press, 2010) & Tim Benton, 'Arengario to Lictor's Axe: Memories of Italian Fascism' in Marius Kwint, Christopher Breward and Jeremy Aynsley eds. *Material Memories: Design and Evocation* (Oxford: Berg, 1999).
40 Camera dei Deputati, *Atti Parlamentari*, CCII, 10613. 'Le scritte al Foro Italico non verrebbero cancellate', *Corriere della Sera*, 26 September 1959, 7.
41 Camera dei Deputati, *Atti Parlamentari*, CCII, 10613.
42 Corriere della Sera, 'Commemorato da Leone e Segni il primo Presidente della Repubblica', *Corriere della Sera*, 7 October 1959, 2.
43 Manlio Lupinacci, 'Stolto epurare le pietre a ogni svolta della storia', *Corriere della Sera*, 10 October 1959, 3.
44 Benton, 'Heritage and Changes in Regime', 140–1 and 'Arengario to Lictor's Axe', 202–4.
45 Biblioteca Hertziana Fototeca, C193. Roma Edilizia pubblica – Edilizia a destinazione culturale, Sport Foro Italico (III) Varia, 585480, 585479, 585478, 585477.
46 Assicurazioni Generali, Corporate Heritage and Historical Archive, 'La *Latinitas* dell'INA: dal *Providentiae Munus* al Novus Décor', 6 November 2017, https://heritage.generali.com/la-latinitas-dellina-dal-providentiae-munus-al-novus-decor/ (accessed 2 March 2021). See also Ferraironi, *Iscrizioni ornamentali,* 543 who translates *Italiae* as Patria or Fatherland.
47 Arthurs, *'Voleva essere Cesare'*, 293–5.
48 Patrizia Cagiano de Azevedo et al., 'Palazzo della civiltà italiana' in Maurizio Calvesi, Enrico Guidoni and Simonetta Lux eds. *E 42, utopia e scenario del regime* (Venice: Marsilio, 1987), 354. For the original image, see *Illustrazione italiana*, 51, December 1938.

49 Francesco Innamorati and Carlo Bertilaccio, *Eur Spa e il patrimonio di E42: manuale d'uso per edifici e opere* (Rome: Palombi, 2004), 20.

50 Marcello and Gwynne, 'Speaking from the Walls', 325.

51 'al quale l'umanità deve talune delle sue più grandi conquiste', Benito Mussolini, 'Discorso per la prima grande adunata del popolo italiano 26 dicembre 1935' in E. Susmel and D. Susmel ed., vol. 26, *Opera omnia di Benito Mussolini* (Florence: La Fenice, 1972), pp. 356–7

52 Benton, 'Epigraphy and Fascism', 189.

53 Veresani et al., 'Palazzo degli uffici' in Calvesi, Guidoni and Lux eds. *E 42, utopia e scenario del regime*, 297–8.

54 Nastasi, 'Introduction'.

55 Benito Mussolini, 'La nuova Roma' in in E. Susmel and D. Susmel ed., vol. 22, *Opera omnia di Benito Mussolini* (Florence: La Fenice, 1972), 48.

56 Letter from interim Commissioner of EUR to the Cabinet of the Council of Ministers, dated 5 December 1944 in ACS PCM44-47 1/7 f.11240/2.

57 See also Nastasi, 'Introduction'.

58 Quotes for this section are taken from Ferraironi, *Iscrizioni ornamentali* 41, 97–8, 136, 418.

59 Marcello and Gwynne, 'Speaking from the Walls', 331–3 and 339.

60 From an interview with Joyce Lussu at the Biblioteca del Vascello, Rome, in Aglaia Zannetti, *Letture*, Associazione Nazionale Partigiani d'Italia, http://anpi.it/media/uploads/files/2013/03 › media › uploads › files › 2013/03 (accessed 16 March 2021).

61 Gianni Rivolta, 'Ritrovate scritte sovversive contro il Re, il fascismo e i tedeschi', *Cara Garbatella*, 26 June 2020, https://caragarbatella.it/ritrovate-scritte-sovversive-contro-il-re-il-fascismo-e-i-tedeschi/ (accessed 17 March 2021).

62 Filippo Colombara, 'Guerra anche sui muri tra partigiani e repubblichini', *Patria indipendente*, April 2013, 36.

63 Lefebvre, *The Production of Space*, 160–1.

64 'L'arte dello scalpellino che martella via le pietre segnate e vuol renderle effimere come l'orgoglio di chi le segnò, in Campidoglio ha operato assai poco, e un fascio littorio che ti capiti sotto gli occhi non sai mai capire di quand'è, e ti domandi se lo ha ordinato un console, un imperatore, un senatore di Roma, il sindaco Nathan o il governatore Bottai'. Manlio Lupinacci, 'Stolto epurare le pietre a ogni svolta della storia'. *Corriere della Sera*, 10 October 1959, 3.

Conclusion

1 Benito Mussolini, 'Al popolo di Roma per il 28 ottobre' in E. Susmel and D. Susmel eds., vol. 22, *Opera omnia di Benito Mussolini* (Florence: La Fenice, 1972), 243.

2   Angela Giuffrida, '"She's very charismatic": Could Giorgia Meloni Become Italy's First Far-Right Leader since Mussolini', *The Observer,* 25 July 2022, https://www.theguardian.com/world/2022/jul/24/italy-summer-snap-elections-far-right-brothers-of-italy-giorgia-meloni (accessed 29 July 2022).

3   Aristotle Kallis, *The Third Rome, 1922–43 the Making of the Fascist Capital* (London: Palgrave Macmillan UK, 2014), 264.

4   Tim Benton and Clementine Cecil, 'Heritage and Public Memory' in Tim Benton ed. *Understanding Heritage and Memory* (Manchester, UK: Manchester University Press, 2010), 7–9 & 15.

5   Tale commissione dovrà tener conto del significato politico e del valore artistico dell'opera, della possibilità o meno di rimuoverla senza arrecar danno estetico troppo marcato all'assieme edificio cui essa appartiene, suggerirà eventualmente gli accorgimenti necessari, e (trattandosi di opere di rilevante valore) le modalità per la loro conservazione. Letter from Minister for National Education to Minister of the Interior dated 4 July 1944. PCM44-47 1/7 f.11240/2.

6   See, for example, Sharon Macdonald, *Difficult Heritage: Negotiating the Nazi Past in Nuremberg and Beyond* (New York: Routledge, 2009); Tim Benton, ed., *Understanding Heritage and Memory* (Manchester: Manchester University, 2010); Nick Carter and Simon Martin, eds., '"Difficult heritage" of Fascist Monumental Art and Architecture'. Special issue, *Modern Italy* 24 (2019); Kay Bea Jones and Stephanie Pilat, eds., *The Routledge Companion to Italian Fascist Architecture: Reception and Legacy* (Abingdon, Oxon, New York: Routledge, 2020); Håkan Hökerberg, ed., *Architecture as Propaganda in Twentieth-century Totalitarian Regimes: History and Heritage* (Florence: Polistampa, 2018); Håkan Hökerberg, 'The Monument to Victory in Bolzano: Desacralisation of a Fascist Relic', *International Journal of Heritage Studies* 23, no. 8 (2017): 759–74; Hannah Malone, 'Legacies of Fascism: Architecture, Heritage and Memory in Contemporary Italy', *Modern Italy* 22, no. 4 (2017): 445–70; Lucy Maulsby, 'Drinking from the River Lethe. *Case Del Fascio* and the Legacy of Fascism in Postwar Italy', *Future Anterior* 9, no. 2 (2014): 18–39; Joshua Samuels, 'Difficult Heritage: Coming to Terms with Sicily's Fascist Past', in Trinidad Rico and Kathryn Lafrenz Samuels eds. *Heritage Keywords: Rhetoric and Redescription in Cultural Heritage* (Boulder, CO: University Press of Colorado, 2015), 111–28; Tim Benton, 'From the Arengario to the Lictor's Axe: Memories of Italian Fascism' in Marius Kwint, Christopher Breward, and Jeremy Aynsley eds. *In Material Memories: Design and Evocation* (New York: Berg, 1999), 199–218; Joshua Arthurs, '"Voleva essere Cesare, morì Vespasiano": The Afterlives of Mussolini's Rome', *Civiltà romana. Rivista pluridisciplinare di studi su Roma antica e le sue interpretazioni* 1 (2015): 283–302.

BIBLIOGRAPHY

-, '"L'aula Bunker deve tornare allo sport" Chiesto l'intervento del Ministro Veltroni per liberare l'ex palestra di scherma.' *Corriere della Sera. Cronaca di Roma*, 3 February 1998.
-, 'A completamento del più moderno quartiere di Roma. La cascata del lago artificiale all'EUR è da ieri una realizzazione compiuta', unknown newspaper, 30 June 1961. ACS Testa Archive, Box 8, f. 28 'Articoli vari sull'EUR'.
-, 'Accelerare l'abbattimento delle Torri', *Corriere della sera. Cronaca di Roma*, 3 January 2008, 3.
-, 'Anche l'ex assessore e tre funzionari incriminati per l'hotel non costruito', *Corriere della Sera*, 2 April 1982, 20.
-. 'Casa della gioventù italiana del littorio a Roma in Trastevere, architetto Luigi Moretti'. *Architettura. Rivista del Sindacato Nazionale Architetti Fascisti* 20, no. 9–10 (September–October 1941): 360–75.
-, 'Centro congressi, sette in corsa', *Corriere della sera. Cronaca di Roma*, 1 December 1998, 49.
-, 'Ente EUR: il commissario Di Mano sentito dal magistrato', *Corriere della Sera. Cronaca di Roma*, 25 September 1982, 20.
-, 'Foro Italico e non "Foro Mussolini"', *Il pomeriggio. Corriere della Sera*, 26–27 August 1943.
-, 'G20. I leader lanciano la monetina nella Fontana di Trevi', *Rai News*, http://www.rainews.it/dl/rainews/media/G20-I-leader-lanciano-la-monetina-nella-Fontana-di-Trevi-66ac6716-3a86-4cc0-a860-b786177749cc.html. Accessed 5 November 2021.
-, 'Giornalisti e dirigenti inglesi visitano "l'Esposizione permanente"', *Corriere della Sera*, 23 September 1959.
-, 'Gronchi riceverà Coty alla stazione', *Corriere della Sera,* 9 May 1957, 1.
-, 'I "Beatles" canteranno anche a Roma', *Corriere della sera*, 28 May 1965, X.
-, 'Il concorso di secondo grado per la Casa Littoria in Roma', *Architettura. Numero speciale - Architettura e urbanistica nella capitale e nell'impero*, 16, no. 12 (December 1937), pp. 707–52
-, 'Il re e la regina di Grecia accolti da Gronchi a Roma', *Corriere d'Informazione*, 19–20 May 1959, 1–2.
-, 'L'itinerario della visita in Italia di Elisabetta II e del principe Filippo', *Corriere della Sera,* 12 April 1961, 2.
-, 'L'Air Terminal diventerà sede di Eataly', *Corriere della Sera, Cronaca di Roma*, 9 April 2010, 5.
-, 'L'Inail acquista quattro musei e salva il bilancio di Eur Spa', *Corriere della Sera*, 23 December 2015, 5.
-, 'L'istruttoria per la deportazione di tremila carabinieri in Germania', *Corriere d'Informazione*, 19–20 February 1946, 1.

BIBLIOGRAPHY

-, 'Musiche e giochi d'acqua all'EUR', *Il giornale d'Italia*, 1 July 1961.
-, 'Quell'omaggio all'incoerenza', *Corriere della Sera. Cronaca di Roma*, 25 June 2005.
-, 'Rutelli: "Roma più verde pensando al Giubileo Troppe critiche ingiuste"', *Corriere della sera. Cronaca di Roma*, 8 October 1998, 17.
-, 'Saragat consegna le "stelle del lavoro" Moro auspica un "ordinato progresso"', *Corriere d'informazione*, 2–3 May 1966, 2.
-, 'Si alla riqualificazione dell'ex velodromo dell'Eur', *Corriere della Sera. Cronaca di Roma*, 3, 26 June 2007, 5.
-, 'Sotto accusa due assessori per illeciti urbanistici' *Corriere della Sera*, 6 July 1984, 27.
-, '"Hotel du Lac": assoluzione per i tre maggiori imputati', *Corriere della Sera. Cronaca di Roma*, 1 July 1983, 19.

Accasto, Gianni, Vanna Fraticelli and Renato Nicolini, eds. *Architettura di Roma capitale*. Rome: Edizioni Golem, 1976.
Agati, Annapaola. 'La residenza di Mussolini a Villa Torlonia'. In *Villa Torlonia. Guida*, edited by Alberta Campitelli, 183–7. Rome: Electa, 2007.
Agnew, John. '"Ghosts of Rome": The Haunting of Fascist Efforts at Remaking Rome as Italy's Capital City'. *Annali d'Italianistica* 28 (2010): 179–98.
Aicher, Peter. 'Mussolini's Forum and the Myth of Augustan Rome'. *Classical Bulletin* 76, no. 2 (2000): 117–39.
Allum, Percy. 'Italian Society Transformed'. In *Italy since 1945*, edited by Patrick McCarthy, 10–41. Oxford: Oxford University Press, 2000.
Amabile, Flavia. 'Riapre il Museo Coloniale, il gioiello di Mussolini', *La Stampa*, 1 June 2019. https://www.lastampa.it/cronaca/2019/06/01/news/riapre-il-museo-coloniale-il-gioiello-di-mussolini-1.33704991. Accessed 30 September 2020.
Angeleri, Gianfranco, and Umberto Mariotti Bianchi. *Termini. Dalle Botteghe di Farfa al Dinosauro*. Rome: Edizioni Abete, 1983.
Arachi, Alessandra. 'Un errore la chiusura della stazione Ostiense', *Corriere della Sera. Corriere Roma*, 22 April 1987, 24.
Archeologiavocidalpassato, 'Roma-Eur. Il museo delle Civiltà cambia pelle e volto: in quattro anni da museo composto da molti musei diventerà un meta-museo che si propone di riflettere criticamente sulle stratificazioni delle collezioni e delle culture rappresentate. Prime aperture in autunno 2022'. https://archeologiavocidalpassato.com/2022/08/30/roma-eur-il-museo-delle-civilta-cambia-pelle-e-volto-in-quattro-anni-da-museo-composto-da-molti-musei-diventera-un-meta-museo-che-si-propone-di-riflettere-criticamente-sulle-stratificazioni-delle-co/. Accessed 9 February 2023.
Archidiap. Istituto Nazionale Luce. http://www.archidiap.com/opera/istituto-nazionale-luce/. Accessed 18 June 2020.
Archidiap. 'Museo della Civiltà Romana'. http://www.archidiap.com/opera/museo-della-civilta-romana/. Accessed 20 May 2021.
Arthurs, Joshua. '"Voleva Essere Cesare, Morì Vespasiano": The Afterlives of Mussolini's Rome'. *Civiltà Romana. Rivista pluridisciplinare di studi su Roma antica e le sue interpretazioni* 1 (2015): 283–302.
Arthurs, Joshua. *Excavating Modernity: The Roman Past in Fascist Italy*. Cornell University Press, 2012.
Arzilli, Andrea. 'Ecco il nuovo piano per l'area del Velodromo'. *Corriere della Sera*, 2 June 2017, 3.

Arzilli, Andrea. 'Ore 17.50 del 24 luglio di nove anni fa, 120 chili di tritolo lo radono al suolo', *Corriere della Sera*, 2 June 2017, 3.
Associazione Roma Sotterranea. 'Il bunker di Palazzo Venezia'. https://www.bunkertorlonia.it/il-bunker-di-palazzo-venezia.html. Accessed 27 July 2020.
Atelier, Jean Nouvel. 'Eni Head Office. Rome, Italy'. http://www.jeannouvel.com/projets/siege-social-eni/. Accessed 5 July 2022.
B. A. 'La vibrante parola di Mussolini ai fedelissimi della prima adunata'. *Corriere della Sera*, 25 March 1933.
B. P. 'Per la Loren e Clark Gable "ciak" alla stazione Ostiense'. *Corriere d'Informazione*, 18–19 August 1959.
Ballone, Adriano. 'La Resistenza'. In *I luoghi della memoria: strutture ed eventi dell'Italia unita*, edited by Mario Isnenghi. Bari: Laterza, 2010.
Barbiellini Amidei, Rosanna. 'La Casa Madre e le Arti'. In *La Casa Madre dei Mutilati di Guerra*, edited by Franco Borsi, 105–56. Rome: Editalia, 1993.
Ben-Ghiat, Ruth, and Mia Fuller, eds. *Italian Colonialism*. New York: Palgrave Macmillan, 2005.
Benevolo, Leonardo. 'La distruzione del piano'. In *La metropoli 'spontanea': il caso di Roma, 1925–1981. Sviluppo residenziale di una città dentro e fuori dal piano*, edited by Alberto Clementi and Francesco Perego, 69–74. Bari: Dedalo, 1983.
Benjamin, Walter. 'The Work of Art in the Age of Mechanical Reproduction'. In *Illuminations*, edited by Hannah Arendt. New York: Fontana Press, 1992.
Benton, Tim. 'Rome Reclaims Its Empire'. In *Art and Power: Europe under the Dictators 1930–45*, edited by Dawn Ades, Neal Ascherson and E. J. Hobsbawm, 120–7, 126. London: Thames and Hudson, 1995.
Benton, Tim. 'From the Arengario to the Lictor's Axe: Memories of Italian Fascism'. In *Material Memories: Design and Evocation*, edited by Christopher Breward Jeremy Aynsley and Marius Kwint, 199–218. New York: Berg, 1999.
Benton, Tim. 'Epigraphy and Fascism'. *Bulletin–Institute of Classical Studies* 44, no. S75 (2000): 163–92.
Benton, Tim. 'Heritage and Changes of Regime'. In *Understanding Heritage and Memory*, edited by Tim Benton, 126–63. Manchester, UK: Manchester University Press, 2010.
Benton, Tim and Clementine Cecil. 'Heritage and Public Memory'. In *Understanding Heritage and Memory*, edited by Tim Benton, 7–43. Manchester, United Kingdom: Manchester University Press, 2010.
Berezin, Mabel. *Making the Fascist Self: The Political Culture of Interwar Italy*. Ithaca, NY: Cornell University Press, 1997.
Berggren, Lars, and Lennart Sjöstedt. *L'ombra dei grandi. Monumenti e politica monumentale a Roma (1870–1895)*. Rome: Artemide, 1996.
Bernabei, Alfio. *Esuli ed emigrati italiani nel Regno Unito: 1920–1940*. Milano: Mursia, 1997.
Bertoli, Ubaldo. 'Cresce un Palazzo All'E.U.R.' *Gatto Selvatico. Mensile aziendale* vol. 7, no.10 (October 1961): 15–16.
Bettegazzi, Niccolò, Hans Lamers, and Bettina Reitz-Joosse, 'Viewing Rome in the Latin Literature of the Ventennio Fascista: Francesco Giammaria's Capitolium Novum', *Fascism. Journal of Comparative Fascist Studies* 8 (2019): 153–78.
Bisso, Marino. 'A Roma la medaglia d'Oro al Valore Militare, 11 giorni di iniziative dell'Anpi nel nome della libertà e dei diritti', *La Repubblica*, 4 June 2019. https://roma.repubblica.it/cronaca/2019/06/04/news/a_roma_la_medaglia_d_

oro_al_valore_militare_11_giorni_di_iniziative_dell_anpi_nel_nome_della_liberta_e_dei_diritti-227908423/?ref=search. Accessed 5 February 2021.

Boatti, Giorgio. 'Piazza Fontana'. In *I luoghi della memoria: strutture ed eventi dell'Italia unita*, edited by Mario Isnenghi. Bari: Laterza, 2010, 479–92.

Bonfiglietti, Rodolfo. 'Obelischi podisti e una base poltrona'. *Capitolium*, no. August (1924): 347–8.

Borsi, Franco, Gabriele Morolli, and Daniela Fonti. *Il Palazzo dell'industria*. Rome: Editalia, 1986.

Bosworth, R. J. B. *Whispering City Modern Rome and Its Histories*. New Haven: Yale University Press, 2011.

Braun, Emily. *Mario Sironi and Italian Modernism*. Cambridge: Cambridge University Press, 2000.

Brogi, Paolo. 'L'affresco nascosto di Mafai su una parete della ex Gil'. *Corriere della Sera. Cronaca di Roma*., 7 December 2004, 53.

Brunetta, Gianpiero. *Storia del cinema italiano. 2. Il cinema del regime 1929–1945*. Editori Riuniti, 2001.

Bruni, Angela Raffaella. 'Cinema Nuovo-Sacher'. In *Il moderno attraverso Roma: Guida a 200 architetture e alle loro opere d'arte*, edited by Gaia Remiddi, Antonella Greco, Antonella Bonavita and Paola Ferri, H106. Rome: Fratelli Palombi, 2000.

Cagiano de Azevedo, Paola, Maria Silvia Farci, Vincenzo Mazzarella, and Alessandra Muntoni. 'Palazzo Della Civiltà Italiana'. In *E 42, Utopia e scenario del regime*, edited by Maurizio Calvesi, Enrico Guidoni, and Simonetta Lux, 353–70. Venice: Marsilio, 1987.

Calchi Novati, Giampaolo. 'Italy in the Triangle of the Horn: Too Many Corners for a Half Power'. *Journal of Modern African Studies* 32, no. 3 (1994): 371–3.

Calvesi, Maurizio, Enrico Guidoni, and Simonetta Lux, eds. *E 42, Utopia e scenario del regime*. Venice: Marsilio, 1987.

Calzini, Raffaele. '"Non sventrare più" dice il chirurgo di Roma'. *Corriere della Sera*, 29 July 1951, 3.

Canestrari, Manuela. 'Edificio per la mostra dell'agricoltura e bonifiche'. In *E 42, Utopia e scenario del regime*, edited by Guidoni Calvesi, and Lux, 500–2.

Cannistraro, Phillip V. *Historical Dictionary of Fascist Italy*. Westport, CT: Greenwood Press, 1982.

Capomolla, Rinaldo, and Rosalia Vittorini, eds. *L'architettura Ina Casa (1949–1963). Aspetti e problemi di conservazione e recupero*. Rome: Gangemi, 2003.

Caporilli, Memmo, and Franco Simeoni. *Il Foro Italico e lo stadio olimpico: immagini dalla storia*. Rome: Tomo edizioni, 1990.

Carli, Carlo Fabrizio, Gianni Mercurio, and Luigi Prisco. '*E42-Eur: Segno E Sogno Del Novecento*'. Rome: Data Ars, 2005.

Carter, Nick. '"What Shall We Do with It Now?": The *Palazzo Della Civiltà Italiana* and the Difficult Heritage of Fascism'. *Australian Journal of Politics & History* 66, no. 3 (2020): 377–95.

Carter, Nick, and Simon Martin. 'The Management and Memory of Fascist Monumental Art in Postwar and Contemporary Italy: The Case of Luigi Montanarini's Apotheosis of Fascism". *Journal of Modern Italian Studies* 22, no. 3 (2017): 338–64.

Cederna, Antonio. *Mussolini Urbanista. Lo sventramento di Roma negli anni del consenso*. Rome: Laterza, 1979.

Celant, Germano. *Post Zang Tumb Tuuum. Art Life Politics: Italia 1918–1943*. Milan: Fondazione Prada, 2018

Cipriani, Antonio. 'Quando all'Ente EUR decideva la P2' *L'Unità*, 14 January 1993, 24.

Ciucci, Giorgio. *Gli architetti e il fascismo, Architettura e città 1922–1944*. Turin: Einaudi, 1989.

Clementi, Alberto, and Francesco Perego, eds. *La metropoli 'spontanea': il caso di Roma, 1925–1981. Sviluppo residenziale di una città dentro e fuori dal piano.* Bari: Dedalo, 1983.

Colonnelli, Lauretta. 'I trent'anni che sconvolsero la Casa della Scherma'. *Corriere della Sera. Cronaca di Roma*, 25 June 2005.

Colonnelli, Lauretta. 'Arturo Dazzi, l'uomo che plasmò l'obelisco dell'EUR'. *Corriere della Sera*, 30 October 2016, 21.

Consoli, Gian Paolo. 'Istituto Forestale A. Mussolini'. In *E 42, Utopia e scenario del regime*, edited by Guidoni Calvesi, and Lux, 503–5.

Conte, Francesco. 'A Roma c'è un monumento al colonialismo che non dovremmo ignorare'. Termini TV, 26 January 2016. https://www.internazionale.it/video/2016/01/26/monumento-colonialismo-termini-roma. Accessed 31 October 2018.

Cooley, Alison, ed. 'The Afterlife of Inscriptions: Reusing, Rediscovering, Reinventing & Revitalizing Ancient Inscriptions'. Papers presented at *The afterlife of inscriptions: reusing, rediscovering, reinventing & revitalizing ancient inscriptions*, London, 2000.

Cresti, Carlo. *Architettura e fascismo*. Florence: Vallecchi, 1986.

Cristallini, Elisabetta. 'Chiesa dei SS. Pietro e Paolo'. In *E 42, Utopia e scenario del regime*, edited by Guidoni Calvesi, and Lux, 441–4.

Cristallini, Elisabetta. 'La Legge Del 2 Per Cento'. In *1935. Gli artisti nell'università e la questione della pittura murale*, edited by Simonetta Lux and Ester Coen. Rome: Multigrafica editrice, 1985.

Culturale Ordine Architetti Roma. 'Roma: un Museo dello Sport nell'Accademia della Scherma di Luigi Moretti', 2020. https://www.aloarchitettiroma.it/roma-un-museo-dello-sport-nellaccademia-della-scherma-di-luigi-moretti/. Accessed 31 July 2020.

D'Onofrio, Cesare. *Gli obelischi di Roma*. Roma: Bulzoni, 1967.

De Chirico, Fabio. *Mosaici contemporanei nella collezione farnesina. Contemporary Mosaics in the Farnesina Collection*. Milan: Electa, 2021.

De Dominicis, Daniela, Martina De Luca, and Enrica Torelli Landini. 'Chiesa Dei Ss. Pietro E Paolo. La Decorazione'. In *E 42, Utopia e scenario del regime*, edited by Calvesi, Guidoni, and Lux, 444–66.

De Simone, Cesare. 'Alla sbarra gli "squadroni neri". Saranno 164 gli imputati nel più grosso processo ai gruppi terroristici neofascisti'. *Corriere della Sera*, 16 April 1985.

De Simone, Cesare. *Roma, città prigioniera i 271 giorni dell'occupazione nazista: 8 Settembre '43–4 Giugno '44*. Milano: Mursia, 1994.

de Vico, Fallani Maurizio. *Raffaele De Vico e i giardini di Roma*. Florence: Sansoni Editore, 1985, 169–70.

Del Viscovo, Mario. 'Centri direzionali e parcheggi sotterranei. dichiarazioni del Prof. Virgilio Testa, Commissario dell'ente autonomo esposizione universale di Roma al Dr. Mario del Viscovo'. *Automobilismo e Automobilismo Industriale. Rivista bimestrale dell'Ufficio Studi dell'ACI*, no. 1 (January–February 1963): 1–22.

Delcroix, Carlo. *Sette santi senza candele*. With original woodcuts by A.G. Santagata. Florence, Italy: Vallecchi, 1928.

della Rovere, Roberto. 'Roma: il trenino dei Mondiali è già da buttare'. *Corriere della Sera, Cronache Italiane*, 16 January 1993, 17.

Diebner, Sylvia. 'Le trasformazioni di un blocco di granito'. *Bullettino della Commissione Archeologica Comunale di Roma* 112 (2011): 153–70.

Do. Re. 'Palazzo Sturzo all'Eur La storica sede DC si trasforma per Italease'. *Corriere della sera. Cronaca di Roma*, 14 December 2009, 2

Dobler, Ralph-Miklas. 'Die Verarbeitung Des Ersten Weltkrieges in Der Künstlerischen Ausstatung Der Casa Madre Dei Mutilati in Rom (1925–1938)'. *Politische Ikonographie* 10, no. 3 (2010): 1–31.

Docci, Marina. '"Case del Fascio": Forgotten "Fragments" in Contemporary Rome'. In *Digital Modernism Heritage Lexicon*, edited by Cristiana Bartolomei, Alfonso Ippolito and Simone Helena Tanoue Vizioli, 163–88. Cham: Springer International Publishing, 2022.

Dogliani, Patrizia. 'Constructing Memory and Anti-Memory: The Monumental Representation of Fascism and Its Denial in Republican Italy'. In *Italian Fascism: History, Memory and Representation*, edited by R. J. B. Bosworth and Patrizia Dogliani, 11–30. London: Palgrave Macmillan UK, 1999.

Doordan, Dennis. *Building Modern Italy*. Princeton: Princeton University Press, 1988.

Erbani, Francesco, ed. *Antonio Cederna. I vandali in casa. Cinquant'anni dopo*. Bari: Laterza, 2006.

Ercolano, Martina. 'I giocattoli dei figli della borghesia fascista. Uno spaccato sulla Napoli di inizio novecento'. *Rivista italiana di educazione familiare*, no. 1 (2017): 201.

Escobar, Arturo. *Encountering Development: The Making and Unmaking of the Third World*. Princeton: Princeton University Press, 2011.

Etlin, Richard *Modernism in Italian Architecture*. Cambridge, MA: MIT Press, 1991.

EUR. *E. U. R.: la città parco della Roma moderna*. Rome: Rotografica romana, 1953.

EUR Spa. 'Obelisco a Guglielmo Marconi'. http://www.eurspa.it/it/asset-property/patrimonio/arte-e-design/opere-scultoree/obelisco-guglielmo-marconi. Accessed 12 October 2018.

Fagone, Vittorio, Giovanna Ginex and Tullia Sparagni, eds. *Muri ai pittori: pittura murale e decorazione in italia 1930–1950*. Milan, Italy: Mazzotta, 1999.

Feltri, Mattia. 'Veltroni: "I luoghi del fascismo"'. *La Stampa*, 23 March 2013.

Ferraironi, Francesco. *Iscrizioni ornamentali su edifici e monumenti di roma: con appendice sulle iscrizioni scomparse*. Rome: Industria Tipografica Romana, 1937.

Ficquet, Eloi. 'La stèle éthiopienne de Rome'. *Cahiers d'études africaines* (2004): 369–85.

Fiorletta, Serena. 'Il museo negato. Narrazione nazionale e museografia' *Roots – Routes. Research on Visual Cultures* 9, no. 30 (May–August 2019). https://www.roots-routes.org/museo-negato-narrazione-nazionale-museografia-serena-fiorletta/. Accessed 30 September 2020.

Fogu, Claudio. 'Fascism and Historic Representation: The 1932 Garibaldian Celebrations'. *Journal of Contemporary History* (1996): 317–45.

Fonti, Daniela. 'La decorazione'. In *Il Palazzo dell'industria*, edited by Franco Borsi, Gabriele Morolli and Daniela Fonti, 145–208. Rome: Editalia, 1986.

Foot, J. *Italy's Divided Memory*. Basingstoke: Palgrave Macmillan, 2011.

Francescangeli, Laura. 'I trasporti pubblici a Roma. Dall'omnibus alla metropolitana'. 2003. http://www.archiviocapitolino.it/cdrom/i_trasporti_pubblici_a_roma/. Accessed 10 May 2019.

Fried, Robert C. *Planning the Eternal City; Roman Politics and Planning since World War II*. New Haven: Yale University Press, 1973.

Frutaz, Amato Pietro. *Le piante di Roma*. Roma: Istituto di studi romani, 1962.

Fulloni, Alessandro. 'Il tritolo spazza via l'antico Velodromo'. *Corriere della Sera. Cronaca di Roma*, 25 July 2008, 5.

Garrone, Lilli. 'Le Torri dell'Eur alla cordata da 160 milioni'. *Corriere della sera. Cronaca di Roma*, 18 March 2005.

Garrone, Lilli. 'Roma, rinasce la stazione Termini'. Cronache, *Corriere della Sera*, 30 January 2000.

Garrone, Lilli. 'Trastevere, quanti bei progetti'. *Corriere della Sera. Cronaca di Roma*, 18 May 2000.

Gennaro, Angela. 'Roma, fiori per i "martiri fascisti" al cimitero del Verano. La comunità di avanguardia non gradisce i giornalisti: "come vi permettete?"'. *Il fatto quotidiano*, no. 28, October (28 October 2017). https://www.ilfattoquotidiano.it/2017/10/28/roma-fiori-per-i-martiri-fascisti-al-cimitero-del-verano-la-comunita-di-avanguardia-non-gradisce-i-giornalisti-come-vi-permettete/3941735. Accessed 22 October 2019.

Gentile, Emilio. *Il culto del littorio: la sacralizzazione della politica nell'Italia fascista*. Rome: Laterza, 1993.

Gentile, Emilio. *Fascismo di pietra*. Rome: Laterza, 2007.

Geraldini, Arnaldo. 'Da oggi si viaggia a cento all'ora sotto i palazzi dei cesari e dei papi'. *Corriere d'Informazione*, 9–10 February 1955, 7.

Gh.G. 'Bomba a Roma contro la DC'. *Corriere della sera*, 16–17 November 1964, 1–2

Gigli Padellaro, Paola, and Mario Panizza. *Roma formale e informale*. Napoli: Editoriale scientifica, 1976.

Ginsborg, Paul author. *A History of Contemporary Italy: Society and Politics, 1943–1988*. New York: Palgrave Macmillan, 2003.

Golan, Romy. *Muralnomad: The Paradox of Wall Painting, Europe 1927–1957*. New Haven: Yale University Press, 2009.

Grandesso, Stefano. 'Il monumento ad Anita Garibaldi a Roma'. In *Garibaldi. Un eroe nel bronzo e nel marmo*, edited by Cristina Beltrami, Giovanni C. F. Villa and Anna Villari, 170–88. Cinisello Balsamo: Silvana Editoriale, 2012.

Greco, Antonella. 'Eur 1953. La mostra dell'agricoltura'. In *Il segno delle esposizioni nazionali e internazionali nella memoria storica delle città. Padiglioni alimentari e segni urbani permanenti*, edited by S. Aldini, C. Benocci, S. Ricci and E. Sessa, 162–71. Rome: Kappa, 2014.

Griffin, Roger. *Modernism and Fascism: The Sense of a Beginning under Mussolini and Hitler*. 1st ed. 2007. London: Palgrave Macmillan UK, 2007. doi:10.1057/9780230596122.

Grilli, Fabio. '"Comune ed Eur spa spieghino cosa intendono fare dell'ex Velodromo". E spunta l'ipotesi stadio della Roma'. *Roma Today*, 3 March 2021. https://www.romatoday.it/zone/eur/altre/stadio-della-roma-dove-ex-velodromo-eur.html. Accessed 7 October 2021.

Guerriero, Augusto. 'Il Presidente Gronchi oggi a Parigi per rinsaldare l'amicizia fra Italia e Francia'. *Corriere della Sera*, 25 April 1956, 1.

Guerzoni, Monica. 'Fiumicino s'allontana'. *Corriere della Sera, Cronaca di Roma*, 27 September 1993, 48.

Guerzoni, Monica. 'Eur, le "Torri" delle Finanze diventeranno un maxialbergo?'. *Corriere della sera. Cronaca di Roma*, 27 August 2001, 45

Halbwachs, Maurice. *On Collective Memory*. Edited by Lewis A. Coser. Chicago: University of Chicago Press, 1992.

Hibbert, Christopher. *Benito Mussolini. The Rise and the Fall of Il Duce*. Harmondsworth: Penguin, 1986.

Homewood, David. 'Exhuming the Archive: Interview with Rossella Biscotti'. *Un Magazine* 5.2. http://unprojects.org.au/magazine/issues/issue-5-2/exhuming-the-archive-interview-with-rossella-biscotti/. Accessed 1 March 2021.

Huyssen, Andreas. 'Monument and Memory in a Postmodern Age'. In *The Art of Memory. Holocaust Memorials in History*, edited by James E. Young, 9–17. Munich: Prestel Verlag, 1994.

Innamorati, Francesco, and Carlo Bertilaccio. *Eur Spa e il patrimonio di E42: manuale d'uso per edifici e opere*. Rome: Palombi, 2004.

Insolera, Italo. 'Le Borgate'. *Urbanistica. Rivista trimestrale dell'Istituto Nazionale di Urbanistica* 28–9, no. June (1959): 45–60

Insolera, Italo. *Roma fascista nelle fotografiie dell'Istituto Luce*. Rome: Editori Riuniti, 2001.

Insolera, Italo. *Roma Moderna. Da Napoleone I al XXI secolo*. Turin: Piccola Biblioteca Einaudi, 2011.

Insolera, Italo, and Alberto Mancini. 'Roma. La "variante generale" del 1942'. *Urbanistica. Rivista trimestrale dell'Istituto Nazionale di Urbanistica* 62, no. April (1974): 63–106.

Insolera, Italo, and Luigi Di Majo. *L'Eur e roma dagli anni trenta al duemila*. Bari: Laterza, 1986.

Isnenghi, Mario. *Le guerre degli italiani: parole, immagini, ricordi 1848–1945*. Milan: Mondadori, 1989.

Isnenghi, Mario. *Italia in piazza: i luoghi della vita pubblica dal 1848 ai giorni nostri*. Milan: Mondadori, 1994.

Italia, Regno di. 'Legge 17 agosto 1942, n. 1150 Legge urbanistica'. *Gazzetta Ufficiale del Regno d'Italia*, 83, 244, 16 October 1942.

Kallis, Aristotle. *The Third Rome, 1922–43 the Making of the Fascist Capital*. 1st ed. 2014. ed. London: Palgrave Macmillan UK, 2014.

King, Amy. 'Antagonistic Martyrdom: Memory of the 1973 Rogo di Primavalle'. *Modern Italy: journal of the Association for the Study of Modern Italy* 25, no. 1 (2020): 33–48. https://doi.org/10.1017/mit.2019.35.

Kirk, Terry, *The Architecture of Modern Italy, Vol. II: Visions of Utopia, 1900s to Present*. New York: Princeton University Press, 2005.

Kostof, Spiro. 'The Emperor and the Duce: The Planning of the Piazzale Augusto Imperatore in Rome'. In *Art & Architecture in the Service of Politics*, edited by Henry A. Millon and Linda Nochlin, 270–325. Cambridge, MA: MIT Press, 1978.

Lamers, Han, and Bettina Reitz-Joosse. *The Codex Fori Mussolini: A Latin Text of Italian Fascism. Bloomsbury Studies in Classical Reception*. Vol. 9. London: Bloomsbury Publishing, 2016.

La Torre, Antonella and Marco Noccioli. 'Piazza ed edifici delle forze armate. Mostra dell'autarchia, del corporativismo e della previdenza sociale'. In *E 42, Utopia e scenario del regime*, edited by Guidoni Calvesi, and Lux, 423–7.

La Torre, Antonella. 'La mostra dell'abitazione'. In *E 42, Utopia e scenario del regime*, edited by Guidoni Calvesi, and Lux, pp 524–8.

LC, Redazione. 'Rino Daus, i miti del fascismo e la fine della memoria'. *il lavoro culturale*, 21 April 2017. https://www.lavoroculturale.org/rino-daus/redazione-lc/2017/. Accessed 8 July 2022.

Lefebvre, Henri. *The Production of Space*. Translated by Donald Nicholson-Smith. Oxford: Blackwell, 1991.

Leone, Rossella. 'La cripta del milite ignoto e le scelte propagandistiche del regime fascista'. In *Il Vittoriano. Materiali per una storia*, edited by Pier Luigi Porzio, 43–52. Rome: Fratelli Palombi, 1986.

Locci, Massimo. 'Palazzo delle poste all'EUR'. *AR. Bimestrale dell'ordine degli architetti di Roma e provincia* 42, no. July–August (2007): 9–11.

Lupano, Mario. *Marcello Piacentini* Bari: Laterza, 1991.

Lupinacci, Manlio. 'Stolto epurare le pietre a ogni svolta della storia'. *Corriere della Sera*, 10 October 1959, 3.

m.b. '"Manifestazioni del XXI Aprile. Viaggio inaugurale di un convoglio S.T.E.F.E.R. sul tratto della metropolitana tra le stazioni della Magliana e l'E.U.R."' *Trasporti pubblici. Rivista mensile a cura dell'ispettorato generale della motorizzazione civile e dei trasporti in concessione* 9, no. 1 (January 1952): 461.

Madea Alfonso, 'Due momenti difficili in una giornata di tensione'. *Corriere della Sera*, 29 Novembre 1969, 1–2.

Maggi, Angelo. 'Architecture of Light and Water at the Universal Exhibition of Rome of 1942'. In *Architecture of Great Expositions 1937–1959: Messages of Peace, Images of War*, edited by Rika Devos, Alexander Ortenberg and Vladimir Papernyi, 99–114. London: Routledge, 2016.

Malone, Hannah. 'Fascist Italy's Ossuaries of the First World War: Objects or Symbols?'. *RIHA Journal*, no. 166 (2017).

Malone, Hannah. 'Legacies of Fascism: Architecture, Heritage and Memory in Contemporary Italy'. *Modern Italy* 22, no. 4 (2017): 445–70.

Mangione, Flavio. *Le case del fascio in italia e le terre dell'oltremare*. Rome: Ministero per i beni e le attività culutruali, Direzione generale per gli archivi, 2003.

Marcello, Flavia. '"The Politics of Place: Siting and Re-Citing Mussolini's New Party Headquarters, the Palazzo Littorio"'. *Architectural Theory Review* 12, no. 2 (2007): 146–72.

Marcello, Flavia. 'Mussolini and the Idealisation of Empire: The Augustan Exhibition of *Romanità*'. *Modern Italy. The Journal of the Association for the Study of Modern Italy* 16, no. 3 (August 2011): 223–47.

Marcello, Flavia. 'All Roads Lead to Rome: The Universality of the Roman Ideal in Achille Funi's Incomplete Fresco Cycle for the Palazzo dei Congressi in Eur, 1940–43'. *Civiltà Romana. Rivista pluridisciplinare di studi su Roma antica e le sue interpretazioni* 3 (2016): 151–77.

Marcello, Flavia. 'Forma Urbis Reconsidered: The Making of Fascist Rome'. In *Companion to Classical Reception in Fascist Italy and Nazi Germany*, edited by Helen Roche and Demetriou Kyriakos, 325–69. Leiden: Brill Academic Publishers, 2017.

Marcello, Flavia. 'Between Censure and Celebration: The Decorative Plan of the *Casa Madre Dei Mutilati* in Rome (1926–1939)'. *Modern Italy* 24, no. 2, Special Issue: The Difficult Heritage of Italian Fascism (2019): 179–98.

Marcello, Flavia and Aidan Carter. 'The Axum Obelisk: Shifting Concepts of Colonialism and Empire in Fascist and 21st-Century Rome'. In *The Colonial Past in the Neocolonial Present: Inherited Built Environments in Africa, Asia, the Middle East and Europe*, edited by Daniel Coslett, 42–64. London: Routledge, 2019.

Marcello, Flavia and Paul Gwynne. '"Speaking from the Walls: Militarism, Education and Romanità in Rome's Città Universitaria (1932–35)"'. *Journal of the Society of Architectural Historians* 75, no. 3 (2015): 323–42.

Marchetti, Patrizia. 'Il vincolo del foro italico nel cinquantesimo anno dal termine dei lavori'. *Monumenti di Roma* 2, nos. 1–2 (2004): 133–47.

Martin, Simon. 'Rebranding the Republic: Rome and the 1960 Olympic Games'. *European review of history = Revue européene d'histoire* 24, no. 1 (2017): 58–79.

Maulsby, Lucy. 'Drinking from the River Lethe. *Case Del Fascio* and the Legacy of Fascism in Postwar Italy'. *Future Anterior. Journal of Historic Preservation History Theory & Criticism* 9, no. 2 (2014): 18–39.

Mazzanti, Gastone. *Roma violata: dagli archivi segreti angloamericani i bombardamenti della seconda guerra mondiale*. Roma: Teos, 2006.

Mechelli, Sara. 'Restyling completo per la Palestra Agnini: sarà polo dello sport del Montesacro'. Romatoday, 29 August 2014. https://www.romatoday.it/zone/montesacro/ex-gil-ristrutturata-. Accessed 8 July 2022.

Mechelli, Sara. 'A Montesacro arriva Salagnini: il nuovo spazio della cultura e del "Tempo Insieme"'. *Romatoday*, 19 October 2018. https://www.romatoday.it/zone/montesacro/montesacro-sala-agnini-polo-culturale-viale-adriatico.html. Accessed 8 July 2022.

Menicucci, Ernesto. 'Eur, la Nuvola c'è e facciamo utili'. *Corriere della Sera. Roma*, 15 October 2011, 1.

Menicucci, Ernesto. 'Prestiti bloccati, cantiere fermo la Nuvola rischia lo stop definitivo', *Corriere della sera. Cronaca di Roma*, 24 November 2014, 3.

Menicucci, Ernesto. 'Quattro palazzi storici in cambio della Nuvola'. *Corriere della sera. Cronaca di Roma*, 17 February 2015, 3.

Menicucci, Ernesto. 'Sbagliato vendere gioielli del razionalismo per coprire spese folli'. *Corriere della sera. Cronaca di Roma*, 17 February 2015, 3.

Mocci, Paola. 'Palazzo degli uffici. L'arredamento'. In *E 42, Utopia e scenario del regime*, edited by Guidoni Calvesi, and Lux, 303–5.

Monelli, Paolo. *Roma 1943*. Rome: Migliaresi, 1945.

Montanelli, Indro. 'Una sfida ai secoli con aquile e "bustarelle"'. *Corriere della Sera*, 30 August 1959, 3.

Mosse, George L. *Masses and Man: Nationalist and Fascist Perceptions of Reality*. New York: H Fertig., 1980.

Muntoni, Alessandra. 'Piazza con le esedre e porta imperiale. Il progetto'. In *E 42, Utopia e scenario del regime*, edited by Guidoni Calvesi, and Lux, 472–5.

Mussolini, Benito. 'Le città tentacolari'. In *Opera omnia di Benito Mussolini*, edited by E. Susmel and D. Susmel. Vol. 2, 209–11. Florence: La Fenice, 1972.

Mussolini, Benito. 'Per la vera pacificazione'. *Opera omnia di Benito Mussolini* 17, 289–300. Florence: La Fenice, 1972.

Mussolini, Benito. 'Il primo anniversario della marcia su Roma'. *Opera omnia di Benito Mussolini* 20, 61–70. Florence: La Fenice, 1972.
Mussolini, Benito. 'Al popolo di Roma'. *Opera omnia di Benito Mussolini* 20, 227–30. Florence: La Fenice, 1972.
Mussolini, Benito. 'La nuova Roma'. *Opera omnia di Benito Mussolini* 22, 47–9. Florence: La Fenice, 1972.
Mussolini, Benito. 'Al popolo di Roma per il 28 ottobre'. *Opera omnia di Benito Mussolini* 22: 241–4. Florence: La Fenice, 1972.
Mussolini, Benito. 'La Roma di Mussolini'. *Opera omnia di Benito Mussolini* 25: 84–8. Florence: La Fenice, 1972.
Nappi, Renato. 'Foro Italico, la Casa delle Armi non sarà più aula bunker'. *Corriere Roma. Cronaca/Sport/Spettacoli*, 17 June 2000.
Nemiz, Andrea. *Studium Urbis Roma novembre 1935, il Duce inaugura la città universitaria laurea 'honoris causa' al re*. Rome: Litografia Covi, 1985.
Noccioli, Marco. 'Edificio per la mostra della romanità'. In *E 42, Utopia e scenario del regime*, edited by Guidoni Calvesi, and Lux, 481–4.
Olivieri, Mauro. '1925–1981: La città abusiva'. In *La metropoli 'spontanea'*, edited by Clementi and Pregeo, 290–331.
Pagano, Giuseppe. 'L'esposizione universale di Roma'. *Casabella* 114 (June 1937): 6.
Pan, M. 'Treni in partenza sull'"anello"'. *Corriere della Sera. Corriere Roma*, 6 June 1990, 30
Pertica, Domenico. 'Il nuovo lago dell'E.U.R. e il vecchio laghetto di Villa Borghese'. *Capitolium* 37, no. 1 (January 1962): 21–6.
Petrucci, Stefano. 'Casa della scherma, stesso iter della Galleria Borghese'. *Corriere della Sera. Cronaca di Roma*, 16 April 2005.
Phillips, Ralph. *FAO: Its Origins, Formation and Evolution*. Rome: Food and Agriculture Organisation of the United Nations, 1981.
Piacentini, Marcello. 'Piano dell'Esposizione Universale di Roma 1941'. *Architettura* 16, no. 4 (1937): 184–8.
Pieri, Giuliana. 'Portraits of the Duce'. In *The Cult of the Duce: Mussolini and the Italians*, edited by Christopher Duggan and Giuliana Pieri Stephen Gundle, 161–77. Manchester: Manchester University Press, 2013.
Pignatti Morano, Monica. 'Palazzo dell'istituto Italo-Latino Americano'. In *Eur. Guida degli istituti culturali*, edited by Antonella Alberini, Nadia Di Santo, Monica Pignatti Morano and Annalisa Zanuttini, 63. Rome: Leonardo Arte, 1995.
Pollard, John F. *The Vatican and Italian Fascism, 1929–32*. Cambridge: Cambridge University Press, 1985.
Ponti, Gio. 'Stile dell'architetto Adalberto Libera'. *Stile* 20, no. 17 (May 1942): 17.
Pontiggia, Elena. '*Novecento* and State Art'. In *Post Zang Tumb Tuuum. Art Life Politics: Italia 1918–1943*, edited by G. Celant, 148–53. Milan, Italy: Fondazione Prada, 2018.
Poretti, Sergio. 'Dal piano al patrimonio INA-Casa'. In *L'architettura Ina Casa (1949–1963). Aspetti e problemi di conservazione e recupero*, edited by Rinaldo Capomolla and Rosalia Vittorini, 9–17. Rome: Gangemi, 2003.
Pullara, Giuseppe. 'Centro congressi Eur appuntamento al 2003'. *Corriere della sera. Cronaca di Roma*, 5 November 1999, 50.
Pullara, Giuseppe. 'Eur, il mistero della Quadriga'. *Corriere della Sera, Cronaca di Roma*, 8 July 2003, 50.

Pullara, Giuseppe. 'La "Casa Della Regione" nel cuore di Trastevere'. *Corriere della Sera. Cronaca di Roma*, 17 May 2007, 9.
Pullara, Giuseppe. 'La "Nuvola" aspetta ancora la prima firma'. *Corriere della sera. Cronaca di Roma*, 8 May 2003, 51.
Pullara, Giuseppe. 'Raggi fischiata alla festa della Nuvola di Fuksas'. *Corriere della sera. Cronaca di Roma*, 30 October 2016, 21.
Ragazzi, F. 'Cronache della pittura murale. Antonio Santagata, Il "Giotto dei soldati"'. In *Muri ai pittori: pittura murale e decorazione in Italia 1930–1950*, edited by G. Ginex and T. Sparagni V. Fagone, 83–95. Milan: Mazzotta, 1999.
Remiddi, Gaia, Antonella Greco, Antonella Bonavita, and Paola Ferri, eds. *Il moderno attraverso Roma: guida a 200 architetture e alle loro opere d'arte*. Roma: Fratelli Palombi, 2000.
Rivolta, Gianni. 'Ritrovate scritte sovversive contro il re, il fascismo e i tedeschi'. *Cara Garbatella*, 26 June 2020 https://caragarbatella.it/ritrovate-scritte-sovversive-contro-il-re-il-fascismo-e-i-tedeschi/. Accessed 17 March 2021.
Romana Stabile, Francesca. *Regionalismo a Roma. Tipi e linguaggi: il caso Garbatella*. Rome: Editrice Librerie Dedalo, 2001.
RomaToday. 'Museo della civiltà romana: servono otto mesi per riaprire il plastico dell'Antica Roma'. *RomaToday*, 27 April 2022 https://www.romatoday.it/politica/museo-civilta-romana-data-riapertura-plastico.html. Accessed 7 February 2023.
Rose, Steve. 'When in Rome …'. *The Guardian*, 1 May 2006. https://doi.org/ http://www.guardian.co.uk/travel/2006/may/01/travelnews.museums. Accessed 14 November 2019.
Rossi, Piero Ostilio, and Ilaria Gatti. *Roma: guida all'architettura moderna 1909–2000*. Bari: Laterza, 2005.
Russo, Giovanni. 'Gronchi visita gli impianti sportivi in costruzione a Roma per le Olimpiadi'. *Corriere della Sera*, 5 March 1959.
Russo, Giovanni. 'Gronchi inaugura a Roma la mostra dello sport nell'arte'. *Corriere della sera*, 15 July 1960.
S. D. 'Il Papa accompagna all'EUR una "processione della pace"'. *Corriere della sera*, 18 June 1965, 7.
Salsano, Fernando. 'La seconda vita dell'Eur: da expo a centro direzionale'. In *Esposizione Universale Roma: una città nuova: dal fascismo agli anni'60*, edited by Vittorio Vidotto, Rome: De Luca 2015.
Salvagnini, Sileno. 'Art in Action. The Organization of Italian Artistic Culture'. In *Post Zang Tumb Tuuum. Art Life Politics: Italia 1918–1943*, edited by G. Celant, 78–87. Milan, Italy: Fondazione Prada, 2018.
Salvatori, Nadia. *Il palazzo della Farnesina e le sue collezioni*. Rome: Palombi, 2011.
Sassi, Edoardo. 'Ma è in abbandono l'altro capolavoro di Moretti: l'ex Gil a Trastevere'. *Corriere della Sera. Cronaca di Roma*, 25 June 2005.
Scaglione, Pino. *Eur a Roma controguida d'architettura*. Vicenza: Testo & Immagine, 2000.
Scego, Igiaba, and Rino Bianchi. *Roma negata. Percorsi postcoloniali nella città*. Rome: Ediesse, 2014.
Scriba, Ferdinand. 'Archaeology as History – the Mostra Augustea della *Romanità* 1937/38 as an Example of the Relation between Archaeology and Fascism'. In *Archaeology, Ideology, Method: Inter-Academy Seminar on Current*

Archaeological Research, edited by K. Gilliver, W. Ernst and F. Scriba, 55–75. Rome: Canadian Academic Centre in Italy, 1996.

Sert, Josep Lluis, Ferdinand Léger, and Siegfried Giedion. 'Nine Points on Monumentality'. In *Architecture You and Me. Diary of a Development*, edited by Siegfried Giedion, 48–51. Cambridge, MA: Harvard University Press, 1943.

Seton-Watson, Christopher. 'Italy's Imperial Hangover'. *Journal of Contemporary History* 15, no. 1 (January 1980): 169–79.

Sironi, Andrea. 'L'elemento monumentale nelle opere murali di Sironi'. In *1935. Gli artisti nell'università*, edited by Lux and Coen, 26–7.

Somma, Paola. 'The *Palazzo Della Civiltà Italiana*. From Fascism to Fashion'. In *The Routledge Companion to Italian Fascist Architecture: Reception and Legacy*, edited by Kay Bea Jones and Stephanie Pilat, 79–91. Abingdon: Oxon, 2020.

Sovrintendenza capitolina ai beni culturali, direzione interventi su edilizia monumentale, D.D._n._408_del_13-07-2020. DIRE. '2022, Il museo della civiltà romana riapre con il planetario'. *QA. Turismo, cultura e arte*, 30 September 2021. https://www.qaeditoria.it/details.aspx?idarticle=170414&AspxAutoDetectCookieSupport=1. Accessed 5 July 2022.

Steimatsky, Noa. 'The *Cinecittà* Refugee Camp (1944–1950)'. *October* 128 (2009): 23–50.

Strappa, Giuseppe, and Gianni Mercurio. *Architettura moderna a Roma e nel Lazio: 1920–1945: Atlante*. Rome: Edilstampa.

Tafuri, Manfredo. 'Giuseppe Terragni: Subject and Mask'. *Oppositions* 11 (Winter 1977): 1–24.

Tafuri, Manfredo. *History of Italian Architecture, 1944–1985*. Translated by Jessica Levine. Cambridge, MA: MIT Press, 1989.

Testa, Virgilio. *Relazione sull'attività svolta nel decennio 1951–1961*. Rome: Ente autonomo Esposizione Universale di Roma. E.U.R., c. 1962.

Testa, Virgilio. *La vita di un urbanista e un capolavoro*. Spoleto: Arti grafiche Pavetto & Petrelli, 1976.

Testa, Virgilio. *Considerazioni economiche e criteri generali per la valutazione del patrimonio immobiliare dell'E.U.R.* Rome: Ente autonomo Esposizione Universale di Roma. E.U.R., n.d.

Tobia, Bruno. 'Il Vittoriano'. In *I luoghi della memoria*, edited by Isnenghi, 288–300.

Trillò, Teresa. 'Hotel au Lac, un processo insabbiato'. *L'Unità*, 14 January 1993, 24.

Tulli, Alberto. 'Il "Leone di Giuda" e l'obelisco di Dogali'. In *Atti del V congresso. Nazionale di Studi Romani*, 182–7. Rome: Istituto dei Studi Romani, 1942.

Tymkiw, Michael. 'Floor Mosaics, *Romanità*, and Spectatorship: The Foro Mussolini's Piazzale dell'Impero'. *The Art Bulletin* 101, no. 2 (2019): 109–32.

Venè, Gian Franco. *mille lire al mese: vita quotidiana della famiglia nell'Italia fascista*. Milan: CDE, 1991.

Versari, Maria Elena. 'Living among the Duce's Words: The Visual Materialization of Political Rhetoric in Italian Public Space, from the Risorgimento to Fascism'. *Word & Image* 34, no. 3 (2018): 251–67.

Vidotto, Vittorio. *Roma contemporanea*. Bari: Laterza, 2001.

Vidotto, Vittorio. 'Palazzi e sacrari: il declino del culto littorio'. *Roma moderna e contemporanea*, no. settembre-dicembre (2003): 577–8.

Vidotto, Vittorio. 'I luoghi del fascismo a Roma'. *Urbs: Concepts and realities of public space/Concetti e realtà dello spazio pubblico*, l'Istituto Olandese di Roma, 2–4 aprile 2003.

Visentini, Gino. 'Centomila romani abiteranno la città satellite delle Tre Fontane'. *Corriere della Sera*, 10 June 1953, 6.
Wegil. 'Wegil – Storia'. Updated 2021. https://wegil.it/la-storia/. Accessed 11 July 2022.
Wilkins, Ann Thomas. 'Augustus, Mussolini and the Parallel Imagery of Empire'. In *Donatello among the Blackshirts: History and Modernity in the Visual Culture of Fascist Italy*, edited by Claudia Lazzaro & Roger Crum, 53–65. Ithaca: Cornell University Press, 2004.
Zamagni, Vera. 'Evolution of the Economy'. In *Italy since 1945*, edited by Patrick McCarthy, 42–68. Oxford: Oxford University Press, 2000.
Zambenedetti, Alberto. 'Filming in Stone: Palazzo Della Civiltà Italiana and Fascist Signification in Cinema'. *Annali d'Italianistica* 28, no. Special issue 'Capital City: Rome 1870–2010' (2010): 119–214.
Zanini, Luca. 'Roba alla guerra dei sapori Eataly contro Città del Gusto'. *Corriere della Sera, Cronaca di Roma*, 3.
Zevi, Adachiara, ed. *Una guida all'architettura moderna dell'EUR*. Rome: Fondazione Bruno Zevi, 2008.

Newsreels

Istituto Luce, 'A Roma l'inaugurazione del monumento ad Anita Garibaldi' (Giornale Luce B009805, 1932)
Istituto Luce, 'Inizio delle demolizioni per l'isolamento del Mausoleo di Augusto' (Giornale Luce B056205, September 1934)
Istituto Luce, 'Nuovi ariosi imponenti quartieri sorgono nella zona di P Bologna. – ex Quartiere Italia'. (Giornale Luce B0576, November 1934)
Istituto Luce, 'Scoperto il Leone di Giuda portato da Addis Abeba' (Giornale Luce B1094, May 1937)
Nuova Luce, 'Piazza Santi Apostoli: manifestazione del CLN dell'Italia dell'Alta Italia; partecipano militanti del partito comunista e democristiano', Notiziario Nuova LUCE, NL00101, 26/7/1945.

Archival sources

ACS E42 B306 f.4922 sf. 5
ACS E42 B306. f. 4922 sf. 6
ACS E42 B309 f. 4933 sf. 4.
ACS E42 B307 f. 4927 sf. 3.
ACS E42 B565 f. 6842/2
ACS PCM44-47 1/7 f.11240/1.
ACS PCM44-47 1/7 f.11240/2.
ACS PCM 1944–47, 7/2 55915 – 433.
ACS PCM 1951–54 B4467 7.2 50058 2/16
ACS PCM 1951–54, 7.2 50058 2/16.
ACS Testa Archive Box 8.
ACS Testa Archive Box 31.

INDEX

abusivismo. See rogue development
Abyssinia. *See* Ethiopia
Accademia della Scherma. See Fencing Academy
Acilia 46, 70
Addis Ababa 121, 157
Adowa/Adwa 9, 122, 157
Aeroporto di Fiumicino. *See* Fiumicino Airport
African Museum 121
after–work circles *(Dopolavoro)* 11, 73, 76, 143
Agnini, Ferdinando 75
Agriculture Exhibition 1953, *Esposizione di Agricoltura* (EA53) 47, 49, 84–5, 89, 91, 126
air-raid shelters 25, 55–6, 92
Aksum Stele 58, 115, 122–5, 137
Alemanno, Giovanni (Mayor) 110–11, 118, 124
Alexander VII (Fabio Chigi), Pope 32
Allied bombing 14, 55, 58, 69–70, 78
Allied military 56, 70, 82–3, 122, 164
Altare della patria. See Victor Emanuel Monument
Altar of Peace *(Ara Pacis)* 115–18, 145–7, 162
Altar of the Fascist Martyrs *(Ara Caduti Fascisti)* 128–30, 137, 139
Altar of the Fatherland. *See* Victor Emanuel Monument
amnesties *(sanatorie)* 48
Andreotti, Giulio 58, 107
Anita Garibaldi Monument *(Monumento ad Anita Garibaldi)* 127–8
anni di piombo. See Lead/Bullet Years
anno santo. See Holy Year
anti-fascistazzione. See de-fascistization

Aosta, Amedeo Duke of 116, 161, 173
apartment buildings 74, 100, 143, 165, 169
Ara Caduti Fascisti. See Altar of the Fascist Martyrs
Ara Pacis. See Altar of Peace
Ara Pacis Museum 115, 117–18, 147
Archivio Centrale di Stato (ACS). *See* State Central Archives
Ardeatine Caves massacre 36, 75, 134
Arengario. See speaker's platform
Argan, Giulio Carlo 25
Armed Forces Exhibition *(Edifici delle Forze Armate)* 98–9
Aschieri, Pietro 96–7
asse attrezzato. See social infrastructure axis
Associazione Nazionale Partigiani d'Italia (ANPI). *See* National Association of Partisans of Italy
Associazione Nazionale Mutilati e Invalidi di Guerra (ANMIG). *See* National Association of War Wounded
Augustan Exhibition of *Romanità* 94, 96
Augustan Mausoleum 17, 53, 115–18, 145
Augustus 12, 17, 37, 96, 115–17, 122, 129, 136, 145–6, 162
Autonomous Worker Housing Institute, *Istituto Autonomo per Case Popolari* (IACP) 29–30, 72
Autostrada del Sole 23
autunno caldo. See Hot Autumn
Azienda Tramvie e Autobus del Governatorato/Comune di Rome (ATAG/C). *See* Tram and Bus Agency of the Governorate/City of Rome

INDEX

Bacigalupo, Marco 105–6
Badoglio, Pietro 142
Banda della Magliana. See Magliana Band
Basilica dei Santi Pietro e Paolo. See Basilica of Saints Peter and Paul
Basilica of Saint Peter 20, 28, 37–8, 42, 94, 100, 107, 114
Basilica of Saints Peter and Paul *(Basilica dei Santi Pietro e Paolo)* 14, 81, 98, 100–1, 173
Battaglia del Grano. See Battle for Grain
Battle Fasces *(Fasci di combattimento)* 8
Battle for Grain *(Battaglia del Grano)* 48, 155
BBPR Group (Banfi, Belgioioso, Peressutti and Rogers) 102
Bersaglieri. See Riflemen of the Italian army infantry corps
Biblioteca Nazionale. See National Library
Bianchi, Salvatore 59
Biscotti, Rossella 67
Borgate. See Outer suburbs
Boccea 40, 48
Bonomi, Ivanoe 143
Borgata Gordiani 23
Borromini, Francesco 148
Bosworth, Richard 47
Bottai, Giuseppe 21, 29, 170
Brasini, Armando 85, 133
bribes *(tangenti)* 104
Bribesville *(Tangentopoli)* 2, 41, 104
Brigate rosse. See Red Brigades
Brothers of Italy *(Fratelli d'Italia)* 111, 132, 171
Brusa, Luigi 95
Buozzi, Bruno 131

Caduti per la Rivoluzione. See Fallen for the [Fascist] Revolution
Cafiero, Vittorio 41, 58
Campidoglio as hill. *See* Capitoline Hill
Campidoglio as Rome City Council. *See* Rome City Council
Cancellotti, Gino 95
Capitoline Hill 17, 129–30, 133, 137, 163

Capizzano, Achille 76
carabinieri. See Military Police
cardo. See North-South axis
Casa delle Armi. See Fencing Academy
Casa Madre dei Mutilati. See Mother House of the War Wounded
Case Balilla. See Fascist Youth headquarters
Case del Fascio. See Fascist Party headquarters
Case GIL. See Fascist Youth headquarters
Castel Sant'Angelo 37, 62
Castelli, Roberto 68
Catholic Power 3–5, 12–14, 32, 36, 38, 52, 61, 63, 81, 98, 100, 114, 172–3
Cecchignola military base 83
Cederna, Antonio 20, 37, 117
Centocelle 22, 70
centro direzionale. See development centre
centro storico. See Historic Centre
Christian Democrat Party Headquarters *(Palazzo della DC)* 109–10
Christian Democrat Party, *Democrazia Cristiana* (DC) 14, 29, 37–8, 41, 63, 109–10, 154
Ciano, Galeazzo 56, 65–6
Cicero, Marcus Tullius 141, 150, 165, 167, 170
Cinecittà. See Cinema City
Cinema City *(Cinecittà)* 3–4, 10, 18, 28, 42–3, 53, 69–71, 172
Cini, Vittorio 82
Città Giardino Aniene. See Montesacro Garden City
Città Parco della Roma Moderna. See Park-City of Modern Rome
Civilisation of Work Building. *See* Italian Civilisation Building
Clearing the Cities *(Sfollare le Città)* 48
Cloud Congress Centre *(Centro Congressi la 'Nuvola')* 110–11
Col, Valentina 75
Colosseum 14, 54, 64, 66, 72, 94, 129
Columbus, Christopher 45, 81
Comitato di Elaborazione Tecnica (CET). *See* Technical Drafting Committee

Comune di Roma. See Rome City Council
Conference and Receptions Building, *Palazzo dei Ricevimenti e Congressi* 88–90
Comitato Olimpico Nazionale Italiano (CONI). *See* Italian National Olympic Committee
Corso Rinascimento 160–1
Council Plan (*Giunta* plan) 23–4
Cremonesi, Filippo 17, 29
Cult of the *Duce* 3–4, 8, 12–13, 17, 32–3, 37, 48–9, 53–7, 64–5, 77, 81–2, 114, 116–17, 122, 126, 133, 136–8, 142–4, 146, 148, 158–60, 162, 164, 172–3

Dante Alighieri 141
Dazzi, Arturo 125–6
De Chirico, Giorgio 59
decumanus. See East-West Axis
de-fascistization *(anti-fascistazzione)* 21–2, 138
Defender of the City *(defensor civitatis)* 14
defensor civitatis. See Defender of the City
De Gasperi, Alcide 30, 47, 60, 72
Del Debbio, Enrico 39, 63–5, 100, 136, 201
Democrazia Cristiana (DC). *See* Christian Democrat Party
demolitions 8, 17–18, 20, 33, 37, 42, 53, 60–1, 68, 74–5, 80, 84, 106, 145–6, 166, 171
Deress, Zerrai 122
detailed plans *(piani particolareggiati)* 19, 22
de Vico, Raffaele 102–4
development centre *(centro direzionale)* 22–3, 45
Diana, Francesco 24
Diaz, Armando 150
difficult heritage 14, 155, 174
Dogali monument 120–2, 129
Donati, Ines 132
Dopolavoro. See after-work circles
Doria Pamphilj, Prince Filippo Andrea 21
Draghi, Mario 171

East-West Axis *(decumanus)* 88, 90
Economic Miracle *(miracolo economico)* 2, 11–12, 17, 43, 53, 85, 96, 105
Edifici delle Forze Armate. See Armed Forces Exhibition
Einaudi, Luigi 45
Empire 3–4, 8–10, 12, 32, 43, 58, 69, 81, 93, 114–16, 120–4, 136, 142–3, 157–64, 172–3
Ente Nazionale Idrocarburi (ENI) skyscraper 83, 85, 103–5
Eritrea 9, 58, 120, 122
Esposizione di Agricoltura (EA53). *See* Agriculture Exhibition 1953
Ethiopia 9–10, 58, 76, 95, 115, 120–4, 138, 143, 151, 157–8, 162, 168, 173
E42. *See* Rome Universal Exposition
E42 train *(Ferrovia dell'E42)* 25, 28
EUR. *See* Rome Universal Exposition
European Recovery Program (ERP) 30
Exhibition Building *(Palazzo delle Esposizioni)* 96, 116, 119
Exhibition of the Fascist Revolution *(Mostra della Rivoluzione Fascista)* 132

Fallen for the [Fascist] Revolution *(Caduti per la Rivoluzione)* 128–30, 137, 139
Fanfani, Amintore 24, 72
Farinetti, Oscar 80
Farnesina. See Ministry of Foreign Affairs Building
fasci di combattimento. See Battle Fasces
Fascist conscription *(leva fascista)* 9, 155
Fascist crack squads *(squadristi)* 132, 142
Fascist Party Headquarters *(Case del Fascio)* 11, 52, 72–4, 126, 129, 143, 149
Fascist Youth Headquarters *(Case Balilla/GIL)* 11, 72–7, 126, 143, 149, 154–5, 160, 167
Fascist Youth Organisation, *Gioventù Italiana del Littorio* (GIL) 9, 63–4, 74–7, 136, 154–5

INDEX

Fascist Youth Organisation, *Opera Nazionale Balilla* (ONB) 9, 74, 136, 154–5
Fatherland *(patria)* 12, 133, 166
Fellini, Federico 42, 69, 71, 91, 110
Fencing Academy *(Accademia della Scherma/ Casa delle Armi)* 63, 66–8, 76, 155
Ferrovia dell'E 42. *See* E42 train
Fédération Internationale de Football Association (FIFA). *See* International Federation of Football Associations
FIAT car company 83, 85, 96–7
FIFA World Cup 1990 30, 39, 41, 49, 63, 79
Fiera di Roma. *See* Rome Trade Fair
Figini, Luigi 99
First Republic 2, 9, 11–12, 14, 20, 22, 25, 35–6, 55, 58, 65, 83, 114, 126, 139, 142, 146, 158–9, 163
First World War 8–9, 12, 15, 35, 54, 74, 113–16, 119–20, 129, 133, 135, 150, 152–3, 155, 173
Fiumicino Airport 24, 40–1, 60, 100, 124
Food and Agriculture Organisation (FAO) 57–9
Food and Agriculture Organisation Building *(Palazzo FAO)* 54, 57–9, 122
Foschini, Arnaldo 64–5, 148–9, 161
Fosse Ardeatine. *See* Ardeatine Caves massacre
Foster, Norman 110
Fratelli d'Italia. *See* Brothers of Italy
Fuksas, Massimiliano 95, 110–12, 118, 124

Gambara, Filippo Maria 95
Garbatella 45, 144, 168–9
Garibaldi, Anita, 115, 127–8, 139
Garibaldi, Ezio 119–20, 151–2
Garibaldi, Giuseppe 12, 113, 115, 119, 127–8, 133, 141, 151–2
General Real Estate Development Agency, *Società Generale Immobiliare* (SGI) 14, 22, 29, 38, 40–1, 45, 48, 83, 109

General Variant (VG41-2) *Variante Generale* 1941–2 19–21, 25, 40, 47–8
Giammaria, Francesco 129
Giedion, Sigfried 114
Giglioli, Giulio Quirino 96–7, 117
Giovannoni, Gustavo 37, 75
Giunta plan. *See* Council Plan
governatorato di Roma. *See* Governorate of Rome
Government Palace *(Palazzo del Governo)* 33, 54–5
Governorate of Rome 17, 19–21, 25, 29, 45, 106, 112, 120, 129
graffiti 76, 159–60, 168–9
Greenaway, Peter 91, 134
Gropius, Walter 75
Gronchi, Giovanni 78–9, 107
Gruppi Azione Patriottica (GAP). *See* Patriotic Action Groups
Guerrini, Giovanni 90, 162

Halbwachs, Maurice 2
Hilton Hotel 41
Historic Centre *(centro storico)* 3–4, 8–10, 12, 17–18, 20, 33–7, 52–4, 116, 142, 164, 172–3
Hitler, Adolf 41, 77–8, 169
Holy Year 14, 30, 37, 42, 46, 49, 55, 60, 63, 83–4, 120, 173
Horace (Quintus Horatius Flaccus) 150, 165–8, 170
Hot Autumn *(autunno caldo)* 2
Hotel du Lac. *See* Lakeside Hotel
housing 3, 11, 18, 20, 22, 29–30, 32, 40–1, 43, 45, 48–9, 53, 70–2, 80, 84, 87, 91, 100–1, 108, 143, 165–6

Imperial Theatre *(Teatro Imperiale)* 93, 109
inner suburbs *(quartieri)* 3–4, 12, 14, 16–18, 31, 48–9, 51, 71–2, 141, 172
Insolera, Italo 21, 124
Istituto Autonomo per Case Popolari (IACP). *See* Autonomous Worker Housing Institute
Istituto per Case Popolari (ICP). *See* Worker Housing Institute

Istituto Italo-Africano (IAA). *See* Italo-African Institute
Istituto Italo-Latino Americano. See Latin American-Italian Institute
Istituto LUCE. See Union of Educational Cinema, *L'Unione Cinematografia Educativa*
Istituto Nazionale Assicurazioni (INA). *See* National Insurance Institute
Istituto Nazionale Assicurazioni-Casa (INA-Casa). *See* National Insurance Housing Institute
Istituto Nazionale Case per Impiegati di Stato (INCIS). *See* National Housing Institute for Public Servants
Istituto Nazionale di Previdenza Sociale (INPS). *See* National Social Security Institute
Istituto Nazionale di Urbanistica (INU). *See* National Institute of Urban Planning/Design
International Federation of Football Associations, *Fédération Internationale de Football Association* (FIFA) 30, 39, 41, 49, 63
Italian Civilisation Building *(Palazzo della Civiltà Italiana/ Palazzo della Civiltà del Lavoro/ Palazzo Fendi)* 7, 85, 90–1, 112, 119, 146, 161–4, 170
Italian National Olympic Committee, *Comitato Olimpico Nazionale Italiano* (CONI) 41, 63, 66, 68, 94, 106
Italiani brava gente. See Italians, the Good People
Italians, the Good People *(Italiani brava gente)* 10, 173
Italo-African Institute, *Istituto Italo-Africano* (IIA) 95

Jacobucci, Giovanni 119–20
Janiculum Hill 37, 115, 118, 127
Janiculum Ossuary *(Ossario del Gianicolo)* 7, 118–20, 128, 150–2, 166
Julius Caesar 12, 83, 115, 130

Kanetaka, Kaoru 158
kickbacks *(tangenti). See* bribes
Kickback City *(Tangentopoli). See* Bribesville

Lakeside Hotel *(Hotel du Lac)* 104, 106
La Padula, Bruno 90, 162
La Sapienza university 3, 10, 43, 69, 143, 146, 148
Lateran Pacts 13, 36
Latin American-Italian Institute 94
Laurentina 25
Lead/Bullet Years *(anni di piombo)* 2, 9, 66, 67–9, 109, 134, 139
League of Nations 59, 143, 157–9, 162
Lefebvre, Henri 49
Léger, Ferdinand 114
leva fascista. See Fascist conscription
Libera, Adalberto 41, 88–9, 100, 109–10
Liberal State 9, 12, 59, 127, 141
Lictory Style *(Stile littorio)* 53, 57, 60, 91, 144–5
Lictory Tower *(Torre Littoria)* 65, 73–4, 76, 155
Livy (Titus Livius) 145, 151
Lo Giudice, Andrea 155
Lupinacci, Manlio 138, 158, 170

Mafai, Mario 76
Magliana Band 67
Mameli, Gofredo 120, 128, 131
Mancini, Alberto 21
Mangiarotti, Edoardo 66, 68
Mantakas, Michele (Mikis) 132
Marconi, Guglielmo 116, 125–7
Marconi Obelisk *(Obelisco Marconi)* 85, 125–6
Marconi, Plinio 105
Marshall Plan 11, 30, 63, 84
Masina, Giulietta 71
Mattei, Stefano & Virgilio 132
Matteotti, Giacomo 158
Mausoleo dei Martiri Fascisti. See Mausoleum of the Fascist Martyrs
Mausoleum of the Fascist Martyrs *(Mausoleo dei Martiri Fascisti)* 131–3

Mazzini, Giuseppe 133, 152
Mazzoni, Angiolo 59, 61
Meier, Richard 117–18, 147
Melandri, Giovanna 68
Meloni, Giorgia 138, 171
militarism 3–4, 8–9, 12, 32, 35, 52, 62–3, 68–9, 74, 81, 91, 98, 114–15, 118–20, 126, 128–9, 133, 141–3, 149–50, 172
Military Police *(carabinieri)* 52, 66, 74, 94, 149–50
Milizia Volontaria per la Sicurezza Nazionale (MVSN). *See* Voluntary Militia for National Security
Ministry of Aeronautics 53, 144
Ministry of Corporations/Business and Made in Italy 53–4
Ministry of Cultural and Environmental Heritage 63
Ministry of Education 75, 94, 138
Ministry of Finance 103, 108–9
Ministry of Foreign Affairs/Foreign Affairs and International Co-operation 40, 42, 56, 63–6, 72, 74, 122, 172
Ministry of Foreign Affairs Building *(Farnesina)* 64–6
Ministry of Foreign Trade 108
Ministry of Grace and Justice 66, 68
Ministry of the Interior 130, 143
Ministry of Italian Africa 57–9, 65, 123
Ministry of Popular Culture 125
Ministry of Post and Communications 58, 70, 102
Ministry of Post-war Assistance 58
Ministry of Public Works 42, 126
Minnucci, Gaetano 75–6, 92
miracolo economico. *See* Economic Miracle
Modernity/Democratic achievement 12, 172
Modernity/Fascist achievement 3–4, 10–11, 25, 32–3, 59, 64, 72, 87, 90–1, 98, 114, 125–7, 155, 172
Montanelli, Indro 30
Monte Mario 18, 40–1, 65, 136
Montesacro Garden City *(Città Giardino Aniene)* 74–6

Montuori, Eugenio 95
Monumento a Vittorio Emanuele. *See* Victor Emanuel Monument
Monumento ad Anita Garibaldi. *See* Anita Garibaldi Monument
moral behaviour/social control 3–4, 11–12, 19, 32, 73–4, 114, 126–9, 136, 141–3, 165–7, 172–3
Moretti, Luigi 41, 63, 66–8, 75–7, 109, 155, 157, 159–60
Moretti, Nanni 73
Moro, Aldo 67, 122
Morpurgo, Vittorio 64–5, 109, 117
Mostra Augustea della Romanità. *See* Augustan Exhibition of Romanità
Mostra della Rivoluzione Fascista. *See* Exhibition of the Fascist Revolution
Mother House of the War Wounded *(Casa Madre)* 62–3, 149, 152–4, 172
Muratori, Saverio 109–10
Murcia, Filippo 102
Musei della Piazza Imperiale/Marconi. *See* Piazza Imperiale/Marconi Museums
Museo Africano. *See* African Museum
Museo Coloniale. *See* Piazza Imperiale/Marconi Museums
Museo della Civiltà Romana. *See* Museum of Roman Civilisation
Museo dell'Ara Pacis. *See* Ara Pacis Museum
Museo dell'Astronomia e Planetario. *See* Museum of Roman Civilisation
Museo delle Civiltà. *See* Piazza Imperiale/Marconi Museums
Museo di Palazzo Venezia. *See* Palazzo Venezia Museum
Museo Pigorini. *See* Piazza Imperiale/Marconi Museums
Museum of Civilisations. *See* Piazza Imperiale/Marconi Museums
Museum of Roman Civilisation *(Museo della Civiltà Romana)* 47, 83, 85, 93, 95–8, 173
Mussolini, Edda 56
Mussolini, Rachele 56

Mussolini Forum *(Foro Mussolini/ Italico)* 3–4, 9–11, 18, 24, 38–42, 53, 63–4, 72, 75, 79, 83, 106, 136, 141–2, 149, 155–60, 172
Mussolini Obelisk (*Obelisco Mussolini*) 136–8
Muzio, Giovanni 87–8

Napolitano, Giorgio 135
Narducci, Roberto 78
Nathan, Ernesto (Mayor) 131, 170
National Association of Partisans of Italy, *Associazione Nazionale Partigiani d'Italia* (ANPI) 36
National Association of War Wounded, *Associazione Nazionale Mutilati e Invalidi di Guerra* (ANMIG) 62, 149, 153–4
National Fascist Party Headquarters *(Palazzo Littorio)* 63–6, 73–4
National Fascist Party, *Partito Nazionale Fascista* (PNF) 65, 73–4, 132
National Housing Institute for Public Servants, *Istituto Nazionale Case per Impiegati di Stato* (INCIS) 41, 166
National Institute of Urban Planning/ Design, *Istituto Nazionale di Urbanistica* (INU) 43
National Insurance Housing Institute, *Istituto Nazionale Assicurazioni-Casa* (INA-Casa) 46, 72, 87
National Insurance Institute, *Istituto Nazionale Assicurazioni* (INA) 29, 33, 53, 86–8, 161
National Library 42, 90
National Liberation Committee, *Comitato di Liberazione Nazionale* (CLN) 22, 35
National Social Security Institute, *Istituto Nazionale di Previdenza Sociale* (INPS) 86–8
National Unity 3–4, 12, 32–3, 36, 52, 62–4, 66, 81, 114–15, 120, 133–5, 172–3
Nazi Army *(Wehrmacht)* 69, 70, 78, 82, 90, 92, 103, 134, 142, 146

Nazi Germany 10, 151, 158
Nazi massacre 134
Nazi occupation 2, 34–5, 45–6, 56, 69, 80, 82, 142, 146
Nervi, Pier Luigi 41, 88, 106–7
North-South axis 43, 88
Nouvel, Jean 106
'*Nuvola*', la. *See* Cloud congress centre

Obelisco Marconi. See Marconi Obelisk
Obelisco Mussolini. See Mussolini Obelisk
Office Building *(Palazzo degli Uffici)* 7, 18, 84, 87–8, 91–3, 161, 163–4
Olympic bids 39, 42
Olympic Plan 24
Olympic Velodrome *(Velodromo olimpico)* 108
Olympic Village *(Villaggio olimpico)* 40–1
Olympics, Rome 1960 11, 30, 39–41, 47, 53, 63, 81, 83, 85, 89, 94, 104, 106–8, 112, 126, 158–9, 170
Olympics of Civilization. *See* Rome Universal Exposition
Organisation armée secrete (OAS). *See* Secret Armed Organisation
Ossario del Gianicolo. See Janiculum Ossuary
Ostiense 77, 101, 168, 192
Ostiense station 41, 77–80
Outer suburbs 3, 12, 18, 20, 22–3, 25, 31, 45–6, 48–9, 69–73, 75, 118, 141, 172

Pacelli, Marcantonio 29
Pagano, Giuseppe 74, 108
Palace of Sports *(Palazzo dello Sport)* 47, 102, 104, 106–7
Palace of Water and Light *(Palazzo dell'Acqua e della Luce)* 85
Palazzo Chigi 65–6
Palazzo del Governo. See Government Palace
Palazzo del Collegio Romano 94
Palazzo dei Ricevimenti e Congressi. See Conference and Receptions Building

Palazzo dell'Acqua e della Luce. See Palace of Water and Light
Palazzo della Civiltà Italiana. See Italian Civilization Building
Palazzo della Civiltà del Lavoro. See Italian Civilization Building
Palazzo della DC. See Christian Democrat Party Headquarters
Palazzo delle Esposizioni. See Exhibition Building
Palazzo dello Sport. See Palace of Sports
Palazzo FAO. See Food and Agriculture Organisation Building
Palazzo Fendi. See Italian Civilization Building
Palazzo Littorio. See National Fascist Party Headquarters
Palazzo Madama 33
Palazzo Quirinale. See Quirinal Palace
Palazzo Uffici. See Office Building
Palazzo Venezia 33–4, 48, 53–5, 57, 133, 144, 157
Palazzo Venezia Museum 54
Pantheon 17, 32, 89
Paniconi, Mario 58, 87–8, 108
Parco e Laghetto dell'EUR. See Park and Lake, EUR
Paris Peace Treaty 122–3
Park and Lake, EUR *(Parco e Laghetto dell'EUR)* 102–4
Park-City of Modern Rome *(Città Parco della Roma Moderna)* 21, 39
Parpagliolo, Maria Teresa 102
Partito Nazionale Fascista (PNF). *See* National Fascist Party
patria. See Fatherland
Parri, Ferruccio 35
Patriotic Action Groups, *Gruppi Azione Patriottica* (GAP) 69
Paul VI (Alessandro Farnese), Pope 100
Pediconi, Giulio 58, 87–8, 108
Permindex 47, 94, 104
Petacci, Clara 131
Piacentini, Marcello 21, 37–8, 43, 45, 62, 84, 94, 96, 102, 106–8, 125, 148, 152, 162, 167
piano nobile 53, 109, 153
Piano, Renzo 109

piani particolareggiati. See detailed plans
Piano Regolatore 1931 – PR31. *See* Regulatory Plan 1931
Piano Regolatore 1962 – PR62. *See Piano Regolatore* 1962 – PR62
Piano Regolatore del Ventennale. See Regulatory Plan, 20th Anniversary
Piazza Augusto Imperatore 145–6
Piazza d'Armi 41
Piazza Imperiale/Marconi Museums (*Musei della Piazza Imperiale/ Marconi & Museo delle Civiltà*) 47, 93–6
Piazza San Pietro 37, 93
Piazza Venezia 13, 20, 22, 32–6, 60, 64, 77, 129, 134, 172
Piazzale Foro Italico (Piazzale dell'Impero) 7, 10, 63–4, 137, 155–60
Piazzale Clodio 47, 67
Piazzale dell'Impero. See Piazzale Foro Italico
Piccinato, Luigi 22, 100
Pietralata 18, 22, 41–2
Pintontello, Achille 60
Pius IX, Pope (Giovanni Mastai-Ferretti) 38
Pius XII, Pope (Eugenio Pacelli) 14, 37
planning legislation 14, 18–19, 25, 43
Pollini, Gino 99
Ponti, Gio 90, 91
Pontine Marsh towns 46, 155, 157
Post and Telegraph Office, EUR *(Ufficio Poste e Telegrafi dell'EUR)* 102
Poste italiane. See Ministry of Post and Communications
Prati 150
Primavalle 48, 74, 132
Prini, Giovanni 132
public transport networks 14, 22, 25–8

Quadraro 18, 42, 49, 69
Quartiere Africano 18, 41, 173
Quartieri. See inner suburbs
Quintilian (Marcus Fabius Quintilianus) 150
Quirinal Palace *(Palazzo Quirinale)* 54

Raggi, Virginia (Mayor) 42, 110–11
Rationalism 10, 41, 52, 63, 66, 72, 75, 93, 106, 141, 172
Ratti, Ugo 105–6
Rebecchini, Salvatore (Mayor) 37
Rebibbia 25, 67
Red Brigades *(Brigate rosse)* 67
Reggiani, Antonio 151
Regulatory Plan 1931 (*Piano Regolatore* 1931 – PR31) 19–24, 28–9, 42, 49
Regulatory Plan 1962 (*Piano Regolatore* 1962 – PR62) 21–5, 27
Regulatory Plan, 20th Anniversary *(Piano Regolatore del Ventennale)* 20–1, 25, 40, 47–8
Renzi, Matteo 42
Resistance 9, 14, 36, 74, 82, 114, 131, 142, 149, 152, 154, 168–9, 170, 173
resurgence *(Risorgimento)* 8–10, 12, 15, 35, 113–16, 119–20, 133, 135, 141, 151–2, 173
Riflemen of the Italian army infantry corps 35–6, 115, 139
Risorgimento. See resurgence
rogue development *(abusivismo)* 18, 25, 30–2, 41, 48–9
Roman Republic 1848–50 114, 119, 131
Roman Republic 5th C BCE 141
Romanità. See Roman-ness
Roman-ness *(Romanità)* 3–9, 19, 32–3, 59, 81, 87, 89–91, 94, 96, 114–17, 129, 136, 141–3, 145–8, 161, 167, 172–3
Romano, Mario 90
Rome City Council *(Comune di Roma)* 19, 21–5, 29, 37, 43, 45, 76, 83, 97, 104, 120, 170
Rome Trade Fair 47, 94
Rome Universal Exposition, 1942 *Esposizione42/Esposizione Universale Roma* (E42/EUR) 3, 8, 10–11, 14, 18, 22, 24–5, 29, 39–40, 43–8, 54, 59, 65, 70, 81–93, 96–8, 100–3, 105–12, 119, 122, 125–6, 141–2, 161–4, 170, 172–3

Rossi, Ettore 73
Rutelli, Francesco (Mayor) 37, 107, 110, 117–18

Sacconi, Giuseppe 135
sacrari. See shrines
Salò, Republic of 55
Samonà, Giuseppe 105
San Basilio 23, 25
sanatorie. See amnesties
Santarelli, Raffaello 161
Santayana, George 124
Sant'Elia, Antonio 55
Saragat, Giuseppe 91
Savoia Royal Family 150, 159
Scalpelli, Alfredo 95
Scego, Igiaba 122, 124
Scotti, Luigi 68
Second Republic 2, 41, 139
Second World War 25, 34, 37, 56, 58, 69, 82, 114, 126, 134, 141–2, 151, 154, 158
Secret Armed Organisation, *Organisation armée secrete* (OAS) 104
Sert, Josep Lluís 114
Severini, Gino 163
Sfollare le Città. See Clearing the Cities
Sgarbi, Vittorio 118
Sixtus V, Pope (Felice Peretti) 37, 136
shrines *(Sacrari)* 129
SNIA Viscosa 83, 165
social infrastructure axis *(asse attrezzato)* 22–3
Somalia 9, 58
Società Generale Immobiliare (SGI). *See* General Real Estate Development Agency
Spaccarelli, Attilio 37
Spanish Civil War 9, 151
speaker's platform *(arengario)* 55, 73–4, 76, 155
Special Office for the New Regulatory Plan, *Ufficio Speciale per il Nuovo Piano Regolatore* (USNPR) 22
squadristi. See Fascist crack squads
Square Colosseum. *See* Italian Civilisation Building

State Central Archives, *Archivio Centrale di Stato* (ACS) 98–100, 138, 168
Stazione Ostiense. *See* Ostiense station
Stazione Termini. *See* Termini station
Stile littorio. *See* Lictory Style
sventramenti. *See* Demolitions

Tafuri, Manfredo 60
Tamburi, Orfeo 76
Tangenti. *See* bribes and kickbacks
Tangentopoli. *See* Bribesville or Kickback City
Taymor, Julie 91, 98
Technical Drafting Committee, *Comitato di Elaborazione Tecnica* (CET) 22–4
Termini Station 3, 25, 42, 47, 54, 59–61, 77, 115, 120, 135
Testa, Virgilio 21, 23, 29, 39, 43, 45–7, 49, 54, 82–4, 89–92, 94, 96–100, 102–4, 106–110, 112, 164
Testaccio 75–6
Third Rome 2–3, 11, 17, 21, 25, 43, 45, 49, 82, 163–4, 174
Tiber 3, 37, 40, 42, 65, 117–8, 136, 155, 158, 163–4
Todt Construction Company 83
Tomb of the Unknown Soldier. *See* Victor Emanuel Monument
Tomba del milite ignoto. *See* Victor Emanuel Monument
Tor Marancio 45
Tor di Quinto 74
Tor Vergata University 43
Torre Littoria. *See* Lictory Tower
Tot, Amerigo 60
Tram and Bus Agency of the Governorate/City of Rome, *Azienda Tramvie e Autobus del Governatorato* (ATAG) 25
Trastevere 50, 75, 155
tribunal *(Palazzo della Giustizia)* 62
Togliatti, Palmiro 138
Troisi, Massimo 76
Tufello 23, 41, 75
Tupini, Umberto 107

Ufficio Poste e Telegrafi dell'EUR. *See* Post and Telegraph Office, EUR
Ufficio Speciale per il Nuovo Piano Regolatore (USNPR). *See* Special Office for the New Regulatory Plan
Unification of Italy. *See* resurgence
Union of Educational Cinema, *L'Unione Cinematografia Educativa*, (Istituto LUCE) 10, 35, 69
United Nations Relief and Rehabilitation Administration (UNRRA) 30, 70, 84, 90
University City *(Città Universitaria)* 3, 7, 9–10, 18, 42, 53, 69, 141–3, 145, 146–50, 164, 167–8, 170, 172
urban development 1, 14, 18–19, 22, 29–30, 33, 39–40, 42–3, 47–8, 50, 82

Val Melaina 75
Valco San Paolo 46
Valletta, Vittorio 97
van der rohe, Mies 59, 106, 109
Variante Generale 1941–2. *See* General Variant (VG41-2)
Vatican 3, 13–4, 28, 36–8, 50, 52, 61–3, 83–4, 100, 117, 172–3
Veltroni, Walter (Mayor) 55–6, 68, 110–11
Velodromo olimpico. *See* Olympic Velodrome
ventennio 1–2, 10–11, 17–18, 33, 48, 52, 66, 72, 114, 143, 158, 168
Via dell'impero/dei Fori Imperiali 32, 35–6, 50, 115, 134
Via della Conciliazione 20, 37–8, 42, 61–2, 83, 92, 106, 173
Via Imperiale/Viale Cristoforo Colombo 45, 47, 58, 81, 88, 93, 106, 108
Via Olimpica 25, 40, 46, 173
Via Tuscolana 3, 18, 42–3, 69
Viale Africa/Aventino 57–8
Viale Trastevere 75

Victor Emanuel II King of Italy 12, 33, 115, 133
Victor Emanuel III King of Italy 54, 146, 148, 163–4
Victor Emanuel Monument *(Vittoriano)* 9, 33, 54, 69, 115, 120, 129–30, 133–5
Vigna Clara 41
Villaggio olimpico. See Olympic Village
Villani, Andrea 96
Villa Torlonia 54–7
Virgil (Publius Vergilius Maro) 143, 166
Vitruvius, Marcus Pollio 166

Vittoriano. See Victor Emanuel Monument
Voluntary Militia for National Security, *Milizia Volontaria per la Sicurezza Nazionale* (MVSN) 132, 149, 155

Wehrmacht. See Nazi Army
Wimmer, Kurt 91
Worker Housing Institute, *Istituto per Case Popolari* (ICP) 72, 143, 165

Zevi, Bruno 102